Mending
The World

Mending The World

Stories of Family by Contemporary Black Writers

Edited by
Rosemarie Robotham

BASIC
CIVITAS
BOOKS

A Member of the Perseus Books Group

Published by BasicCivitas Books,
A Member of the Perseus Books Group

Designed by Michael Walters and Sue Canavan

Photography credits:
p. 1 © Paul Kuroda/SuperStock; p. 67 © Masterfile;
p.139 Courtesy of Mrs. Winifred Price; p. 185 Courtesy of
Mr. and Mrs. Radford Arrindell; p. 249 © Rosemarie
Robotham-Arrindell

Library of Congress Cataloging-in-Publication Data is available.

ISBN 0-465-07062-0

02 03 04 / 10 9 8 7 6 5 4 3 2 1

To the Robothams, Stiebels and Arrindells,
from whom I received my true education.

With gratitude and love.

contents

THE SHIFTING SELF

A TASTE OF EDEN

MENDING THE WORLD

Great Expectations

by Maya Angelou

This important and timely book is called *Mending the World*, and we can all agree that our world needs mending. Anthropologists, biologists, and historians tell us that all human life began with the black family. It is likely that what we as black people have learned over the millennia could be, must be, of use in mending the world. And as the seminal people, Africans, wherever we are in the world, must be prominent in righting the wrongs of history. The knowledge of healing is in us, as surely as wonder drugs are to be found in the bark of a tree.

So it is timely to approach black people, and indeed brown, yellow, red, beige, and white people, with great expectations. We can be effective as healers only if we expect it of ourselves. If you say to a person, "Well, you can't do anything," that person will respond, "Okay, I'll show you that I really can't." But if you lift a person up, if you expect more of that person—if we expect more of each other—then it seems to me we can uplift not just ourselves but everyone.

We appear to have lost sight of this important truth. One of the most poisonous ideas brought to our community was a statement made in the Sixties that the black woman was the root of the black family's problem. She was too bold, too strong; she really ought to step back; she was crushing the African-American male genitalia. The statement was made by a politician, but the *idea* was

introduced long before. It was said some four hundred years earlier by Machiavelli in his slim volume, *The Prince*. Separate and rule,
he said. Divide and conquer. This poison is still worming its way
through our families, which explains some of the monster rap,
vulgarity, and violence that we live with.

The result is a widening gap in the African-American community between the dual-headed families and the single-headed families and their progeny. This is critical, because more often than
not, people who come from homes where two parents are present
will be supported by the family, will receive more education, will
earn their degrees, will more than likely go on to become a part of
the middle and upper-middle class. And more than likely, those
who come from the single-parent homes will not make it as far.
There will always be those who push through, but too often, the
mother in the single-parent household is working too hard to give
the children the discipline and attention they need, and sometimes even to give them love. It could be she doesn't love herself
very much, which makes it very hard for her to love somebody who
looks like her, who came from her. Sometimes she's just plain
tired. Her children grow up with few toys, or none at all. They
learn to depend on other people rather than themselves for what
they need. They know best the feel of other people's property. But
we must understand that these children, too, are our own. When
we speak about the black family, we must recognize that we are
speaking about all of us, brothers and sisters, branches of the same
tree, sharing the same sky.

Of course, our experiences are not all the same. My grandson
lives in Atlanta with his wife and two children. He recently gradu-
ated from Georgia State University, Magna Cum Laude. He spent
last summer as a Ron Brown Fellow in Washington, D.C. And he
goes back to school in a couple of weeks to work on his MBA. Now
his children will have something in common with the great-
grandchildren of a black woman who raised her children alone,
with very little help. What my great-grandchildren, ages four and
one, will have in common with those children is that they're black.
They'll share the culture, the music, the foods, the body behavior,

all of those things. But intellectually, they will be worlds apart. And I don't mean in intelligence. I mean in academic training. In opportunities. In the ability to care for themselves. To love themselves. To find themselves quite admirable.

What can we do to heal this yawning gap between those who have and have not in our community? Stop the separation. Volunteer. Go into the community. Give one day or some hours a month to a school, to a children's ward, to a church. We can love each other. It's very simple. Love liberates. Love rescues. Love reclaims. I know this from experience.

When I was three and my brother was five, we were, for all intents and purposes, abandoned. Our parents were breaking up their marriage, and they sent us from Los Angeles, California, to the little village of Stamps, Arkansas. We went to live with my father's mother, Grandmother Henderson, whom we called Mama. She would put her hands on me—it seemed to me her hands were big as heaven itself—and she'd rub me, my arm, my back, my hair, my face, hug me to her talcumed bosom. And you know, I don't remember her ever kissing me. Many white sociologists would make a big thing of that: "There's no tactile love in the black community," they'd say, but that's not true. It's just that old black people don't often kiss children. But they do put their hands on you and let you know that you are loved.

Later, my brother and I were taken to St. Louis, where my mother was living. I was raped there, and after that I stopped talking. For years I did not speak. I thank the Lord now that my mother's family sent me back to Mama in Arkansas. When I got there, Mama said, "Sister, Mama don't care what these people say about you, that you must be an idiot, a moron, 'cause you can't talk. Mama don't care about that, because Mama knows when you and the Good Lord get ready, you're gonna be a teacher." At the time I just thought, *She's crazy. I'm never gonna talk. You can't teach like that, you can't teach without speaking.*

But she loved me so. And I healed.

And that's what each child needs—a safe haven of love. If you can't do any more, if you cant feed them more than beans, give them love. Give them a reflection of themselves they can be proud of. I always tried to do that with my son, so much so that when he was twenty, a friend of mine, an English aristocrat, said that he was very intelligent and handsome. "But you know, Maya," my friend said, "he's terribly, terribly arrogant." "Well," I said, "I didn't have a great mansion to give him, or the storied names to make people shiver in the marketplace, and I didn't have large packets of everlasting earth, and I didn't have bank accounts and cash. So I told him, 'You're the best, you're the greatest, you're the finest, by gosh.' And he was. And he is. And he *believed* it."

We need to give all children this message of love if we are to mend the gashes in our world. In the struggle for the soul of our families, black writers have a special role to play. I think it would be dangerous for us to ignore the rift, the tear in the fabric of the family— dangerous and foolhardy. But it is imperative that black writers stand on the good foot, speak the good truth, too. We need the love stories, the stories of courage, the humor. We need the James Baldwin stories, the Paule Marshall stories. We need all of it, because the majority of black people go to church, send their kids to school, live rather uneventful lives. And because they are uneventful, not sensational, the media does not even report them. So it is up to us to report them. It is up to us to create a reflection of ourselves that we are proud of. A vision of ourselves that we can love.

Now by love I don't mean indulgence. I don't mean sentimentality. By *love* I mean a condition that we are capable of and desperate for, which envelops and sustains and supports and encourages and doesn't even have to touch. I mean I love you if you're in Alabama, I love you if you're in Afghanistan. I mean love that passes all understanding, that recognizes that if we are the source of all humanity, then we are sisters and brothers to those in Afghanistan and in Tel Aviv and in Kyoto and in Lagos.

Yes, absolutely.

I mean love that says, *I free you.*

Because only when we are free can we do the work of mending the world.

Reflections on Family

by Pearl Cleage

Sometimes family is like the air you breathe. Because it's always around, you take for granted that it always will be. You forget the birthdays you used to take care to remember. You don't send a card when your niece graduates from high school or call to say be careful when your nephew goes to war. You find reasons not to be a part of the boisterous holiday gatherings where your uncle always drinks too much, and your cousin can't stop bragging about his latest professional accomplishment, and your great aunt wonders aloud why you're still not married, just before your mother pulls you aside to tell you she thinks your father is having an affair and has he said anything to you?

The family news you get comes secondhand and once removed until it almost seems like background noise. You realize with a shock that you probably know more about the personal lives of celebrities you will never meet than the people to whom you are connected by blood and bone and memory. And then you have a grandchild and the fact of family suddenly comes charging back into your life, promising the only immortality of which we can be sure. So you take a deep breath and look into the future's face to see what you can see.

First, there are the obvious things. Color of the hair. Shape of the mouth. Size of the ears. After the ritual counting of the fingers and marveling at the ten tiny toes, the search begins for who he looks like. Is that the beginning of his daddy's determined chin? Is that really just gas or the faint, but unmistakable glimmer of his mama's sweetest smile? Opinions are offered in hushed tones over the crib where the baby lies, blissfully unaware, or, with a bit more volume and perhaps a bit more confidence, over cake and coffee in the proud new grandmother's kitchen.

To them all, I simply smile and nod, murmuring something non-committal and offering another cup of this or slice of that. Their opinions, although lovingly offered, are quite beside the point. The details of my grandson's face and form will reveal themselves in due time, but for right now, his tiny body curled against his mother's breast or nestled in his father's arms is all the proof I need that he is one of us: family.

This is still new to me, this business of grandmothering, and I hope I'm going to be good at it. Unlike the almost unbearably intense mixture of emotions I felt when my own daughter was born—exhilaration, anticipation, relief, tenderness, and terror— my grandson's appearance produced in me a profound feeling of peace and connection unlike any I have ever known. Watching my baby have a baby was somehow more miraculous and more myste- rious than my own birth experience. After I had my daughter, I wanted to laugh and cry and dance around the delivery room. Watching my grandson emerge after that last big push, all I wanted to do was pray.

Which is what family will make you do when you're finally able to understand it, finally able to see past the constant demands and the endless dramas; the hidden agendas and the secret heartaches; the external pressures and the internal fortitude. My grandson may never understand the story of how his great-great-great-grand- mother Jenny often wore her high-button shoes on the wrong feet all day because she refused to change them once she discovered her mistake, but that same stubbornness is as much his birthright as his father's love of basketball and his mother's sense of style. He may never march in demonstrations or exhort a crowd to action, but his great-grandfather's determination to live free will be as much a part of who he is as the tiny brown birthmark on the back of his hand. He is already marked and coded by the long line of love that produced him and by the generations of his family, seen and unseen, who now hover around his crib, clucking and cooing, surrounding him with light.

As my grandson will learn soon enough, our families are not perfect, as much as we might wish them to be. But as the years go by, and we clutch each others' hands as we bury our elders, and call no matter what the hour to announce a new arrival, the more I realize that perfection is not required. Because a family is always greater than the details that come to define it. Always the best example of the whole being so much more than the sum of its parts. It is our families that push us so energetically out into the world to make our mark and then provide us with a place to regroup when the world just as energetically pushes back. It is our families that first show us the power of love and forgiveness and, just as clearly, the destructive force of anger and bitterness and wounds that never heal.

That's why this collection is so important. Because it allows our imperfections; it recognizes that we are works-in-progress. It understands that mending the world is not an overnight task. It is a way of living; a way of seeing; a way of being. This putting back together of what has been torn asunder is a delicate and demanding process that must take place block by block, house by house, one family at a time. This book is an important part of that movement toward the wholeness that comes only from understanding the power of love, the necessity of truth, and the possibility of rebirth.

For African-American families, born by the rivers of Babylon, the journey we have taken has often been perilous, filled with danger and defeat, separation and the silence of all those unmarked graves. And however tempting, it would be naive to suggest that we have emerged unscathed, to pretend that the desperation of the Middle Passage, the horrors of slavery, and the continuing legacy of Jim Crow, did not shake our family structure to its very core. Such pretending would only dishonor the courage of those whose struggles have allowed us to survive.

Because, ultimately, our true legacy is not their triumph over a seemingly implacable foe, but their determination to assert their humanity through the nurturing of families in the face of all they were forced to endure. That is the legacy we share and the foundation of our ability to continue to grow, and grow stronger.

It is that strength that I pray will manifest in my grandson. It is that spirit that I hope will bind him, across the miles and the generations, to those who came before and those who will come after. It is that life force that I hope will guide his feet as he takes his place among us, with his daddy's ears and his mama's smile, and his head full of the family stories that will be his grandmother's greatest gift, his living connection to who we were, who we are, and who we will be.

Amen.

Introduction

Making Up the Truth

by Rosemarie Robotham

As I sit down to write this introduction, I find that I cannot consider the experiences of Black families without first considering my own family, without first recognizing how they opened the door of possibility—in particular *this* possibility, this book of literature about the Black family—when I was still just a solemn girl with a secret love of stories.

It happened the year I turned fourteen. In a matter of one week my paternal grandfather would be dead of a heart attack. No one expected it. Grandpa had been so hearty just the Saturday before, his sphere-like brown head gleaming with vitality as he looked around the dinner table at his grandchildren. It was the last weekend of the Easter vacation, and my brother and I, and five of our cousins, were spending it at our grandparents' farm in the sleepy rural town of Mandeville. The next day our parents would come to get us for the drive back to Kingston, the capital of Jamaica, where we lived. School would begin the following week.

Grandma had been the one everyone worried about. She was small and stooped, her coiled hair fully white, her memory of recent occurrences less reliable than her recollection of events that had happened in her twenties. As she drifted in and out of the hazy mists of her youth, she had become increasingly difficult to connect with. She would gaze at us grandchildren as we tumbled into her kitchen, barefoot and sweaty and streaked with dirt, as if wondering idly who we were. She thought sometimes that we were her own children, but why were there seven of us instead of five, and who were those grown ones calling her "Mother?" Grandpa alone remained substantial and familiar to her. "Viv," she would say, "call the children in for dinner." Or "Viv, tell the children to get ready for bed." Then, mercifully, the mists would clear, and our identities would shift back into place for a while.

Grandpa, on the other hand, was keen and discerning till the day he died. The Saturday before his heart attack—the first and only he would ever suffer—he had gone around the table, interrogating each grandchild about his or her plans for the future. Grandpa, having been a teacher and later an inspector of schools, wanted to be sure that his grandchildren were being properly instructed, and that our attitudes about education and our ambitions for the future were appropriate to his mind.

He looked first at my older brother, whom I'd always suspected was his favorite. "And what will you become, young Lascelles?" Grandpa often referred to us by our parents' names, so that Gordon was "young Lascelles" and I was "little Gloria."

"A scientist, Grandpa," Gordon piped up, his cheeks bulging with mashed potatoes.

Grandpa nodded approvingly. "Yes," he said. "You have a scientist's inquisitive mind. You'd make a good doctor."

Next came Christopher, David, and Paul, an architect, a lawyer, and a linguist, respectively. Then Laurie-Anne, who wanted to be a teacher—Grandpa beamed at that—then her sister Nicky, who wanted to be a chef. "You want to be a businesswoman," Grandpa corrected. "*Own* the restaurant, then you can cook in its kitchen if you choose to."

Nicky was the youngest cousin at the table, only ten years old, with a shy voice and downcast eyes. "Yes, Grandpa," she conceded.

Then it was my turn. "I want to be an artist," I said.

Grandpa frowned. "What kind of an artist?"

"A painter," I clarified. "On canvas."

"Who will buy your paintings?" Grandpa asked. This, for Grandpa, amounted to affectionate indulgence, since it was already clear from his follow-up questions that he didn't hold with the notion of becoming anything so vague as "an artist." A civil servant all his life, Grandpa had arrived at certain conclusions about adult conduct and responsibility.

I shrugged, a touch of defiance in my shoulders.

"It doesn't matter," I said. "Nobody has to buy them."

Grandma, who had been busy spooning second helpings of her beef stew onto our plates, glanced up briefly. She knew that I had displayed about as much impracticality as Grandpa could stand.

Grandpa was true to form. "Nonsense!" he announced. "Little Gloria, it makes no sense for you to be a burden to your parents because you can't make any money. They'll sacrifice whatever they have to educate you, young lady, and the way you will pay them back is to become *self-sufficient*. Make a *living*." Grandpa thought for a moment, then he continued imperiously. "Leave painting on canvas to those who are truly born to it. You, little Gloria, are always scribbling in those notebooks of yours. You carry them everywhere. Look around this table at your family. You should aspire to tell their stories. Make it *literature*."

He spoke the last word with such respect, such worship, that it made me sit up and listen. That single word, in my grandfather's mouth, in my ear, swelled with the purest resonance and possibility.

A week later, Grandpa's heart stopped beating. After his funeral, my father told me that Grandma had decided I should have Grandpa's desk, the great old mahogany behemoth that stood in the corner of his study, across the room from the bookcase with the crumbling encyclopedias my brother loved. How had Grandma known that I loved Grandpa's desk, loved its faint smell of sawdust and lemon oil? I said a silent prayer of thanks for the whisper of clarity that had allowed her to notice. Sitting at Grandpa's desk was like steering a huge ship, its scarred surface so expansive that I felt it could take me on any journey, accommodating a lifetime of *literature*. This, after all, was what my grandfather had seen for me as he hovered, without our realizing it, at the margin of his life. And senile or not, Grandma had somehow managed to recognize the light of the future breaking over me.

So it is in families. So it is that most of us, if we stop to consider it, can trace who we become to some defining moment within the crucible of the family. This is certainly true for people of African descent, who centuries ago were wrested from our first families by a cruel transatlantic trade. For us, kinship relationships have been critical to our survival, helping us to create entirely new definitions of who we are—and who we might yet become in a world that does not always admit our possibilities or welcome our vision.

Ironically, for Black writers, this lack of welcome has been a kind of gift. It has forced us to set our own table, to invite wholly original muses to sit down with us, giving voice to our truths. Marginalized as we were in the societies of the New World, Black writers were faced with "making up" the truth, literally writing ourselves and our experiences into being. In doing so, we chose to reject the more negative images of ourselves reflected by others in favor of defining our own realities. As a consequence, African-American and Caribbean-born writers have managed to stake out definitive new territory on the American literary landscape, and we have done this by finding value in what is real and true *for us*.

Indeed, even as my grandfather exhorted me to "make it literature," gifted Black writers were taking their place at center stage—and even on bestseller lists. In the weeks, months, and years after my grandfather issued his challenge, Maya Angelou, James Baldwin, Nikki Giovanni, Toni Morrison, Derek Walcott, Alice Walker, and Audre Lorde exploded into my consciousness. Here were writers who looked like me, telling stories about people whose experiences resonated with mine. Here were men and women holding up a mirror to the world I knew. With great boldness and poetry, they were filling that gaping hole at the center of our collective consciousness that had been there for centuries. Patiently and courageously, they were "mending the world."

Through the work of these and so many other Black writers, the myriad ways in which people of African descent have managed to redefine themselves and the lives of their families are finally being understood as evidence of resourcefulness and resiliency rather than as proof of weakness and dysfunction. Yes, we lost much when we were brought, chained, to America in the holds of ships, but we have also gained much by virtue of our survival. For people of African descent in the New World, it is the family—bonded by blood and by love—that has been the supreme source of our ability to persevere and triumph in the face of unimaginable odds.

Yet the positive aspects of Black family life have not always been fully visible in American literature. Nor have past portrayals always recognized the ways in which Black writers understand the word *family*. The roots of today's Black family reach back centuries, and many familial patterns created in the past persist to this day. Five hundred years ago, when the first enslaved Africans set foot on Western shores, they were barred by law from seeking to sustain traditional family life. Despite a reverence for kinfolk that our ancestors brought from Africa, in those bleak days of slavery, Black families could not count on living out their lives close to their loved ones. A husband, a wife, a mother, a child could be sold away to a distant plantation at a moment's notice, and so we learned to hold family members close when we could, and to preserve and cherish their memories when we couldn't. Over time, we devised new and extended definitions of kinship to cope with uncertainty and loss. A cousin, for example, is simply a cousin, whether first, second, or third. A neighbor may take in a child and become more "Mama" to that child than its own kin. Close elders unrelated by blood may be called "aunt" and "uncle" and are treated with the regard those titles suggest.

Social scientists have traced the marks left on the psyche by the whip of slavery and by the twin scourges of prejudice and poverty that continue to haunt our families. But scholarly renditions of Black family life, while they can do much to expand our understanding, lack the poetry, the passionate immediacy, and the intimate range of personal truths that Black fiction writers, poets, and memoirists bring to the experience. Only by appreciating that there is no one truth about the Black family, but many individual and subjective truths, can we begin to understand how far we've come, and where we yet dream of arriving.

This, then, is the gift of this anthology—to transform how we see our kinship experiences by creating a lens through which we can view today's Black family anew.

Mending the World is divided into five sections, each revealing the Black family in all its complicated brilliance and pain, with stories of faith and allegiance, forgiveness and perseverance, heartbreak and loss, radiant realization and harsh, even bitter, discovery.

In the book's opening section, FIRST LIGHT, young people, some still in childhood, confront a definitive loss of innocence, a tearing apart of the protective fantasies of youth. But this awakening also has the power to transform, often in surprising ways. MYTH-MAKING, the book's second section, follows characters seeking lost or illusive elders, believing that the discoveries they make will unlock the truth of their own identities. By contrast, the characters in the book's third section, THE SHIFTING-SELF, explore the stereotypes that attach to Black folk in the larger world and the ways in which outside perceptions can alter the dynamics within a family. The fourth section, A TASTE OF EDEN, reveals the ways in which family members can wound and even devastate each other, and yet these stories also illuminate the many faces of unconditional love. MENDING THE WORLD, the book's final section, examines what happens when family members reach deep within themselves to preserve and honor the bonds of kinship.

The stories in these pages—tender, disturbing, funny, fierce—attest to the fact that within the embrace of our families, Black people have fashioned worlds of possibility from near-nothingness.

Now, through the weaving of memories and imaginings into compelling narratives, contemporary Black writers bear witness to that truth above all others. In *Mending the World,* the story of today's Black family emerges through the extraordinary work of men and women who have set themselves the task of interpreting the nature of kinship. And, as my grandfather commanded, they have made it *literature.*

First Light

Rachel

By Tina McElroy Ansa

Four-time novelist **Tina McElroy Ansa** (1949–) weaves the supernat-
ural and the natural into compelling tales of family and community.
"It's important to claim our spirituality and our connection to
Mother Earth," she says. "These are the things that got us through
slavery and up into freedom." A Georgia native, Ansa is collaborating
with her husband Jonee on the film of her bestselling novel *Baby of
the Family*. In this excerpt from *Baby*, seven-year-old Lena encoun-
ters a spirit of the past who imparts an utterly modern message.

This trip to the beach was different. It was to be the longest trip
the family had ever undertaken. Lena's father calculated it
would take them all about eight hours, with rest, comfort,
and lunch stops. He had calculated just about everything they were
likely to encounter between their house and the Georgia shore. He
didn't tell anybody, but he had even allowed time for them to
get lost because he was to be at the head of the caravan leading
three cars and ten people across the state. And he almost always got
lost at least once during every road trip he took. He couldn't
explain it or understand it really, but there was just something
about a road map that seemed to dare him to strike out in his own
direction regardless of what the lines and signs told him to do. In
private Lena's mother said it was just so he could get mad when
things didn't go according to his schedule. But Lena had noticed
that it was her mother who always got anxious and angry when they

got lost. Her father seemed to enjoy it, taking it as an opportunity to explore an area that they wouldn't have normally seen.

"Well, what do you know? I never knew that there was this little lake back here off this road," he'd say, sounding sincerely intrigued.

Her father had already told them that there would be no reading during this trip. They could do that as soon as they got back home from vacation and started school. He wanted them to pay particular attention during the next two weeks to the things around them.

"As soon as we get out of this county," he told them over his shoulder as they pulled away from the house, their grandmother still waving to them from the steps of the side porch, "you'll start noticing how things are gonna change. The land, the way things look, the way they smell. Just watch."

Lena and the boys, wide-eyed with excitement over the trip and with no comic books to read, had to admit that he was right. Out the windows of the station wagon, they watched the familiar red Georgia clay of their own region gradually change to the rich black loam farther south and then to the light friable sandy soil of the coast.

The peach trees they were so used to seeing by the sides of the roads on their Sunday drives gave way to the broad pecan trees of south Georgia. After a hundred miles or so, the tall pines they knew so well seemed to grow shorter, into the knobby loblolly pines of the coastal region. Then, to their amazement, the trees seemed to take on an even stranger form.

The majestic oak trees they were familiar with began spreading their limbs and growing curly appendages like an old man's beard, which their father told them was Spanish moss. Then the sandy ground began sprouting palm trees, like those they had seen in pictures of desert islands.

The caravan of cars—first their big green station wagon, then Lena's aunt and uncle's black Ford sedan, and finally the Stevenses' brand-new 1956 red Cadillac—arrived at their small motel across the road from the beach long after dark because they had made so many stops across the state to eat and pee and stretch and rest. Lena could smell the sharp salty scent that her father told her was the smell of the marshes and the ocean, and she could hear the waves crashing against the shore, but it was too dark to see anything. And her mother insisted that the children get right into bed after a bath in putrid water that smelled like rotten eggs so they would be rested and ready to start their vacation early the next morning.

The motel they stayed in was owned by a short fat black man with a square fleshy face, who said his people came from Savannah. He had the unsettling habit of slapping his palm to his forehead, then slowly pulling his hand over his face and down the curve of his throat before he spoke. He wrapped up this ritual by thumping the middle of his chest with his fist once where his hand's journey ended. After seeing him do this the first night when he showed each family to its flat concrete block bungalow, Lena avoided him as much as possible. She lived in fear of watching the man pull his features into his hand like a cartoon character and seeing them snap back like rubber into the shape of another face altogether.

The sulphur of the bath water made them all smell like old-time beachcombers before they even saw the ocean. And that night Lena dreamed of the beach—or at least what she imagined it to look like from pictures she had seen.

The next morning Lena's father was the first to rise, getting the rest of them out of bed by singing loud choruses of "Shake, Rattle, and Roll."

"Get out of that bed, wash your face and hands. Get into that kitchen, rattle them pots and pans," he sang in his smooth tenor voice. "Shake, rattle, and roll."

He had them all laughing and dancing in the tiny kitchen of the small motel suite as grits bubbled in the pot and bacon fried in the skillet. Then they all dressed in their swimsuits and covers and headed across the street for the beach.

It was like going on a treasure hunt.

They started out walking in a group, but by the time they reached the wind-blown rickety fence along the well-worn path into the dunes, they were walking single-file. They all stopped every few steps to admire something completely new to their inland eyes: the wild white fiddle-leaf morning glories that crawled on dark green vines all over the dunes, the tiny sand crabs that ran from their approaching feet, the big holes in the sand that the men, sissy-like and skittish, swore were made by some kind of beach snakes. Raymond and Edward ran over to the biggest hole they could find in the sand, expecting to find a huge snake sticking its head out. Disappointed to discover no signs of life around the hole, Edward started to stick his hand down the wide opening. Four or five adults yelled at the same time. "Boy, don't you stick your hand down there! You may draw back a nub!" his father cautioned harshly.

Even for those in the group who had been to the beach before, this trip seemed like a whole new excursion into an unknown territory, an exotic exploration by pretty brown-skinned creatures perfectly at home under the burning midmorning sun.

Lena loved everything about the beach: the way the gulls and pelicans squawked and swooped above her, the way the air cooled the closer she got to the water, the salt she tasted on her lips when she licked them, the way the sea oats swayed gently in the ocean breeze, the tiny sanderlings scurrying away from the surf trying not to get their feet wet. She felt that she somehow belonged there at the shore, even though it was her first time even seeing the ocean.

She followed her first impulse when her group topped the final tertiary dunes and caught their first sight of the greenish-brown waters of the Atlantic. She threw down her bundles, kicked off her rubber thongs, and ran into the water, her many braids flying behind her like a bridal train. An incoming wave met her head-on and kissed her right in her face. She giggled like a flirtatious teenager and shook her head so her wet braids swung around her like a dog flinging water off its body.

By midday everyone was spent from the sun, the playing, the sea air, and the big picnic lunch of fried chicken, potato salad, deviled eggs, ham and pimento cheese sandwiches, and lemon Coke that the women had found time to prepare during the morning. There were times when Lena hated the idea of having to grow into an adult woman on whose shoulders so much work seemed to fall. But like everyone else she sat down on the spread and ate until her face was greasy.

After lunch, while the women and men half-dozed under the big beach umbrellas, the children played on the sandy beach, careful not to go into the water without an adult or until an hour after they had eaten.

It was in this half-dazed state that Lena wandered away from her brothers and cousins, who were playing near the surf, kicking up sand and salt water in each other's faces in their exuberance. Her brothers had already forgotten the instructions given to them just that morning.

"Now, boys," their mother had said, trying to sound serious and stern as she beat eggs in a bowl for breakfast, "we want you to enjoy yourselves during this trip, but we also want you to take on some responsibility."

Lena, standing in the doorway of the small kitchenette, saw both sets of her brothers' shoulders sag at the news.

"Lena is just a little thing and doesn't understand like you two boys the respect you have to have for the water. Now, like I said, we want you to have a good time down here, too, but don't forget it's just like at home. Keep an eye out for Lena. She's our baby."

Lena found it easy to understand sometimes why the boys said they hated her. She hated it herself: always being considered a burden no matter how good she tried to be.

But when the idea hit her, she still wandered down the beach by herself without a thought to how the boys would have to pay for her absence when her mother discovered it.

It was low tide. Lena didn't know it was called that, but she knew the ocean was different because she could now see the big brown pelicans congregate out on a long narrow sandbar that was not even visible a few hours before. Every now and then another three or four would glide by her, flying just inches above the waves, and swoop down on the island, insisting every time that their brothers and sisters find room for them to land. To Lena the birds looked ancient, like something from another time, before creatures like her mama and daddy and brothers walked the beaches.

As she strolled down the beach, she stopped for a while to watch a school of mullet leap and splash not three feet from where she stood at the water's edge. Lena could see the dragonflies and sand flies and gnats hovering above the water's smooth still surface. Each time a big fat mullet, going after an insect, jumped out of the muddy water, the sun turned it silver-colored as it fell back in on its side, and Lena let out a little cry of appreciation.

When the fish moved on to another feeding spot, the girl looked down at her feet sunk nearly ankle-deep in the muddy sand of the ocean floor and saw the darting figures of minnows swimming fearlessly over her toes and behind her heels. She tried to keep her feet as still as possible because the smallest wiggling of her toes would produce clouds of mud in the water and disturb the tiny fish. To Lena there seemed to be hundreds of them, but then she saw that their shadows on the ocean floor near the water's edge doubled their numbers.

The child really enjoyed the feeling of communion with other creatures that the small fish playing around her ankles gave her. Bugs and small crawly things didn't bother her. The only thing that crawled on the ground she was truly afraid of was the black crusty roll-up bugs that her brothers delighted in throwing in her hair and dropping down the back of her blouse.

If Raymond and Edward were here, she thought as she watched the tiny fish play with her toes, they would feel called upon to go whooping and running through the water trying to catch the poor little things. Boys! Then she sucked her teeth in disgust the way her grandmother did and walked on.

The fine white sand, sparkling with glints of light like the glitter her mother sprinkled over her hair and on the costumes for her dance teacher's annual recitals, was hot between her bare brown toes. She wandered in and out of the surf to cool them off from time to time. To someone watching her from a spot in the dunes farther inland, Lena would have appeared to be wandering idly down the beach with no particular destination in mind, but the appearance would have been misleading.

Lena was looking for a particular place just a little farther down the beach, where the big rocks that lined part of the coast formed a low overhang facing the ocean. At that spot, she was sure, there was a curve in the beach that created a protected little cove where she could sit on the dry pure sand and feel the ocean breeze blow over her face and chest. She had dreamed about that very spot the night before as she slept with the smell of the sea in her throat.

When she saw the spot, she wasn't a bit surprised that it looked exactly like she had dreamed it would, with a big tree stump bleached white wedged among the rocks. In her seven years she had occasionally dreamed about places and things and events before they came to pass.

But she was a bit startled to find a barefoot black woman dressed in a long filmy maroon dress sitting on the huge stump of driftwood with her knees pulled up to her chin and her arms wrapped tightly around her bent legs.

The woman's hair, coming loose from short nappy braids, was wild and free in the wind. A heavy dark gray scarf of some rough cotton material, caught on one of the tree's short broken branches, blew just as wildly in the breeze beside her.

The woman was staring out at the water. She acted as though she didn't see Lena, but something inside the child told her she had. Lena continued walking toward the woman, although her best instincts told her to run back in the direction she had come. Her heart began to beat rapidly.

The strange figure continued to look out to sea as Lena walked toward her spot on the beach.

There was something familiar about the way the woman sat there. She looked as if she belonged there, but she also looked unaffected by her surroundings. The July sun, blazing like a hot tin plate in the sky, hadn't even raised a sweat on the woman's face and throat, which looked like they were made of old brown leather. But Lena could feel the rays burning her own scalp in the tiny parts between her braids.

Lena stopped and just stood there for a moment, digging her toes into the sand a few yards from the woman. The woman's washed-out-looking eyes swept away from some point far out to sea and moved around to Lena.

"Hey, Lena," the woman in the long thin maroon dress said in an easy, natural way. "My name is Rachel. I been waiting for you."

"Waiting for me?" Lena asked, her voice cracking with fear before she even felt it. "How you even know who I am? I don't know you."

"Oh, I knows all kinds of t'ings," the woman said. "Why don't you come over chere and set down by me?"

Lena was about to answer, "Do I have to?" when the woman said, "Or do you want me to come visit you in your bed tonight?"

The image of the woman coming to haunt her in the middle of the night instead of there on the sunny beach made Lena walk up to the apparition and sit down beside her immediately.

They sat there in silence for a long while, looking out at the baby waves gently lapping the sandy shore as the ocean breeze, soft as her grandmother's kiss, blew around them and lightly lifted Rachel's thin skirts around her knees. Hundreds of dragonflies zipped and darted through the air, going after the large mosquitoes, with the squawking gulls right on their tails looking for lunch. All the animal activity filled the air with humming, buzzing, and flapping.

The woman appeared calm and untroubled. Lena felt just the opposite. Now that she was sitting up close to the woman, the vise that had gripped her chest on first seeing her had tightened even more. The tightness made it hard for her to breathe and made the thumping of her heart against her rib cage seem more pronounced. Lena thought everybody on the beach would be able to hear her heart beat.

But when she looked up and down the beach, she realized for the first time that she had walked so far that her family and friends were no longer even in sight. And she began to panic.

"What's wrong wif you, gull? What you scared of?" Rachel sounded a bit annoyed.

"Lady, I'm scared of you."

"Shoot," the woman snorted and pulled the child closer to her on the tree. Rachel smelled like something out of the ocean: salty and wet all the way through, and her skin was scratchy with grains of sand.

"You ain't got no cause to be scared of me. A child like you. You gonna see a heap more like me before you dead, too."

Lena shuddered at the thought and the feel of Rachel's clammy skin and clothes pressed next to her face, arm, and thigh.

"Feel good here on this log, don't it?" Rachel said as she slipped her arm from around Lena's shoulders and leaned her head back to catch the breeze on her throat. "Me and the peoples 'round here used to call the wind Tony. We used to sing, 'Blow, Tony, blow.' "

Lena just nodded dumbly. Her heart was still thumping like the machines at the paper plant, and when she tried to swallow, no spit came up in her mouth.

"When I was 'live, I used to love to come sit on this chere very spot. But I wasn't here much, much as I loved it, 'cause when I was 'live I was a slave."

"A slave?" Lena wanted to know.

"Yeah," Rachel answered.

"A slave? A slave like I read about in school?"

"A little thing like you can read?" Rachel asked with wonder in her voice. "How old you is, Lena?"

"Seven," Lena said.

"Seven. Hummmpph, I always wanted to read."

She just sat there a moment looking at the child, who sat next to her scratching mosquito bites on her thigh and staring back at her with big eyes. Then the woman seemed to remember what she was talking about and continued speaking.

"Years and years ago we peoples, black peoples, was all slaves up along in through this chere area. All up in through Georgia and down on through Alabama and 'ssippi and on up the coast, too.

"I wasn't born here. I was born on a place up 'round Macon, where I was a slave, too, but they sold me off down chere when I was just 'bout a growed 'oman. I don't know why, just one day they just sold me, put me on a wagon with some pigs and goats and rode me off to this chere place . . . still to be a slave but a slave 'way from my ma and my pa and everybody I know."

"A slave?" Lena repeated in wonderment.

"The big house and barns and outbuildings and our cabins where us slaves stayed was set way back there," Rachel explained as she pointed inland past the sand dunes and sea grass that rose, then dipped out of sight. "The white man that say he owned us owned a whole lot of land and he grew rice 'long the river up the coast. You ever see fields where they grows rice, Lena?"

"No," Lena answered. She didn't know how to address the woman. Do you call a ghost ma'am? she wondered.

"Well, let me tells you, you don't never want to see it either. I didn't know not'ing 'bout no rice till I was brought down chere, but I had to learn mighty quick.

"And, Lena, if you ain't clearing a field, you planting or you weeding or you cutting and hauling. Every day."

"Every day? Even Sundays?" Lena wanted to know.

"Every day and some nights too, when the moon was big and bright. Going out in that marsh at night used to scare me to death. Sometimes there wouldn't even be no moon, and they send us out there to work with somebody holding a flambeau.

"But onst in a while, I take a chance and I slip off and come down chere to set. All I wanted to do was go by myself, set with my feets in this sand and let those cool, cool, moist breezes brush all over my tired body. I wanted the wind to blow right through me.

"I warn't trying to run away. Not then. Down chere I didn't even know which a-way to run. All I wanted was a little time down by the water. No working and sweating and hauling and caring for folks that wasn't my own.

"This land right chere looked like the onliest place I was ever gonna know, the onliest home I was ever gonna have. I knew I had another home 'way, 'way 'cross the waters, but I ain't never been there or set foot on that soil. This all I know and I wanted it for my own. I wanted to feel and taste and hear this place that was all I knew.

"But the white folks say I warn't nothing but a slave. The missus she say, 'How dare you think you can just go to the ocean when you feels like it?' Just like that, she say it, 'How dare you? The onliest reason for you to go to the shore is to bring me a cool breeze back. Can you do that? Can you?' I'd say no, I can't do that. Then she say, 'Then what use is you going there wasting time?'

Rachel stopped speaking and seemed to catch her breath. Lena remembered to breathe for the first time since the ghost started talking, it seemed, and Rachel continued.

"They beat me the first time they caught me chere. Beat me bad, too. But I still come back. I had to breathe this air. I had to let it play with my skin. Shoo things out my body."

"You were a little girl to get a whipping?" Lena asked.

"No, I was a growed 'oman like I is now."

"And they still whipped you like you wasn't but a child?"

"They whipped me like I wasn't nothing. That what it mean to be a slave—you ain't nothing."

"What you mean, you ain't nothing?" Lena really wanted to know. She couldn't comprehend what Rachel was trying to tell her.

Rachel just looked at her. "Lots of people loves you, don't they, Lena?" she asked after a little while. "Don't they?"

Lena thought a second or two, then nodded her head.

"I'm glad. I'm glad you loved. Most times I don't think I was loved. Mebbe I was. My ma and pa loved me, I knows that, but they couldn't save me none. Sitting down chere at the ocean made me feel loved a little."

Sadness was overtaking Lena's feeling of fear. She wanted to tell Rachel, "I'm just a little girl. I don't want to hear all this. I don't want to know all this. Please, don't tell me any more." But Rachel just looked at the child's big brown eyes welling up with tears and slipped inside her head and thoughts again.

"Child," she said softly. "Do you know how long I been waiting for somebody like you to come along so I can tell them all of this, so I can share some of this? You t'ink I'm not gonna tell you now I got you here on my beach?"

Then Rachel threw her head back and began to shake all over, her short nappy braids quivering with her. She opened her mouth wide, wider than Lena thought anyone was capable of doing. Her lips stretched back farther and farther, exposing more and more of her brown-and-pink gums. Then she started moaning and howling like something from the grave, long and low like a were-wolf out of a scary movie. Lena started to cover her eyes with her hands and bring her knees up to her ears, the way she always did during the scary part of movies when she sat in the balcony of the Burghart Theatre with her brothers, but she couldn't move her hands to her face. She couldn't move at all.

At last Rachel settled down and sat quietly on the log, rocking from side to side.

"But I didn't feel so bad when I took a chance and come down here to set awhile," Rachel finally said.

"Did they beat you some more when they caught you down here again?" Lena couldn't understand why she asked these questions. She didn't really want to know the answers. They seemed to pour out of her mouth without her permission.

"No, little girl, they didn't beat me." Rachel lifted her chin in the air. "This is where I was setting when them two white mens—the man which owned the place where I was a slave to and the man which worked for him—come riding up on their big snorting hosses. In the dark they sound to me like they was come riding from hell.

"I could feel those hosses' hoofbeats hitting the earth and echoing through my chest, but I wasn't scared. Not a bit that time, 'cause I knew I warn't gonna go nowhere. They reined in them hosses and come to a stop right up there above us," Rachel continued, jerking her head over her shoulder in the direction of the overhang behind them.

" 'Rachel!' one of 'em screamed down at me. I was surprised they could see me in the dark. They most likely couldn't. They must a' just knowed I was down here.

" 'Rachel, you black bitch, who the hell you think you is, making us come out here in the dark to look for your black ass? Get on back to the house, you gon' regret the day you ever saw this here water.'

"But I didn't say a word. The tide was coming in fast, I could feel it around my feets already. And I knew that the path leading up to the overhang where they stood was under water itself by then. I just sat there listening to the ocean, to what she had to say to me 'bout what coulda been.

"I reached up and pulled this chere scarf off my head. Wropped one end of it 'round my right arm here at the wrist, then wropped the other end onto this branch of the log. Had this here long apron. I ripped it off from 'round my waist and tied my other arm best I could to the other side of this log.

"By then the water was almost up to my waist, and it felt good and cool on my body.

" 'We oughta just leave your black ass down there,' one of the mens said.

"I didn't say nothing. I just smiled. It happened real quick, faster than I thought it would. The tide rose so fast I hardly had time to t'ink of my ma and pa back at the place up 'round Macon, then I thought 'bout this here man name Daniel and how his eyes look when they drove me away from up there. He looked so sad that I was going away.

"And the last thing I remember as I heard them two mens trying to ride down that watery path and cursing when they find out they can't get down there to me is I hope don't nobody's eyes never look that sad for me again. 'Cause I was glad to be going. I was going to the ocean and couldn't nobody ever stop me from going there again.

"I been chere ever since, but you the onliest one I ever talked to. You special, Lena."

Rachel settled back on the log so solidly and contentedly that Lena thought the ghost might just disappear into the wood. The child sat as still she had before. When a big stinging deer fly landed on her left arm and began biting her, she swatted it with the palm of her right hand. The swift movement of her own hand surprised her. She could move once again. Get up and

walk away, she told herself, since Rachel was back to looking out
to sea as she had been when Lena first saw her. But now it was
Lena who held herself there. She knew in her heart there was
something she still had to share with Rachel, just as the woman
had shared her story with her.

"Grandmama say colored folks don't belong on the beach."
Lena's voice was barely a whisper.

Rachel turned her whole body around so she was facing Lena.
Then she reached out with her damp leathery hands and grabbed
the child's shoulders firmly and dipped her face down until it was
level with Lena's. She spoke right into the girl's mouth.

"Don't you believe that," she said very slowly. "Don't you believe
that, Lena. Black folk belong here. You belong here. Don't believe
black folks don't belong on the beach. Don't never believe black
folks don't belong nowhere. Don't be afraid, Lena. Claim what is
yours. I died to be here on this beach, Lena. Don't never forgit
that. You belong anywhere on this earth you want to."

The smell of the ocean—salty, fishy, alive, green—was so strong
on Rachel's breath blowing into Lena's face that it made the girl a
little dizzy. And the woman was holding the child's shoulders so
tightly in her hands that it was beginning to hurt.

"Lena!" her brother Raymond's harsh voice broke through the
sea air.

"Girl, where you been?"

Lena jumped up from the log, breaking Rachel's grip on her.
She was in a state of confusion. For a while she had forgotten that
her brothers even existed. Seeing them running up the beach
toward her and Rachel's protected cove seemed to make stars spin
before her eyes, as if two worlds had collided before her.

"Lena, wh-wh-what you doing up h-here all by yourself?"
Edward demanded angrily as he reached her first and grabbed her
skinny bare arm so hard it made her wince. But Lena could see the
relief in his eyes.

"Good God, Lena, what made you go off by yourself like that?"
Raymond asked. He was as mad as Edward.

Lena didn't know what to say. She saw the boys looking right at her where she stood next to the log, but they didn't say a word about Rachel.

Just to make sure, Lena turned around and looked at the woman in the thin maroon dress. She was still there and had gone back to staring out to sea.

"Lena, pay attention." Raymond grabbed her hand and pulled her sharply toward him. "Do you know you almost got us killed? What you wander off for by yourself like that? Mama an' 'em still 'sleep, so they don't know you gone."

"Yeah, if th-th-they did, they'd b-b-be makin' two little wo-wo-wooden overcoats for us right now. Daddy woulda sk-skinned us alive."

"Yeah. You're more damn trouble than you'll ever be worth," Raymond agreed as he took her other arm and pulled her away from the log back down the beach in the direction of the motel. "Come on, let's get back. And quick too."

Coming behind them, Edward gave Lena a push and muttered, "You old pop-eyed fool."

Lena couldn't take any more. Seeing Rachel, hearing the ghost's story, knowing she was the only one who saw her and that she better not tell anyone, then having Raymond and Edward shoving and pinching her like she was nothing. It was all too much.

She pulled away from her brothers' grasp and flung herself down on the hot beach sobbing, the ends of her hundreds of plaits falling into the sand.

The sight stopped Raymond and Edward in their tracks. They had never seen anything like it, had never heard their baby sister cry like that before: deep heart-rending sobs that shook her whole body. They were immediately repentant.

Dropping to the sand beside her, they sat her up and tried brushing the sand off her face and arms and swimsuit.

"Shhhh, don't cry, Lena, we sorry. Come on, stop crying, we sorry we yelled at you," Raymond said in gentle tones.

"Yeah," Edward added, as contrite as his brother, "we were just scared you had gone off and got in the water and drowned. You know you ain't got no business going off by yourself on this beach."

"Yes, I do. Yes, I do, I belong on this beach. We all do. We do, too, belong down here," Lena kept repeating to her puzzled brothers.

"Lena, you know you don't have any business going off being by yourself, especially down here where you don't know anybody," Raymond tried to reason with her.

"Yes, I do, yes, I do," Lena kept saying. "I belong down here on this beach. This ocean is just as much mine as anybody's. It's yours too, Raymond. We colored folks, we belong on the beach."

"Girl, what you talking about?" Raymond demanded.

"I do, too, belong down here. I belong on this beach, Raymond, I belong anywhere on this earth I want to be," she insisted.

The boys exchanged glances and decided not to press their baby sister about what she meant. They knew she was as likely as not to say something that would confuse and scare them. And they had had enough of a scare for one day.

"Okay, okay, y-y-you right, Lena, w-we do belong here. I know w-wh-what you mean. Now, stop crying."

Lena was calming down some now. She was trying to stop her sobs. But they kept escaping from her chest in little hiccuping sounds that shook her whole body. And her face was red and strained. The boys knew that their mother would be able to tell right away that Lena had been crying.

"Come on," Raymond suggested. "Let's get in the water and cool off."

The sudsy waves rolling into the shore with the tide were like a refreshing cool drink against their bodies. But Lena couldn't help shuddering a bit at the feel of the salty water on her skin. It made her think of Rachel, whom she could still see sitting up on the beach on her bleached-out tree stump. And when an especially big wave came in while Lena wasn't looking, covering her head and face, going up her nose, and putting a salty taste in her throat, she had to fight a panicky feeling that she knew must have been like the one Rachel felt when the tide came in and she was tied underwater to that tree.

When she emerged from the wave, spitting and sputtering, her heart racing, her eyes stinging, she heard the boys laughing at her histrionics. She was about to get angry with them because they obviously didn't understand the importance of what she had just experienced. She was going to tell them that they were stupid and unfeeling and didn't care about anything but not getting a whipping. Then she looked up at Rachel and saw a smile on the woman's leathery face. She was laughing, too, just like the boys. Throwing her head back, showing her throat and teeth. She was laughing at Lena flopping around in the water's edge like a clown doll trying to find her footing in the shifting sands under her feet, hundreds of plaits heavy with ocean water trailing down around her ears.

It was the first time Lena had seen a smile on the visage of the ghost, and it raised so many emotions in the girl that she didn't know whether to laugh herself or cry. Instead she threw her head back into the next oncoming wave with her braids dangling behind her and flopped her entire body spread-eagle like a puppet into the surf. The ocean rushing into her ears filled her head with salty water, grains of sand, and what Lena knew had to be the sound of Rachel's laughter.

The Circling Hand

By Jamaica Kincaid

Jamaica Kincaid (1949–), born Elaine Potter Richardson in the Caribbean island of Antigua, left home at sixteen for New York. She eventually became a staff writer for the *New Yorker,* where the stories that evolved into her early books were first published. The author of novels, memoirs, short stories, and essays, as well as meditations on gardening, Kincaid now lives in Vermont. In this excerpt from her novel, *Annie John,* she looks into the heart of a young girl who must "break up" with the mother she has so adored to begin a new love affair with herself.

During my holidays from school, I was allowed to stay in bed until long after my father had gone to work. He left our house every weekday at the stroke of seven by the Anglican church bell. I would lie in bed awake, and I could hear all the sounds my parents made as they prepared for the day ahead. As my mother made my father his breakfast, my father would shave, using his shaving brush that had an ivory handle and a razor that matched; then he would step outside to the little shed he had built for us as a bathroom, to quickly bathe in water that he had instructed my mother to leave outside overnight in the dew. That way, the water would be very cold, and he believed that cold water strengthened his back. If I had been a boy, I would have gotten the same treatment, but since I was a girl, and on top of that went to school only with other girls, my mother would always add some hot water to my bathwater to take off the chill. On Sunday afternoons, while I was in Sunday school, my father took a hot bath; the tub was half filled with plain water, and then my mother would add a large caldronful of water in which she had just boiled some bark and leaves from a bay leaf tree. The bark and leaves were there for no reason other than that he liked the smell. He would then spend hours lying in this bath, studying his pool coupons or drawing examples of pieces of furniture he planned to make. When I came home from Sunday school, we would sit down to our Sunday dinner.

My mother and I often took a bath together. Sometimes it was just a plain bath, which didn't take very long. Other times, it was a special bath in which the barks and flowers of many different trees, together with all sorts of oils, were boiled in the same large caldron. We would then sit in this bath in a darkened room with a strange-smelling candle burning away. As we sat in this bath, my mother would bathe different parts of my body; then she would do the same to herself. We took these baths after my mother had consulted with her obeah woman, and with her mother and a trusted friend, and all three of them had confirmed that from the look of things around our house—the way a small scratch on my instep had turned into a small sore, then a large sore, and how long it had taken to heal; the way a dog she knew, and a friendly dog at that, suddenly turned and bit her; how a porcelain bowl she had carried from one eternity and hoped to carry into the next suddenly slipped out of her capable hands and broke into pieces the size of grains of sand; how words she spoke in jest to a friend had been completely misunderstood—one of the many women my father had loved, had never married, but with whom he had had children was trying to harm my mother and me by setting bad spirits on us.

When I got up, I placed my bedclothes and my nightie in the sun to air out, brushed my teeth, and washed and dressed myself. My mother would then give me my breakfast, but since, during my holidays, I was not going to school, I wasn't forced to eat an enormous breakfast of porridge, eggs, an orange or half a grapefruit, bread and butter, and cheese. I could get away with just some bread and butter and cheese and porridge and cocoa. I spent the day following my mother around and observing the way she did everything. When we went to the grocer's, she would point out to me the reason she bought each thing. I was shown a loaf of bread or a pound of butter from at least ten different angles. When we went to market, if that day she wanted to buy some crabs she would inquire from the person selling them if they came from near Parham, and if the person said yes my mother did not buy the crabs. In Parham was the leper colony, and my mother was convinced that the crabs ate nothing but the food from the lepers' own plates. If we were then to eat the crabs, it wouldn't be long before we were lepers ourselves and living unhappily in the leper colony.

How important I felt to be with my mother. For many people, their wares and provisions laid out in front of them, would brighten up when they saw her coming and would try hard to get her attention. They would dive underneath their stalls and bring out goods even better than what they had on display. They were disappointed when she held something up in the air, looked at it, turning it this way and that, and then, screwing up her face, said, "I don't think so," and turned and walked away—off to an other stall to see if someone who only last week had sold her some delicious christophine had something that was just as good. They would call out after her turned back that next week they expected to have eddoes or dasheen or whatever, and my mother would say, "We'll see," in a very disbelieving tone of voice. If then we went to Mr. Kenneth, it would be only for a few minutes, for he knew exactly what my mother wanted and always had it ready for her. Mr. Kenneth had known me since I was a small child, and he would always remind me of little things I had done then as he fed me a piece of raw liver he had set aside for me. It was one of the few things I liked to eat, and, to boot, it pleased my mother to see me eat something that was so good for me, and she would tell me in great detail the effect the raw liver would have on my red blood corpuscles.

We walked home in the hot midmorning sun mostly without event. When I was much smaller, quite a few times while I was walking with my mother she would suddenly grab me and wrap me up in her skirt and drag me along with her as if in a great hurry. I would hear an angry voice saying angry things, and then, after we had passed the angry voice, my mother would release me. Neither my mother nor my father ever came straight out and told me anything, but I had put two and two together and I knew that was one of the women that my father had loved and with whom he had had a child or children, and who never forgave him for marrying my mother and having me. It was one of those women who were always trying to harm my mother and me, and they must have loved my father very much, for not once did any of them ever try to hurt him, and whenever he passed them on the street it was as if he and these women had never met.

When we got home, my mother started to prepare our lunch (pumpkin soup with droppers, banana fritters with salt fish stewed in antroba and tomatoes, fungie with salt fish stewed in antroba and tomatoes or pepper pot, all depending on what my mother had found at market that day). As my mother went about from pot to pot, stirring one, adding something to the other, I was ever in her wake. As she dipped into a pot of boiling something or other to taste for correct seasoning, she would give me a taste of it also, asking me what I thought. Not that she really wanted to know what I thought, for she had told me many times that my taste buds were not quite developed yet, but it was just to include me in everything. While she made our lunch, she would also keep an eye on her washing. If it was a Tuesday and the colored clothes had been starched, as she placed them on the line I would follow, carrying a basket of clothespins for her. While the starched colored clothes were being dried on the line, the white clothes were being whitened on the stone heap. It was a beautiful stone heap that my father had made for her: enormous circle of stones, about six inches high, in the middle of our yard. On it the soapy white clothes were spread out; as the sun dried them, bleaching out all stains, they had to be made wet again by dousing them with buckets of water. On my holidays, I did this for my mother. As I watered the clothes, she would come up behind me, instructing me to get the clothes thoroughly wet, showing me a shirt that I should turn over so that the sleeves were exposed.

Over our lunch, my mother and father talked to each other about the houses my father had to build; how disgusted he had become with one of his apprentices, or with Mr. Oatie; what they thought of my schooling so far; what they thought of the noises Mr. Jarvis and his friends made for so many days when they locked themselves up inside Mr. Jarvis's house and drank rum and ate fish they had caught themselves and danced to the music of an accordion that they took turns playing. On and on they talked. As they talked, my head would move from side to side, looking at them. When my eyes rested on my father, I didn't think very much of the way he looked. But when my eyes rested on my mother, I found her beautiful. Her head looked as if it should be on a sixpence. What a beautiful long neck, and long plaited hair, which she pinned up around the crown of her head because when her hair hung down it made her too hot. Her nose was the shape of a flower on the brink of opening. Her mouth, moving up and down as she ate and talked at the same time, was such a beautiful mouth I could have looked at it forever if I had to and not mind. Her lips were wide and almost thin, and when she said certain words I could see small parts of big white teeth—so big, and pearly, like some nice buttons on one of my dresses. I didn't much care about what she said when she was in this mood with my father. She made him laugh so. She could hardly say a word before he would burst out laughing. We ate our food, I cleared the table, we said goodbye to my father as he went back to work, I helped my mother with the dishes, and then we settled into the afternoon.

When my mother, at sixteen, after quarreling with her father, left his house on Dominica and came to Antigua, she packed all her things in an enormous wooden trunk that she had bought in Roseau for almost six shillings. She painted the trunk yellow and green outside, and she lined the inside with wallpaper that had a cream background with pink roses printed all over it. Two days after she left her father's house, she boarded a boat and sailed for Antigua. It was a small boat, and the trip would have taken a day and a half ordinarily, but a hurricane blew up and the boat was lost at sea for almost five days. By the time it got to Antigua, the boat was practically in splinters, and though two or three of the passengers were lost overboard, along with some of the cargo, my mother and her trunk were safe. Now, twenty-four years later, this trunk was kept under my bed, and in it were things that had belonged to me, starting from just before I was born. There was the chemise, made of white cotton, with scallop edging around the sleeves, neck, and hem, and white flowers embroidered on the front—the first garment I wore after being born. My mother had made that herself, and once, when we were passing by, I was even shown the tree under which she sat as she made this garment. There were some of my diapers, with their handkerchief hemstitch that she had also done herself; there was a pair of white wool booties with matching jacket and hat; there was a blanket in white wool and a blanket in white flannel cotton; there was a plain white linen hat with lace trimming; there was my christening outfit; there were two of my baby bottles; one in the shape of a normal baby bottle, and the other shaped like a boat, with a nipple on either end; there was a thermos in which my mother had kept a tea that was supposed to have a soothing effect on me; there was the dress I wore on my first birthday: a yellow cotton with green smocking on the front; there was the dress I wore on my second birthday: pink cotton with green smocking on the front; there was also a photograph of me on my second birthday wearing my pink dress and my first pair of earrings, a chain around my neck, and a pair of bracelets, all specially made of gold from British Guiana; there was the first pair of shoes I grew out of after I knew how to walk; there was the dress I wore when I first went to school, and the first notebook in which I wrote; there were the sheets for my crib and the sheets for my first bed; there was my first straw hat, my first straw basket—decorated with flowers—my grandmother had sent from Dominica; there were my report cards, my certificates of merit from school, and my certificates of merit from Sunday school.

From time to time, my mother would fix on a certain place in our house and give it a good cleaning. If I was at home when she happened to do this, I was at her side, as usual. When she did this with the trunk, it was a tremendous pleasure, for after she had removed all the things from the trunk, and aired them out, and changed the camphor balls, and then refolded the things and put them back in their places in the trunk, as she held each thing in her hand she would tell me a story about myself. Sometimes I knew the story first hand, for I could remember the incident quite well; sometimes what she told me had happened when I was too young to know anything; and sometimes it happened before I was even born. Whichever way, I knew exactly what she would say, for I had heard it so many times before, but I never got tired of it. For instance, the flowers on the chemise, the first garment I wore after being born, were not put on correctly, and that is because when my mother was embroidering them I kicked so much that her hand was unsteady. My mother said that usually when I kicked around in her stomach and she told me to stop I would, but on that day I paid no attention at all. When she told me this story, she would smile at me and say, "You see, even then you were hard to manage." It pleased me to think that, before she could see my face, my mother spoke to me in the same way she did now. On and on my mother would go. No small part of my life was so unimportant that she hadn't made a note of it, and now she would tell it to me over and over again. I would sit next to her and she would show me the very dress I wore on the day I bit another child my age with whom I was playing. "Your biting phase," she called it. Or the day she warned me not to play around the coal pot, because I liked to sing to myself and dance around the fire. Two seconds later, I fell into the hot coals, burning my elbows. My mother cried when she saw that it wasn't serious, and now, as she told me about it, she would kiss the little black patches of scars on my elbows.

As she told me the stories, I sometimes sat at her side, leaning against her, or I would crouch on my knees behind her back and lean over her shoulder. As I did this, I would occasionally sniff at her neck, or behind her ears, or at her hair. She smelled sometimes of lemons, sometimes of sage, sometimes of roses, sometimes of bay leaf. At times I would no longer hear what it was she was saying;

I just liked to look at her mouth as it opened and closed over words, or as she laughed. How terrible it must be for all the people who had no one to love them so and no one whom they loved so, I thought. My father, for intance. When he was a little boy, his parents, after kissing him goodbye and leaving him with his grandmother, boarded a boat and sailed to South America. He never saw them again, though they wrote to him and sent him presents—packages of clothes on his birthday and at Christmas. He then grew to love his grandmother, and she loved him, for she took care of him and worked hard at keeping him well fed and clothed. From the beginning, they slept in the same bed, and as he became a young man they continued to do so. When he was no longer in school and had started working, every night, after he and his grandmother had eaten their dinner, my father would go off to visit his friends. He would then return home at around midnight and fall asleep next to his grandmother. In the morning, his grandmother would awake at half past five or so, a half hour before my father, and prepare his bath and breakfast and make everything proper and ready for him, so that at seven o'clock sharp he stepped out the door off to work. One morning, though, he overslept, because his grandmother didn't wake him up. When he awoke she was still lying next to him. When he tried to wake her, he couldn't. She had died lying next to him sometime during the night. Even though he was overcome with grief, he built her coffin and made sure she had a nice funeral. He never slept in that bed again, and shortly afterward he moved out of that house. He was eighteen years old then.

When my father first told me this story, I threw myself at him at the end it, and we both started to cry—he just a little, I quite a lot. It was a Sunday afternoon; he and my mother and I had gone for a walk in the botanical gardens. My mother had wandered off to look at some strange kind of thistle, and we could see her as she bent over the bushes to get a closer look and reached out to touch the leaves of the plant. When she returned to us and saw that we had both been crying, she started to get quite worked up, but my father quickly told her what had happened and she laughed at us and called us her little fools. But then she took me in her arms and kissed me, and she said that I needn't worry about such a thing as her sailing off or dying and leaving me all alone in the world. But if ever after that I saw my father sitting alone with a faraway look on his face, I was filled with pity for him. He had been alone in the world all that time, what with his mother sailing off on a boat with his father and his never seeing her again, and then his grandmother dying while lying next to him in the middle of the night. It was more than anyone should have to bear. I loved him so and wished that I had a mother to give him, for, no matter how much my own mother loved him, it could never be the same.

When my mother got through with the trunk, and I had heard again and again just what I had been like and who had said what to me at what point in my life, I was given my tea—a cup of cocoa and a buttered bun. My father by then would return home from work, and he was given his tea. As my mother went around preparing our supper, picking up clothes from the stone heap, or taking clothes off the clothes-line, I would sit in a corner of our yard and watch her. She never stood still. Her powerful legs carried her from one part of the yard to the other, and out of the house. Sometimes she might call out to me to go and get some thyme or basil or some other herb for her, for she grew all her herbs in little pots that she kept in a corner of our little garden. Sometimes when I gave her the herbs, she might stoop down and kiss me on my lips and then on my neck. It was in such a paradise that I lived.

The summer of the year I turned twelve, I could see that I had grown taller; most of my clothes no longer fit. When I could get a dress over my head the waist then came up to just below my chest. My legs had become more spindlelike, the hair on my head even more unruly than usual, small tufts of hair had appeared under my arms, and when I perspired the smell was strange, as if I had turned into a strange animal. I didn't say anything about it, and my mother and father didn't seem to notice, for they didn't say anything, either. Up to then, my mother and I had many dresses made out of the same cloth, though hers had a different, more grownup style, a boat neck or a sweetheart neckline, and a pleated or gored skirt, while my dresses had high necks with collars, a deep hemline, and, of course, a sash that tied in the back. One day, my mother and I had gone to get some material for new dresses to celebrate her birthday (the usual gift from my father), when I came upon a piece of cloth—a yellow background, with figures of men, dressed in a long-ago fashion, seated at pianos that they were playing, and all around them musical notes flying off into the air. I immediately said how much I loved the piece of cloth and how nice I thought it would look on us both, but my mother replied, "Oh, no. You are getting too old for that. It's time you had your own clothes. You just cannot go around the rest of your life looking like a little me." To say that I felt the earth swept away from under me would not be going too far. It wasn't just what she said, it was the way she said it. No accompanying little laugh. No bending over and kissing my little wet forehead (for suddenly I turned hot, then cold, and all my pores must have opened up, for fluids just flowed out of me). In the end, I got my dress with the men playing their pianos, and my mother got a dress with red and yellow overgrown hibiscus, but I was never able to wear my own dress or see my mother in hers without feeling bitterness and hatred, directed not so much toward my mother as toward, I suppose, life in general.

As if that were not enough, my mother informed me that I was on the verge of becoming a young lady, so there were quite a few things I would have to do differently. She didn't say exactly just what it was that made me on the verge of becoming a young lady, and I was so glad of that, because I didn't want to know. Behind a closed door, I stood naked in front of a mirror and looked at myself from head to toe. I was so long and bony that I more than filled up the mirror, and my small ribs pressed out against my skin. I tried to push my unruly hair down against my head so that it would lie flat, but as soon as I let it go it bounced up again. I could see the small tufts of hair under my arms. And then I got a good look at my nose. It had suddenly spread across my face, almost blotting out my cheeks, taking up my whole face, so that if I didn't know I was me standing there I would have wondered about that strange girl—and to think that only so recently my nose had been a small thing, the size of a rosebud. But what could I do? I thought of begging my mother to ask my father if he could build for me a set of clamps into which I could screw myself at night before I went to sleep and which would surely cut back on my growing. I was about to ask her this when I remembered that a few days earlier I had asked in my most pleasing, winning way for a look through the trunk. A person I did not recognize answered in a voice I did not recognize, "Absolutely not! You and I don't have time for that anymore." Again, did the ground wash out from under me? Again, the answer would have to be yes, and I wouldn't be going too far.

Because of this young-lady business, instead of days spent in perfect harmony with my mother, I trailing in her footsteps, she showering down on me her kisses and affection and attention, I was now sent off to learn one thing and another. I was sent to someone who knew all about manners and how to meet and greet important people in the world. This woman soon asked me not to come again, since I could not resist making farting-like noises each time I had to practice a curtsy, it made the other girls laugh so. I was sent for piano lessons. The piano teacher, a shriveled-up old spinster from Lancashire, England, soon asked me not to come back, since I seemed unable to resist eating from the bowl of plums she had placed on the piano purely for decoration. In the first case, I told my mother a lie—I told her that the manners teacher had found that my manners needed no improvement, so I needn't come back anymore. This made her very pleased. In the second case, there was no getting around it—she had to find out. When the piano teacher told her of my misdeed, she turned and walked away from me, and I wasn't sure that if she had been asked who I was she wouldn't have said, "I don't know," right then and there. What a new thing this was for me: my mother's back turned on me in disgust. It was true that I didn't spend all my days at my mother's side before this, that I spent most of my days at school, but before this young-lady business I could sit and think of my mother, see her doing one thing or another, and always her face bore a smile for me.

Now I often saw her with the corners of her mouth turned down in disapproval of me. And why was my mother carrying my new state so far? She took to pointing out that one day I would have my own house and I might want it to be a different house from the one she kept. Once, when showing me a way to store linen, she patted the folded sheets in place and said, "Of course, in your own house you might choose another way." That the day might actually come when we would live apart I had never believed. My throat hurt from the tears I held bottled up tight inside. Sometimes we would both forget the new order of things and would slip into our old ways. But that didn't last very long.

In the middle of all these new things, I had forgotten that I was to enter a new school that September. I had then a set of things to do, preparing for school. I had to go to the seamstress to be measured for new uniforms, since my body now made a mockery of the old measurements. I had to get shoes, a new school hat, and lots of new books. In my new school, I needed a different exercise book for each subject, and in addition to the usual—English, arithmetic, and so on—I now had to take Latin and French and attend classes in a brand-new science building. I began to look forward to my new school. I hoped that everyone there would be new, that there would be no one I had ever met before. That way, I could put on a new set of airs; I could say I was something that I was not, and no one would ever know the difference.

On the Sunday before the Monday I started my new school, my mother became cross over the way I had made my bed. In the center of my bedspread, my mother had embroidered a bowl overflowing with flowers and two lovebirds on either side of the bowl. I had placed the bedspread on my bed in a lopsided way so that the embroidery was not in the center of my bed, the way it should have been. My mother made a fuss about it, and I could see that she was right and I regretted very much not doing that one little thing that would have pleased her. I had lately become careless, she said, and I could only silently agree with her.

I came home from church, and my mother still seemed to hold

the bedspread against me, so I kept out of her way. At half past two in the afternoon, I went off to Sunday school. At Sunday school, I was given a certificate of best student in my study-of-the-Bible group. It was a surprise that I would receive the certificate on that day, though we had known about the results of a test weeks before. I rushed home with my certificate in hand, feeling that with this prize I would reconquer my mother—a chance for her to smile on me again.

When I got to our house, I rushed into the yard and called out to her, but no answer came. I then walked into the house. At first, I didn't hear anything. Then I heard sounds coming from the direction of my parents' room. My mother must be in there, I thought. When I got to the door, I could see that my mother and father were lying in their bed. It didn't interest me what they were doing—only that my mother's hand was on the small of my father's back and that it was making a circular motion. But her hand! It was white and bony, as if it had long been dead and had been left out in the elements. It seemed not to be her hand, and yet it could only be her hand, so well did I know it. It went around and around in the same circular motion, and I looked at it as if I would never see anything else in my life again. If I were to forget everything else in the world, I could not forget her hand as it looked then. I could also make out that the sounds I had heard were her kissing my father's ears and his mouth and his face. I looked at them for I don't know how long.

When I next saw my mother, I was standing at the dinner table that I had just set, having made a tremendous commotion with knives and forks as I got them out of their drawer, letting my parents know that I was home. I had set the table and was now half standing near my chair, half draped over the table, staring at nothing in particular and trying to ignore my mother's presence. Though I couldn't remember our eyes having met, I was quite sure that she had seen me in the bedroom, and I didn't know what I would say if she mentioned it. Instead, she said in a voice that was sort of cross and sort of something else, "Are you going to just stand there doing nothing all day?" The something else was new;

I had never heard it in her voice before. I couldn't say exactly what it was, but I know that it caused me to reply, "And what if I do?" and at the same time to stare at her directly in the eyes. It must have been a shock to her, the way I spoke. I had never talked back to her before. She looked at me, and then, instead of saying some squelching thing that would put me back in my place, she dropped her eyes and walked away. From the back, she looked small and funny. She carried her hands limp at her sides. I was sure I could never let those hands touch me again; I was sure could never let her kiss me again. All that was finished.

I was amazed that I could eat my food, for all of it reminded me of things that had taken place between my mother and me. A long time ago, when I wouldn't eat my beef, complaining that it involved too much chewing, my mother would first chew up pieces of meat in her own mouth and then feed it to me. When I had hated carrots so much that even the sight of them would send me into a fit of tears, my mother would try to find all sorts of ways to make them palatable for me. All that was finished now. I didn't think that I would ever think of any of it again with fondness. I looked at my parents. My father was just the same, eating his food in the same old way, his two rows of false teeth clop-clopping like a horse being driven off to market. He was regaling us with another one of his stories about when he was a young man and played cricket on one island or the other. What he said now must have been funny, for my mother couldn't stop laughing. He didn't seem to notice that I was not entertained.

My father and I then went for our customary Sunday-afternoon walk. My mother did not come with us. I don't know what she stayed home to do. On our walk, my father tried to hold my hand, but I pulled myself away from him, doing it in such a way that he would think I felt too big for that now.

That Monday, I went to my new school. I was placed in a class with girls I had never seen before. Some of them had heard about me, though, for I was the youngest among them and was said to be very bright. I liked a girl named Albertine, and I liked a girl named

Gweneth. At the end of the day, Gwen and I were in love, and so we walked home arm in arm together.

When I got home, my mother greeted me with the customary kiss and inquiries. I told her about my day, going out of my way to provide pleasing details, leaving out, of course, any mention at all of Gwen and my overpowering feelings for her.

The Driving Lesson

By Gerald Early

Gerald Early (1952–) is the Merle Kling Professor of Modern Letters and Director of the International Writers Center at Washington University in St. Louis, Missouri. His books include *The Culture of Bruising,* which won the 1994 National Book Critics Circle Award, and *Tuxedo Junction,* which earned him the Whiting Foundation Writer's Award in 1988. In "The Driving Lesson," Early's eldest daughter reveals a quiet courage.

About eighteen months ago, I taught my oldest teenage daughter how to drive. It was at the same time that I read to both my daughters J.D. Salinger's *Catcher in the Rye,* which I did largely because I was teaching it to a class and I thought my children would be interested in a book about growing up absurd, so to speak. Not to say that I was trying to rear them that way. Naturally, I had not thought that a book about an upper-class, White teenage boy written in the late 1940s would not be especially relevant. I always assume that people should be interested in learning about two things: themselves and everything that is not themselves.

Teaching Linnet how to drive is, I firmly believe, one of the great accomplishments of my life as a parent, not because it was difficult, although it had its challenging moments, but because I learned a great deal about myself and about my daughter, as well. And even this *Catcher in the Rye* business turned out to be more useful than it seemed at first.

When my daughter turned fifteen and a half, she applied for and received her learner's permit. She had thought of little else since she turned fifteen except learning how to drive. It meant a great deal to her, which struck me, at the time, as odd. When I was her age, I did not know how to drive, and did not apply for a learner's permit to take driver's education at my high school, as I thought it would do me very little good. My mother was too poor to own a car. Besides, she did not know how to drive and I lived in the middle of South Philadelphia, where public transportation was readily available and in many instances more convenient than owning a car. (Where in heaven's name could you park it?) My oldest sister, who has lived in Philadelphia most of her life, still does not know how to drive. But my daughter was living in decidedly different circumstances, in a two-car, middle-class family, and in a suburb where public transportation is sporadic and far from convenient. It certainly doesn't take you anywhere you want to go. In a sense, she understood very rightly that if she were to have a period of her adolescence independent of her parents, she needed to learn to drive. She told me this in no uncertain terms and cut me short when I began to reminisce about growing up in Philadelphia. "I'm not growing up in some cold-water, coal-burning flat in an inner-city neighborhood. I'm not living your childhood and I don't care about it." Well, that's telling me, I thought.

My wife had given Linnet her first driving lesson and came back entirely bemused and out of sorts. Linnet came in crying, marched upstairs, and slammed the door to her room.

"I can't teach that girl to drive," my wife said. "She scares me too much behind a wheel. Why don't you take her out? You're much better at teaching than I am. Remember, you taught me how to drive. Besides, this is something a father should do with his daughter."

My wife was exaggerating for effect and because she wanted to get out of something she found disagreeable. I had not really taught her how to drive. When we began dating, she owned a Nova, a new car at the time with an automatic transmission, and I was driving my mother's Toyota, a somewhat less-than-new car with a standard transmission. She expressed an interest in wanting to learn how to drive a car with a standard transmission, so I taught her. As my wife is a very good driver, and she did, after all, already know how to drive, it was easy to teach her, and I think she was driving my mother's car on the street in a matter of two or three days. For the first ten years of our marriage, we owned nothing but standard transmission cars. And she thought I was the greatest teacher in the world because I was so relaxed and patient, was never the least concerned that she couldn't master the stick shift, was never upset when she made a mistake, and explained things thoroughly and dearly. This was all an act. I was terrified to my toenails the whole time, but I suspected that she thought that, as a man, I should exhibit a certain coolness.

The one prolonged teaching session I had with my mother was when she taught me to drive when I was eighteen. My mother had learned to drive only two years earlier and she seemed very keen that I should learn as well. I don't remember having much enthusiasm for it. To this day, I hate to drive. What compounded my situation was that my mother's car had a manual transmission. The lessons were tense. My mother was extremely nervous and extremely angry, although I picked up driving with relative ease. She kept thinking I would strip the gears, run into something, or get run into, normal fears but in her case pitched at high frequency.

After three lessons, I could drive the car, a Volkswagen Beetle, fairly well. But I hated the lessons. Then, suddenly, one day, she decided to have a male friend continue the instruction. The change was dramatic. He was very laid-back, patient, and had endless confidence, or pretended confidence, in my ability. The lessons were no longer an ordeal. I learned two things from this switch, which I think in part my mother effected because she wanted me to receive instruction from a man. First, I decided I wanted very much to teach people things in the manner of a middle-aged Black man, because I thought all middle-aged Black men taught like my new driving instructor, and all of my life, I have associated good teaching with being middle-aged, Black, and a man. I wanted to be patient, assured, relaxed, with boundless confidence in my student and in my ability to teach him or her.

Second, paradoxically, is that I missed my mother as an instructor. I thought there was something in this cross-gender moment of instruction that helped me understand what being a man was. Perhaps this is why my wife was able, very easily, to talk me into teaching my daughter how to drive. "Men are better teachers at mechanical things than women are," my wife told me in an appeal to my ego. I don't believe it. I am the most hapless man with mechanical contrivances that I know. But it meant something to my male ego to teach my daughter to drive, especially because my wife felt unable to do it.

I went upstairs and talked to Linnet.

"Didn't go too well today, huh?" I asked.

"Daddy," she turned to me with her tear-streaked face, "teach me how to drive. Mommy thinks I can't do it. I know I can learn to drive if you teach me. I think you're the best teacher in the world. Remember how you taught me to play checkers and Monopoly and stuff like that. You always explain stuff well and never get mad if I need to have it explained again. I think most of the stuff I remember you taught me."

It is a terrible weight put on any parent to hear that suddenly and so sincerely from a child, as if the dreadful responsibility of childrearing appears in such vivid relief at such a moment.

I have been a terrible parent, I thought. This kid can't believe what she is saying. Immediately, it struck me that the last thing I wanted to do was teach my daughter to drive. I felt dizzy from the sheer immensity of it, as if, in some surreal moment, I was assigned to teach her the most important task a human being ever could be taught and feeling myself insufficient for the undertaking. After all, I secretly thought that perhaps because of a learning disability, Linnet couldn't learn how to drive. I remember trying to dissuade her from getting her learner's permit, telling her there was "no rush," that she had plenty of time. "You don't know how much time I have," she responded angrily. "Driving isn't everything," I would tell her at other times. "It is to me," she would answer. I felt like a fraud bearing a sickening guilt.

"I'll teach you how to drive," I said.

We went out early every Sunday during early spring. We would drive around the huge empty parking lot on the Washington University campus in St. Louis for about an hour. Turn left. Turn right. Pull into a parking stall. Keep the car straight. Keep your eyes on the road. Check your rearview mirror. The usual instructions. I was calm, collected, coolly explaining everything and giving her tips about various complications that could arise when she actually would drive in traffic, which I promised her week after week but always found some excuse not to fulfill. So, she wound up driving around the parking lot for far longer than most drivers-ed students. After a bit, she wanted to drive on the street, but she never became impatient about it, believing that her father knew best.

One very cold, very sunny Sunday, I decided to have her drive from one parking lot to another. This involved going up a winding, tricky stretch of road. I thought she could handle it. We went up without too much difficulty. But when we returned, matters became very dicey very quickly. Going down the winding road meant hugging a high brick wall that abutted the road. The car started going faster than Linnet could control, the nearness of the wall unnerved her and she couldn't keep the car straight. She turned the steering wheel and it seemed we were going to hit the wall. Maybe she had better control of the car than I thought. Maybe she wasn't going to hit the wall. Until that point, I had been, against my inner urges, very cool, but when I thought she was going to hit the wall, I panicked and grabbed the wheel.

"Goddamnit," I yelled, "you're going to get us killed."

I pushed her out of the way and guided the car down the road, virtually sitting on top of her. When we reached the bottom of the hill, I stopped the car.

"Look," I said, a bit sheepishly, "I'm sorry about that, but it looked like you were about to . . ."

Her head was down. She was crying quietly.

"I wasn't going to crash into the wall," she said. "You don't think I can learn how to drive, do you? You never did. You think I'm too dumb to learn to drive, don't you?"

I was silent for a moment. I didn't quite know what to say. I stammered something, but she wasn't listening. She got out of the car and opened the door on the passenger side.

"I guess you better drive us home," she said.

"Listen, Linnet, I'm sorry. I didn't mean . . ."

"Drive," she yelled at me. I was so startled that I simply obeyed her and got behind the wheel.

I started the car, but I didn't move it. I was trying to formulate something to say, an apology of some sort. I felt so exposed. She knew she had hit a nerve when she said I did not think she could learn to drive. But before I could say anything, she spoke to me in a quiet, choked voice, wiping her face with the heel of her hand.

"Do you know I got out of the Resource Room this year?" she said.

"Yes," I said, "I know that. That's very good for you."

"Hardly any kid gets out of Resource," she said, ignoring my interjection. "Once you get in special education, you stay there. And everybody thinks you're dumb. Even the teachers think you're dumb and they don't help you. They just do the work for you. It's awful to have everybody think you're dumb. I wanted to get out of there so bad. I worked and worked and got out. I'm not dumb, and I was tired of people thinking I was dumb."

"I never thought you were dumb, Linnet," I said.

"You know, there are a lot of Black kids in Resource. I didn't want to be there because I thought, everybody will think I'm dumb because I'm Black."

This was becoming too painful. What goes on in the minds of children is something adults don't want to know about. I didn't want to hear anymore. What was I supposed to say, some trite, unconvincing thing about your great Black ancestry, the wonders of Africa? People who think those recitations make a difference are afraid to plumb the awful and contradictory depths of the human soul. There was no escaping racial pride, in the end, as that was what motivated her to get out of the Resource Room. And there was no escaping race as a burden, a stigma, a form of shame. A Black person is forever caught between a kind of heroism and simply being the nigger. I pressed the accelerator.

"We don't have to go through this now, Linnet," I said.

"It's hard to go to school. A lot of the White kids are racist and can't stand most of the Black kids. And most of the Blacks think you're a sellout if you have White friends and they go around in some kind of clan. They think like their parents. All of them do. I don't want to like something just to make the Black kids happy, make them think I'm Black. They say I act White, but I'm just trying to be myself. What is this being Black? Hanging around complaining about White people all the time. Thinking about your color all the time and how different you're supposed to be? Just being part of a clan? But a lot of White kids do dope, come from messed-up homes, and just act crazy. I don't act like that. I sure don't want to be White. I want to be myself. That's why I wanted to learn to drive. To help me be myself," she said.

I had driven a few blocks, but pulled the car over. I looked at my daughter for a moment and realized that God does indeed give only ironic gifts.

"You know something?" Linnet continued, "I kind of liked the *Catcher in the Rye*. I mean, some of it. But Holden Caulfield was just too crazy. Sometimes I think he's right, though. I think sometimes everybody in the world is phony. I know I think the Black kids and their blackness and the White kids and their whiteness are all phony. They just don't know how to be themselves."

I got out of the car and went around to the passenger side, opened the door and shoved her gently toward the driver's seat.

"I don't feel like driving," I said.

"I don't want to do this, Daddy," she said. She was now completely in the driver's seat.

"Then, I guess, we're not getting home, because I'm not driving," I said.

"I might mess up the car," she said.

"I'll buy another one and take you out next week. There are plenty of car dealers around. Buying another car is easy. As Hemingway said, the world is 'a good place to buy in.' Go ahead and drive."

Holy Cross Hospital

By Toi Derricotte

Toi Derricotte (1941–), co-founder in 1996 of the African-American poetry workshop, Cave Canem, is a professor of English at the University of Pittsburgh. Born in Detroit, she has published four poetry collections and a memoir, *The Black Notebooks,* which won the Annisfield-Wolf Book Award in non-fiction, and the ALA Black Caucus' non-fiction award in 1997. Her poem, "Holy Cross Hospital," follows a young woman in her final weeks of pregnancy.

In my ninth month, I entered a maternity ward
set up for the care of unwed girls and women.

couldn't stand to see these new young faces, these
children swollen as myself. my roommate, snotty,
bragging about how she didn't give a damn about the
kid and was going back to her boyfriend and be a
cheerleader in high school, *could we ever "go back"?*
would our bodies be the same? could we hide among the
childless? she always reminded me of a lady at the bridge
club in her mother's shoes, playing her mother's hand.

i tried to get along, be silent, stay in my own corner.
i only had a month to go—too short to get to know them.
but being drawn to the room down the hall, the t.v. room
where, at night, we sat in our cuddly cotton robes and

fleece-lined slippers—like college freshman, joking
about the nuns and laughing about due dates: jailbirds
waiting to be sprung . . .

one girl, taller and older, twenty-six or twenty-seven, kept
to herself, talked with a funny accent, the pain on her face
seemed worse than ours . . .

and a lovely, gentle girl with flat small bones, the
great round hump seemed to carry *her* around! she never
said an unkind word to anyone, went to church every morning
with her rosary and prayed each night alone in her room.

she was seventeen, diabetic, fearful that she or the baby
or both would die in childbirth. she wanted the baby, yet
knew that to keep it would be wrong. but what if the child
did live? what if she gave it up and could never have another?

i couldn't believe the fear, the knowledge she had of
death walking with her. i never felt stronger, eating
right, doing my exercises. i was holding on to the core,
the center of strength; death seemed remote, i could not
imagine it walking in our midst, death in the midst of
all that blooming. she seemed sincere, but maybe she was lying . . .

she went down two weeks late. induced. she had decided
to keep the baby. the night i went down, she had just
gone into labor so the girls had two of us to cheer about.
the next morning when i awoke, i went to see her. she
smiled from her hospital bed with tubes in her arms. it
had been a boy. her baby was dead in the womb for two
weeks. i remember she had complained *no kicking.* we
had reassured her everything was fine.

meanwhile i worked in the laundry, folded the hospital
fresh sheets flat three hours a day. but never alone.
stepping off the elevator, going up, feeling something,
a spark catch. i would put my hand there and smile with
such a luminous smile, the whole world must be happy.

or out with those crazy girls, those teenagers, laughing,
on a christmas shopping spree, free (the only day they
let us out in two months) feet wet and cold from snow.

i felt pretty, body wide and still in black leotards
washed out at night. my shapely legs and
young body like iron.

i ate well, wanted lamaze (painless childbirth)—i
didn't need a husband or a trained doctor—i'd do it
myself, book propped open on the floor, puffing and
counting while all the sixteen-year-old unwed children
smiled like i was crazy.

one day i got a letter from my cousin, said:

> *don't give your baby up—*
> *you'll never be complete again*
> *you'll always worry where and how it is*

she knew! the people in my family knew! nobody died
of grief and shame!

I *would* keep the child. i was sturdy. would be a better
mother than my mother. i would still be a doctor,
study, finish school at night. when the time came, i
would not hurt like all those women who screamed and

took drugs. i would squat down and deliver just like the
peasants in the field, shift my baby to my back, and
continue . . .

when my water broke, when i saw that stain of pink blood
on the toilet paper and felt the first thing i could not
feel, had no control of, dripping down my leg, i heard
them singing mitch miller xmas songs and came from the
bathroom in my own pink song—down the long hall, down
the long moment when no one knew but me. it was time.

all the girls were cheering when i went downstairs, i was
the one who told them to be tough, to stop believing
in their mother's pain, that poison. our minds were
like telescopes looking through fear. it wouldn't hurt
like we'd been told. birth was beautiful if we believed
that it was beautiful and good!

—*maternity—i had never seen inside those doors.*
all night i pictured the girls up there, at first hanging
out of the windows, trying to get a glimpse of me . . .
when the pain was worst, i thought of their sleeping faces,
like the shining faces of children in the nursery, i held
onto that image of innocence like one light in the darkness.

Bright Thursdays

By Olive Senior

Olive Senior (1941–) is the author of the *Encyclopedia of Jamaican Heritage;* three critically acclaimed works of fiction, *Summer Lightning* (which won the Commonwealth Writers Prize), *Arrival of the Snake-Woman,* and *Discerner of Hearts;* and two poetry collections, *Talking of Trees* and *Gardening in the Tropics.* Born and raised in Jamaica, Senior now divides her time between her homeland and Toronto, Canada. "Bright Thursdays," she says, describes a young girl "starting on a path to self-affirmation which eventually transcends childhood pain."

Thursday was the worst day. While she had no expectations of any other day of the week, every Thursday turned out to be either very good or very bad, and she had no way of knowing in advance which one it would be. Sometimes there would be so many bad Thursdays in a row that she wanted to write home to her mother, 'Please please take me home for I cannot stand the clouds'. But then she would remember her mother saying, "Laura this is a new life for you. This is opportunity. Now dont let yu mama down. Chile, swallow yu tongue before yu talk lest yu say the wrong thing and dont mek yu eye big for everything yu see. Dont give Miss Christie no cause for complain and most of all, let them know you have broughtuptcy."

Miss Christie was the lady she now lived with, her father's mother. She didn't know her father except for a photograph of him on Miss Christie's bureau where he was almost lost in a forest of photographs of all her children and grandchildren all brown skinned with straight hair and confident smiles on their faces. When she saw these photographs she understood why Miss Christie couldn't put hers there. Every week as she dusted the bureau, Laura looked at herself in the mirror and tried to smile with the confidence of those in the photographs, but all she saw was a being so strange, so far removed from those in the pictures, that she knew that she could never be like them. To smile so at a camera one had to be born to certain things—a big house with heavy mahogany furniture and many rooms, fixed mealtimes, a mother and father who were married to each other and lived together in the same house, who would chastise and praise, who would send you to school with the proper clothes so you would look like, be like everyone else, fit neatly into the space Life had created for you.

But even though others kept pushing her, and she tried to ease, to work her way into that space too, she sometimes felt that Life had played tricks on her, and there was, after all, no space allotted for her. How else could she explain this discomfort, this pain it caused her in this her father's house to confront even the slightest event. Such as sitting at table and eating a meal.

In her mother's house she simply came in from school or wherever and sat on a stool in a corner of the lean-to kitchen or on the steps while Mama dished up a plate of food which one ate with whatever implement happened to be handy. Mama herself would more often than not stand to eat, sometimes out of the pot, and the boys too would sit wherever their fancy took them. Everything would be black from the soot from the fireside which hung now like grotesque torn ribbons from the roof. After the meal, Laura would wash the plates and pots in an enamel basin outside and sweep out the ashes from the fireside. A meal was something as natural as breathing.

But here in this house of her father's parents a meal was a ritual, something for which you prepared yourself by washing your hands and combing your hair and straightening your dress before approaching the Table. The Table was in the Dining Room and at least twelve could have comfortably sat around it. Now Laura and the grandparents huddled together at one end and in the sombre shadows of the room, Laura sometimes imagined that they so unbalanced the table that it would come toppling over on to them. At other times, when she polished the mahogany she placed each of the children of the household at a place around this table, along with their mother and father and their bewhiskered and beribboned grandparents who looked down from oval picture frames. When they were all seated, they fitted in so neatly in their slots that there was now no place left for her. Sometimes she didn't mind.

But now at the real mealtimes, the ghosts were no longer there and she sat with the old people in this empty echoing space. Each time she sat down with dread in her heart, for meal time was not a time to eat so much as a time for lessons in Table Manners.

First Mirie the cook would tinkle a little silver bell that would summon them to the dining room, and the house would stir with soft footsteps scurrying like mice and the swish of water in the basin. All the inhabitants of the house were washing and combing and straightening themselves in preparation for the Meal. She tried not to be the last one to the table for that was an occasion for chastisement. Then she had to remember to take the stiffly starched white napkin from its silver ring and place it in her lap.

"Now sit up straight, child. Don't slump so," Miss Christie would say as she lifted the covers off tureens. Miss Christie sat at the table uncovering dishes of food, but by the time Laura was served, her throat was already full and she got so confused that she would forget the knife and start to eat with her fork.

"Now dear, please use your knife. And don't cut your meat into little pieces all at once."

At the sulky look which came over Laura's face, Miss Christie would say, "You'll thank me for this one day you know, Laura. If you are going to get anywhere, you must learn how to do things properly. I just can't imagine what your mother has been doing with you all this time. How a child your age can be so ignorant of the most elementary things is beyond me."

The first time Miss Christie had mentioned her mother in this way, Laura had burst into tears and fled from the room. But now, remembering her mother's words, she refused to cry.

Laura's father had never married her mother. The question never came up for, said Myrtle without even a hint of malice in her voice, "Mr. Bertram was a young man of high estate. Very high estate." She was fond of telling this to everyone who came to her house and did not know the story of Laura's father. How Mr. Bertram had come visiting the Wheelers where Myrtle was a young servant. They had had what she liked to call 'a romance' but which was hardly even imprinted on Mr. Bertram's mind, and Laura was the result. The fact that Mr. Bertram was a man of 'high estate' had in itself elevated Miss Myrtle so far in her own eyes that no one else could understand how she could have managed to bear her sons afterwards for two undoubtedly humble fathers.

Laura had come out with dark skin but almost straight hair which Miss Myrtle did her best to improve by rubbing it with coconut oil and brushing it every day, at the same time rubbing cocoa butter into her skin to keep it soft and make it 'clear'. Miss Myrtle made the child wear a broad straw hat to keep off the sun, assuring her that her skin was 'too delicate'.

Miss Myrtle had no regrets about her encounter with Mr. Bertram even though his only acknowledgement of the birth was a ten dollar note sent to her at the time. But then he had been shipped off to the United States by his angry parents and nothing further had been heard from him.

Miss Myrtle was unfortunate in her choice of fathers for her children for none of them gave her any support. She single-handedly raised them in a little house on family land and took in sewing to augment what she got from her cultivation of food for the pot and ginger for the market. She did not worry about the fate of her sons for they were after all, boys, and well able to fend for themselves when the time came. But her daughter was a constant source of concern to her, for a child with such long curly hair, with such a straight nose, with such soft skin (too bad it was so dark) was surely destined for a life of ease and comfort. For years, Miss Myrtle sustained herself with the fantasy that one day

Laura's father would miraculously appear and take her off to live up to the station in life to which she was born. In the meantime she groomed her daughter for the role she felt she would play in life, squeezing things here and there in order to have enough to make her pretty clothes so that she was the best-dressed little girl for miles around. For the time being, it was the only gift of her heritage that she could make her.

Then after so many years passed that it was apparent even to Myrtle that Mr. Bertram had no intention of helping the child, she screwed up her courage, aided and abetted by the entire village it seemed, and wrote to Mr. Bertram's parents. She knew them well, for Mr. Bertram's mother was Mrs. Wheeler's sister and in fact came from a family that had roots in the area.

> Dear Miss Kristie
> Greetings to you in Jesus Holy Name I trust that this letter will find that you an Mister Dolfy ar enjoin the best of helth. Wel Miss Kristie I write you this letter in fear and trimblin for I am the Little One and you are the Big One but I hope you will not take me too forrard but mr. Bertram little girl now nine year old and bright as a button wel my dear Mam wish you could see her a good little girl and lern her lesson wel she would go far in Life if she could have some Help but I am a Poor Woman! With Nothing! To Help I am in the fidls morning til night. I can tel you that in looks she take after her Father but I am not Asking Mr Bertram for anything I know. He have his Life to live for but if you can fine it in Your Power to do Anything for the little girl God Richest Blessing wil come down on You May the Good Lord Bles and Keep you Miss Kristie also Mas Dolfy. And give you a long Life until you find Eternal Rest Safe in the arms of the Savor
> Your Humble Servant
> Myrtle Johnstone.

The letter caused consternation when it was received by the old people for they had almost forgotten about what the family referred to as 'Bertram's Mistake' and they thought that the woman had forgotten about it too. Although Myrtle was only 17 at the time and their son was 28, they had never forgiven what Miss Christie called the uppity black gal for seducing their son. "Dying to raise their colour all of them," Miss Christie had cried, "dying to raise their colour. That's why you can't be too careful with them." Now like a ghost suddenly materialising they could see this old scandal coming back to haunt them.

At first the two old people were angry, then as they talked about the subject for days on end, they soon dismissed their first decision which was to ignore the letter, for the little girl, no matter how common and scheming her mother was, was nevertheless family and something would have to be done about her. Eventually they decided on limited help—enough to salve their consciences but not too much so that Myrtle would get the idea that they were a limitless source of wealth. Miss Christie composed the first of her brief and cool letters to the child's mother.

> Dear Myrtle,
> In response to your call for help we are sending a little money for the child, also a parcel which should soon arrive. But please don't think that we can do this all the time as we ourselves are finding it hard to make ends meet. Besides, people who have children should worry about how they are going to support them before they have them.
> Yours Truly,
> Mrs. C. Watson

They made, of course, no reference to the child's father who was now married and living in New Jersey.

Myrtle was overjoyed to get the letter and the parcel for they were tangible indications that the child's family would indeed rescue her from a life of poverty in the mountains. Now she devoted even more care and attention to the little girl, taking pains to remind her of the fineness of her hair, the straightness of her nose, and the high estate of her father. While she allowed the child to continue to help with the chores around the house, she was no longer sent on errands. When all the other children were busy minding goats, fetching water or firewood, all of these chores in her household now fell on Laura's brothers. Myrtle was busy grooming Laura for a golden future.

Because of her mother's strictures, the child soon felt alienated from others. If she played with other children, her mother warned her not to get her clothes too dirty. Not to get too burnt in the sun. Not to talk so broad. Instead of making her filled with pride as her mother intended, these attentions made the child supremely conscious of being different from the children around her, and she soon became withdrawn and lacking in spontaneity.

Myrtle approved of the child's new quietness as a sign of 'quality' in her. She sent a flood of letters to Miss Christie, although the answers she got were meagre and few. She kept her constantly informed of the child's progress in school, of her ability to read so well, and occasionally made the child write a few sentences in the letter to her grandmother to show off her fine handwriting. Finally, one Christmas, to flesh out the image of the child she had been building up over the years, she took most of the rat-cut coffee money and took the child to the nearest big town to have her photograph taken in a professional studio.

It was a posed, stilted photograph in a style that went out of fashion thirty years before. The child was dressed in a frilly white dress trimmed with ribbons, much too long for her age. She wore long white nylon socks and white T-strap shoes. Her hair was done in perfect drop curls, with a part to the side and two front curls caught up with a large white bow. In the photograph she stood quite straight with her feet together and her right hand stiffly bent to touch an artificial rose in a vase on a rattan table beside her. She did not smile.

Her grandparents who were the recipients of a large framed print on matte paper saw a dark-skinned child with long dark hair, a straight nose, and enormous, very serious eyes. Despite the fancy clothes, everything about her had a countrified air except for the penetrating eyes which had none of the softness and shyness of country children. Miss Christie was a little embarrassed by this gift, and hid the picture in her bureau drawer for it had none of the gloss of the photos of her children and grandchildren which stood on her bureau. But she could not put the picture away entirely; something about the child haunted her and she constantly looked at it to see what in this child was of her flesh and blood. The child had her father's weak mouth, it seemed, though the defiant chin and the bold eyes undoubtedly came from her mother. Maybe it was the serious, steady, unchildlike gaze that caused Miss Christie sometimes to look at the picture for minutes at a time as if it mesmerised her. Then she would get hold of herself again and angrily put the picture back into the drawer.

Despite her better judgement, Miss Christie found herself intensely curious about this child whose mother made her into such a little paragon and whose eyes gazed out at the world so directly.

Soon, she broached the subject obliquely to her husband. One evening at dusk as the two of them sat on the verandah, she said, "Well, just look at the two of us. Look how many children and grandchildren we have, and not a one to keep our company."

"Hm. So life stay. Once your children go to town, country too lonely for them after that."

"I suppose so. But it really would be nice to have a young person about the house again." They dropped the subject then, but she kept bringing it up from time to time.

Finally she said, as if thinking about it for the first time, "But Dolphie, why don't we get Myrtle's little girl here?"

"What! And rake up that old thing again? You must be mad."

"But nobody has to know who she is."

"Then you dont know how ol'nayga fas'. They bound to find out."

"Well, they can't prove anything. She doesn't have our name. She bears her mother's name."

They argued about it on and off for weeks, then finally they decided to invite the child to stay for a week or two.

When Laura came, she was overawed by the big house, the patrician old couple who were always so clean and sweet-smelling as if laundered each day anew by Mirie the cook. She fell even more silent, speaking only when spoken to, and then in a low voice which could hardly be heard.

Miss Christie was gratified that she was so much lighter than the photograph (indeed, Myrtle had quarrelled with the photographer for just this reason) and although she was exactly like a country mouse, she did fill the house with her presence. Already Miss Christie was busy planning the child's future, getting her into decent clothes, correcting her speech, erasing her country accent, teaching her table manners, getting her to take a complete bath every day—a fact which was so novel to the child who came from a place where everyone bathed in a bath pan once a week since the water had to be carried on their heads one mile uphill from the spring.

In the child Miss Christie saw a lump of clay which held every promise of being moulded into something satisfactory. The same energy with which Miss Christie entered into a 'good' marriage, successfully raised six children and saw that they made good marriages themselves, that impelled her to organise the Mothers Union and the School Board—that energy was now to be expended on this latest product which relatives in the know referred to as 'Bertram's stray shot'.

Although her husband fussed and fumed, he too liked the idea of having a child in the house once more though he thought her a funny little thing who hardly made a sound all day, unlike the boisterous family they had reared. And so, as if in a dream, the child found herself permanently transported from her mother's two-room house to this mansion of her father's.

Of course her father was never mentioned and she only knew it was him from the photograph because he had signed it. She gazed often at this photograph, trying to transmute it into a being of flesh and blood from which she had been created, but failed utterly. In fact, she was quite unable to deduce even the smallest facet of his character from the picture. All that she saw was a smiling face that in some indefinable way looked like all the faces in the other photographs. All were bland and sweet. In none of these faces were there lines, or frowns, or blemishes, or marks of ugliness such as a squint eye, or a broken nose, or kinky hair, or big ears, or broken teeth which afflicted all the other people she had known. Faced with such perfection, she ceased to look at herself in the mirror.

She had gone to live there during the summer holidays and Miss Christie took every opportunity to add polish to her protege whom she introduced everywhere as 'my little adopted'. As part of the child's education, Miss Christie taught her to polish mahogany furniture and to bake cakes, to polish silver and clean panes of glass, all of which objects had been foreign to the child's former upbringing.

The child liked to remain inside the house, which was cool and dark and shaded, for outside, with its huge treeless lawn and beyond, the endless pastures, frightened her.

She had grown up in a part of the mountain cockpits where a gravel road was the only thing that broke the monotony of the humpbacked hills and endless hills everywhere. There were so many hills that for half of the day their house and yard were damp and dark and moss grew on the sides of the clay path. It was only at midday when the sun was directly overhead that they received light. The houses were perched precariously up the hillsides with slippery paths leading to them from the road, and if anyone bothered to climb to the tops of the hills, all they would see was more mountains. Because it was so hilly the area seemed constantly to be in a dark blue haze, broken only by the occasional hibiscus or croton and the streams of brightly coloured birds dashing through the foliage. They were hemmed in by the mountains on all sides and Laura liked it, because all her life was spent in space that was enclosed and finite, protecting her from what dangers she did not even know.

And then, from the moment she had journeyed to the railway station some ten miles away and got on to the train and it had begun to travel through the endless canefields, she had begun to feel afraid. For suddenly the skies had opened up so wide all around her; the sun beat down and there was the endless noisy clacking of the train wheels. She felt naked and anxious, as if suddenly exposed, and there was nowhere to hide.

When she got off the train at the other end, there were no cane-fields there, but the land was still flat and open, for this was all rolling pastureland. Her curiosity about the herds of cattle she saw grazing in the shade of an occasional tree could not diminish the fear she felt at being so exposed.

Her father's parents' house was set on the top of a hill from where they could see for miles in all directions. Whenever she went outside she felt dizzy for the sky was so wide it was like being enclosed within a huge blue bowl. The summer was cloudless. And the hills were so far away they were lost in blue. But then summer came to an end and it was time for her to go to school. The nearest school was three miles away. Her grandmother, deciding that this was too far for her to walk—though walking greater distances had meant nothing in her former life—had arranged for her to travel to and from school on the bus which went by at the right time each day. This single fact impressed her most as showing the power and might of her grandmother.

She was glad of the bus for she did not want to walk alone to school. Now the clear summer days were ending, the clouds had begun to gather in the sky, fat cumulus clouds that travelled in packs and in this strange and empty country became ugly and menacing. They reminded her of the pictures she used to get in Sunday School showing Jesus coming to earth again, floating down on one of these fat white clouds. And because the Jesus of their church was a man who had come to judge and punish sinners, these pictures only served to remind her that she was a sinner and that God would one day soon appear out of the sky flashing fire and brimstone to judge and condemn her. And until he came, the clouds were there to watch her. For why else did they move, change themselves, assume shapes of creatures awesome and frightful, if not to torment her with her unworthiness? Sometimes when she stood on the barbecue and looked back at the house outlined against the sky, the house itself seemed to move and she would feel a wave of dizziness as if the whole earth was moving away off course and leaving her standing there alone in the emptiness.

She would run quickly inside and find Miss Christie or Mirie or somebody. As long as it was another human being to share the world with.

While all day long she would feel a vague longing for her mother and brothers and all the people she had known since childhood, she never felt lonely, for if her mother had given her nothing else, in taking her out of one life without guaranteeing her placement in the next, she had unwittingly raised her for a life of solitude. Here in this big house she wandered from room to room and said nothing all day, for now her lips were sealed from shyness. To her newly sensitised ears, her words came out flat and unmusical and she would look with guilt at the photographs and silently beg pardon for being there.

There were no other children around the house and she was now so physically removed from others that she had no chance to meet anyone. Sometimes she would walk down the driveway to the tall black gate hoping that some child would pass along and talk so that they could be friends, but whenever anyone happened by, her shyness would cause her to hide behind the stone pillar so they would not see her. And although her grandmother said nothing on the subject, she instinctively knew after a while that she would never in this place find anyone good enough to bring into Miss Christie's house.

Although she liked the feeling of importance it gave her to get on and off the bus at the school gate—the only child to do so—most times she watched with envy the other children walking home from school, playing, yelling, and rolling in the road. They wore no shoes and she envied them this freedom, for her feet, once free like theirs except for Sundays, were now encased in socks and patent leather shoes handed down from one or the other of the rightful grandchildren who lived in Kingston or New York.

Most days the bus was on time. Every morning she would wait by the tall black gate for the bus to arrive. The bus would arrive on time every day. Except Thursday. Sometimes on Thursdays the bus wouldn't arrive until late evening. She would nevertheless every Thursday go to the gates and wait, knowing in her heart that the bus would not come. Miss Christie would sometimes walk out and stand by the gate and look the road up and down.

Sometimes Mass Dolphie passing on his way from one pasture to the next would rein in his horse and would also stand by the gate and look up the road. All three would stand silently. The road swayed white in an empty world. The silence hummed like telegraph wires. Her life hung in the air waiting on a word from Miss Christie. Her chest began to swell like a balloon getting bigger and bigger. "The bus isn't coming. You'll have to walk," Miss Christie pronounced with finality.

"Oh Miss Christie, just a few minutes more," she begged. It was the only thing she begged for. But she knew that the bus wouldn't come, and now, at this terribly late hour, she would have to walk alone the three miles to school in a world that was empty of people. She would walk very fast, the dust of the marl road swirling round her ankles, along this lonely road that curved past the graveyard. Above, following every step of the way, the fat clouds sat smirking and smug in the pale blue sky. She hated them for all they knew about her. Her clumsiness, her awkwardness, the fact that she did not belong in this light and splendid place. They sat there in judgement on her every Thursday. Thursday, the day before market day. The day of her Armageddon.

Thursdays the old bus would sit on the road miles above, packed with higglers and their crocus bags, bankras and chickens. The bus would start right enough: somewhere on the road above the bus would start in the dawn hours, full and happy. And then, a few miles after, the bus would gently shudder and like a torn metal bird would ease to a halt with a cough and a sigh and settle down on the road, too tired and worn out to move. It would remain there until evening, the market women sitting in the shade and fanning the flies away with the men importantly gathered around the machine, arguing and cursing until evening when the earth was cool again and the driver would go slowly, everything patched up till next Thursday when the higglers descended with their crocus bags and their bankras, their laughter and their girth and their quarrelling and their ferocious energy which would prove too much for the old bus. Then with a sigh it would again lie still on the road above her. Every Thursday.

Sometimes though if she managed to dawdle long enough Miss Christie would say, "Heavens, It's 10 o'clock. You can't go to school again."

"O Miss Christie" she would cry silently 'thank you, thank you.'

Sometimes when she didn't go to school Mass Dolphie would let her dig around in his Irish potato patch collecting the tiny potatoes for herself.

Digging potatoes was safe. She could not see the sky. And she never knew when a really big potato would turn up among all the tiny ones.

"Like catching fish, eh?" Mass Dolphie said and she agreed though she didn't know how that was having never seen the sea. But she would laugh too.

One day they got a letter from the child's father. He was coming home with his wife on a visit. It wasn't long after their initial joy at hearing the news that the grandparents realised that difficulties were bound to arise with the child. For one thing, they hadn't told their son about her, being a little ashamed that they had not consulted him at all before coming to the decision to take her. Besides, it was a little awkward to write to him about such matters at his home, since from all they had heard of American women they believed that there was a strong possibility that his wife would open his letters.

Their immediate decision, was to send the child home, but that too presented certain problems since it was still during the school term and they couldn't quite make up their minds what they would tell her mother to explain a change of heart. They certainly couldn't tell her the truth for even to them the truth seemed absurd: that they wanted to return the little girl because her father was coming. For once, Miss Christie was at a loss. It was Mr. Dolphie who took a firm line. "Write and ask him what to do," he instructed his wife, "after all, it's his child. If he doesn't want her here when he comes then he can tell us what we should do with her."

They were suprised but not overly so when their son wrote that they should do nothing about the child as he would be greatly amused to see her.

Mr. Dolphie didn't see any cause for amusement in the situation and thought that it was just like his youngest son to take a serious thing and make a joke of it and all in all act in a reckless and irresponsible manner. He had certainly hoped that Bertram had finally settled down to the seriousness of life.

Long before they told the child the news of her father's coming, she knew, for without deliberately listening to their conversations, she seemed to absorb and intuitively understand everything that happened in the house.

Since hearing the news there had been a joy in her heart, for her mother had told her so often that one day this mysterious father of hers would come and claim her as his own that she had grown to believe it. She knew that he would come and rescue her from fears as tenuous as clouds and provide her with nothing but bright Thursdays.

But when she searched out the photograph from the ones on the bureau, his face held that unreadable, bland smile and his eyes gave off nothing that would show her just how he intended to present his love for her.

One day Miss Christie said to her, "Laura, our son is coming on a visit. Mr. Bertram." She said it as if the child and the man bore no relationship to each other. "He is coming with his wife. We haven't seen him for so many years."

Yes. Since I was born, Laura thought.

"Now Laura, I except you to be on your best behaviour when they are here."

"Yes mam."

Laura showed no emotion at all as Miss Christie continued to chat on the subject. How does one behave with a father? Laura thought. She had no experience of this. There were so few fathers among all the people she knew.

Miss Christie turned the house upside down in a frenzy of preparation for her son's visit. Without being told so, Laura understood that such preparation was not so much for the son as for his white wife. She was quite right, for as Miss Christie told Mirie, "These foreign women are really too fresh, you know. Half of them don't really come from anywhere but they believe that everybody from Jamaica is a monkey and live in trees. I am really glad my son is bringing her here so that she can see how we live." Laura silently assented to that, for who in the wide world could keep up a life that was as spotless and well ordered as Miss Christie's?

Laura longed to talk to somebody about her father. To find out what he was really like. But she did not want to ask Miss Christie. She thought of writing secretly to her mother and telling her that Mr. Bertram was coming, asking what he was really like, but she was too timid to do anything behind Miss Christie's back for Miss Christie was so all-knowing she was bound to find out. Sometimes she wanted to ask Mirie the cook who had been working with the family for nearly forty years. But although she got into the habit of dropping into the roomy kitchen and sitting at the table there for hours, she never got up the nerve to address Mirie, and Mirie, a silent and morose woman, never addressed her at all. She believed, though, that Mirie liked her, for frequently, without saying a word, she would give her some tidbit from the pot, or a sample of the cookies, or bread and guava jelly, though she knew that Miss Christie did not approve of eating between meals. But apart from grunting every now and then as she went about her tasks, Mirie said nothing at all on the subject of Mr. Bertram or any other being. Laura wished that Mirie would talk to her, for she found the kitchen the most comforting part of the house.

Her father and his wife arrived one day when she was at school. When she got home, she was too shy to go in, and was hanging around trying to hide behind a post when Miss Christie spotted her.

"Oh Laura, come and meet my son," said Miss Christie and swept her into the living room. "Mina," she said to a yellow-haired woman sitting there, "this is Laura, the little adopted I was telling you about." Laura first vaguely made out the woman, then Mass Dolphie, then a strange man in the shadows, but she was too shy to give him more than a covert glance. He did not address her but gave a smile which barely moved his lips. In days to come she would get accustomed to that smile, which was not as bland as in the photograph. To his daughter, he paid no more attention. It was his wife who fussed over the little girl, asking questions and exclaiming over her curls. Laura could hardly understand anything the woman said, but was impressed at how trim and neat she was, at the endless fascination of her clothes, her jewellery, her laughter, her accent, her perfume, her assurance. Looking at her long polished nails, Laura had a picture of her mother's hands, the nails cracked and broken like a man's from her work in the fields; of her mother's dark face, her coarse shrill voice. And she was bitterly ashamed. Knowing the mother she had come from, it was no wonder, she thought, that her father could not acknowledge her.

She was extremely uneasy with the guests in the house. Their presence strained to the fullest the new social graces that Miss Christie had inculcated in her. Now she had a twofold anxiety: not to let her mother down to Miss Christie, and not to let Miss Christie down in front of this white woman from the United States of America.

For all the woman's attentions, it was the man that she wanted to attend her, acknowledge her, love her. But he never did. She contrived at all times to be near him, to sit in his line of vision, to 'accidentally' appear on the path when he went walking through the pastures. The man did not see her. He loved to talk, his voice going on and on in a low rumble like the waves of the sea she had never seen, the ash on his cigarette getting longer till it fell on his clothes or Miss Christie's highly polished floor. But he never talked to her. This caused her even greater anxiety than Miss Christie's efforts at 'polishing' her, for while she felt that Miss Christie was trying, however painful it was, to build her up, she could not help feeling that her father's indifference did nothing so much as to reduce her, nullify her. Laura would have wondered if he knew who she was if she hadn't known that Miss Christie had written to him on the subject. She decided then that all his indifference was merely part of a play, that he wanted to surprise her when he did claim her, and was working up to one magical moment of recognition that would thereafter illuminate both their lives forever and ever. In the daytime that is how she consoled herself but at nights she cried in the little room where she slept alone in the fearful shadow of the breadfruit tree against the window pane.

Then Thursday came round again and in this anxiety she even forgot about her father. As usual the bus was late and Laura hung around the gate hoping that Miss Christie would forget she was there until it was too late to walk to school. The road curved white and lonely in the empty morning, silent save for the humming of bees and the beating of her own heart. Then Miss Christie and Mina appeared on the verandah and obviously saw her. Talking together, they started to walk slowly towards the gate where she stood, trapped by several impulses. Laura's heart beat faster then almost stopped as her father appeared from the orange grove and approached the two women. Now the three of them were walking towards her. They were now near enough for Laura to hear what they were saying but her eyes were only on her father.

"Oh dear, that old bus. Laura is going to be late again," Miss Christie said.

"Oh for chrissake. Why don't you stop fussing so much about the bloody little bastard," her son shouted.

Laura heard no more for after one long moment when her heart somersaulted once. There was no time for hearing anything else for her feet of their own volition had set off at a run down the road and by the time she got to the school gates she had made herself an orphan and there were no more clouds.

The Myth of Music

By Rachel M. Harper

Rachel M. Harper (1972–), a Boston native who now lives in Providence, Rhode Island, won the 2002 Fellowship in Fiction from the Rhode Island State Council on the Arts for an excerpt from her first novel, *Brass Ankle Blues*. Her poems and short fiction have appeared in *Chicago Review, African American Review,* and *Prairie Schooner.* Her jazz-inspired riff, "The Myth of Music," was written as a Christmas gift for her father, the poet Michael S. Harper.

for my father

If music can be passed on
like brown eyes or a strong
left hook, this melody
is my inheritance, lineage traced
through a title track,
displayed on an album cover
that you pin to the wall
as art, oral history taught
on a record player, the lessons
sealed into the grooves like fact.
This is the only myth I know.
I sit on the hardwood
floors of a damp November,

my brother dealing cards
from an incomplete deck,
and I don't realize that this
moment is the definition
of family, collective memory
cut in rough-textured tones,
the voice of a horn so familiar
I don't know I'm listening,
don't know I'm singing,
a child's improvisation
of Giant Steps or Impressions:
songs without lyrics
can still be sung.

In six months, when my mother
is 2,000 miles away, deciding
if she wants to come home,
I will have forgotten
this moment, the security
of her footsteps, the warmth
of a radiator on my back and you
present in the sound of typing
your own accompaniment,
multiphonics disguised as chords
in a distant room, speakers set
on high to fill the whole house
with your spirit, your call
as a declaration of love.

But the music will remain.
The timeless notes of jazz
too personal to play out loud,
stay locked in the rhythm
of my childhood, memories fading

like the words of a lullaby,
come to life in a saxophone's blow.
They lie when they say
music is universal—this is my song,
the notes like fingerprints
as delicate as breath.
I will not share this air
with anyone
but you.

Myth-Making

Ocean

By Shay Youngblood

Shay Youngblood (1960–), was raised in Columbus, Georgia, and lives in New York. A poet, playwright and the author of two novels, she's been awarded a Pushcart Short Story Prize, the Lorraine Hansberry Playwriting Award, the Quality Paperback Book New Voices Award, and several NAACP Theater Awards. In this excerpt from her first novel, *Soul Kiss*, a child left with spinster aunts calls back memories of the dreamy mother whose sudden unraveling changed everything.

The first evening Mama doesn't come back, I make a sandwich with leaves from her good-bye letter. I want to eat her words. I stare at the message written on the stiff yellowed paper as if the shaky scrawl would stand up and speak to me. *Mama loves you. Wait here for me.* I want her to take back the part about waiting. After crushing the paper into two small balls I flatten them with my fist, then stuff them into the envelope my aunt Faith gave me after Mama had gone. I feel weak as water and stone cold as I sit with my legs dangling over the edge of the thick mattress on the high iron-frame bed, reading by the dim lamplight. I unfold the tiger-print scarf Mama gave me and lay in its center the good-bye sandwich, a small book of rhymes, a biscuit from dinner wrapped in wax paper, and her pink radio that fits in the palm of my hand. I tie the ends of the scarf twice across the body of my treasures and hold it to my heart. I turn off the light by the bed and make my way across the bedroom in the dark.

I tiptoe down the stairs. When I hit the third step from the bottom the wood complains in the darkness. I drop my bundle and the radio comes alive. Elvis Presley singing "Love Me Tender." Aunt Merleen appears like a giant at the top of the stairs in a red union suit with a pair of men's leather mules on her feet, her fine black hair hidden by a lace night cap. Long and lean with fiery skin the color of Georgia dirt, she has a shotgun in her hands pointed at me.

"Make a wrong move and you're dead. Come stand in the light," Aunt Merleen orders.

Aunt Faith emerges from the darkness like a spirit in a white cotton nightgown, big and wide, silver hair wild around her shoulders. Her plump fingers aim a flashlight at the bottom of the stairs. I step into the circle of light and look down at the radio and the stair that betrayed me.

"Mariah!" Aunt Merleen shouts, as if my name was a crime. I take tiny steps backwards, away from the light.

"Child, where are you going this time of night?" Aunt Faith's voice is soft as Mama's scarf.

"My mama's waiting on me. I'm going home," I say to the bottom of the stairs.

"Why don't you stay here and wait for her," Aunt Faith insists.

"You don't like me. I want my mama," I say quietly.

Aunt Faith throws her enormous weight from side to side as she walks. Huge breasts merge with the rolls of flesh wrapped around her waist. Her thighs and legs are long and solid like the trunks of trees. She is warm beige, the color of my mother's pressed face powder, with long, silver hair. Soft, round, and gray. She comes down the stairs and sits on the bottom step. She speaks to me from a distance. Her voice, sweet and sad, floats to me through the darkness. I almost reach out to her. I need the comfort of arms to hold me.

"We're just old. It's been a long time since we been around children. We'll get used to one another. Come on back upstairs. Your mama'll be back soon. She had some . . . " There is hesitation between the sweet threads of her voice. "Some business to take care of."

Aunt Merleen, tall and stormy, repeats the word "business," twisting it into a hard question. She sucks her teeth in disgust like my mama would do when she was disbelieving or fed up. I wonder what kind of business would make Mama leave me with these sour old women.

"You're a big girl," Mama often said, with confidence, when she had left me alone in our apartment for a night or two sometimes. She had never left me with strangers. These are her aunts, she had known them all her life, but I've only met them this morning and I don't like them and it seems they don't like me either.

"Let's get something straight. I don't allow Elvis Presley music to play in my house," Aunt Merleen roars. "He told the world the only thing a nigger could do for him was shine his shoes and buy his records when he stole every note he sing from colored lips. Turn that mess off."

She gives me a cold look from way up there at the top of the stairs, then heads off to bed with the shotgun over her shoulder.

I turn off the radio, then collect the book and the biscuit and the sandwich of words. I follow Aunt Faith back upstairs one sad step at a time and into the room I am to sleep in. I sit on the bed, grinding the biscuit between my fingers until it is fine as dust, letting it fall onto the slip of brown wax paper. I sprinkle the crumbs around the bed so that any ghosts that might come in the night will eat them and not bother me in my sleep. Mama taught me to do this after countless ghosts had slipped past the salt sprinkled across our doorways and windowsills to interrupt my dreams. Mama believes in spirits and knows their ways. After a while I lie down on the bed with the scarf across my face, breathing in the bergamot smell of my mother's hair, tasting bitter tears. I take small bites of the sandwich, careful to taste every word she left me, even the ones I don't understand, then swallow each with a tear or two.

When me and Mama lived together the world was a perfect place to be a little girl. I adored Mama and she adored me in return. No one else mattered. One of my first memories was watching her dress for work. Next to her reddish-brown skin, softened each night with a thin layer of Vaseline and cold cream, she wore a pink satin slip. Pink was romantic, she said, the color of love and laughing. Mama's slanted eyes, a gift, she said, from her Cherokee grandfather, were dreamy remembering how my father told her she looked like a princess when she wore pink. On the outside she wore white. Her nurse's uniform was starched, white-white, a petite size eight, with a tiny white cap perched on her short, tight, nappy curls, dyed blonde not quite down to her dark roots. White silk stockings veiled her long thin legs. Silent crepe-soled white shoes she'd let me lace up held her perfect, size six feet. Every weekday morning, on her way to the military hospital, she would walk me to school past the gray army barracks to the steel, bread-shaped huts, where we lined up for the pledge of allegiance to the flag.

Armed with a sandwich, a piece of fruit, and a word written on a small square of pink paper folded twice, I was ready for anything. The word was written in blue ink in my mother's fancy script . . . *pretty* . . . *sweet* . . . *blue* . . . *music* . . . *dream* . . . Sometimes she gave me words in Spanish . . . *bonita* . . . *dulce* . . . *sueños* . . . *agua* . . . *azul* . . . The word I kept in my mouth, repeated like a prayer when I missed her. Mama told me that she would be thinking of the same word all day. That thought made our time apart bearable. Before she left me at the door of the school she would whisper the word into my ear. I'd close my eyes and she would kiss me quickly on my neck, then let go of my hand. She always watched me through the window as I walked to my seat near the back of the room. We would mouth our word to each other once more before she disappeared. When Mama came for me in the afternoon I would take her hand and swing our arms as if we were both little girls on a walk.

"Blue. B-L-U-E. Blue is the color of sad music. Blue." I would pronounce, spell, and give the meaning of our word. Sometimes on our walks we invented words and spoke to each other in new languages. As praise, Mama would tickle me under my chin, then cup my face in her warm delicate hands and close her eyes. She would press her lips full on mine and give me what she called a soul kiss. My whole body would fever from my mother's embrace.

"I love you, Mama," I would say, looking into her eyes.

"I love you more," she answered every time, looking deep inside me.

I could read books before I could walk, Mama said. By the time I was three years old I was sitting on her lap reading to her from the newspaper. I don't remember all this, but Mama said it's so. I was so smart I got special treatment in school. "Teachers' pet" they called me, and other names I grew to hate. I didn't make friends, but I didn't need them. I had Mama. All my days at school were spent passing the time, waiting for Mama to free me from the steel breadbox. She taught me all the important things there were to know.

We lived on a military base near Manhattan, Kansas. Flat squares of grass occupied by long flat gray squares of apartments one after the other for miles. There was a swing in our backyard where Mama spent hours pushing me into the sky. Sometimes I sang songs into the wind, catching pieces of cloud in my throat and swallowing them for safe keeping.

We lived in a tiny apartment. The bare walls were an unpleasant weak shade of green transformed at night by Mama's colored light bulbs into a pink velvet womb. In the living room an overstuffed red crushed velvet sofa sat in the middle of the room on gray-flecked linoleum tiles. There was a table at one end of the room and a lamp with a red-fringed shade and a big black radio on top of it. The radio's antenna was wrapped with aluminum foil so we could get better reception for the blues and jazz music that came on in the evening from someplace so far away that pulsing static accompanied each song. Mama kept the plain white shades pulled down past the window sills "to keep our business to ourselves," she said. The living room opened onto the kitchen where a bright yellow and pink flowered plastic tablecloth was spread over a wobbly card table surrounded by three silver folding chairs. A bare white bulb hung from the center of the white ceiling. White metal cabinets lined one wall and underneath them, an old-fashioned double sink with one side deeper that the other. Mama said she used to wash me in the deep part of the sink when I was small enough to crawl back inside her stomach where she said I was once small enough to fit. I could imagine no greater comfort. The bedroom was just big enough to fit the queen-sized bed and chest of drawers which held all our neatly folded clothes among fragrant cedar balls. A clean white tiled bathroom had a toilet that ran all night and a sink that dripped but also a deep, creamy white enamel tub that was big enough to fit me and Mama together just right.

At night we would eat directly from tin cans heated on a one-eyed hot plate while we listened to music on the radio. In summer she said it was too hot to light the oven, in winter she said she was too tired to cook. On special days we had picnics, selecting cans of potted meat, stewed tomatoes, fruit cocktail, applesauce, and pork and beans to spread on saltine crackers or spear with sturdy toothpicks and wash down with sweet lemon iced tea. Mama just didn't have any use for cooking and I never missed it because this was all I knew. After supper we would take a bath together, soaping each other with a soft pink sponge. Sometimes she let me touch her breasts. In my tiny hands they felt like holding clouds must. Like delicate overripe fruit. Her nipples were dark circles that grew into thick buttons when I pressed them gently as if I were an elevator operator. I kneeled in the warm soapy water between her legs letting water pour over her breasts from between my small fingers and watched her as she leaned back in the tub, her narrow eyes closed, hair damp and matted, mouth slightly open as if she were holding her breath. I felt so close to her, as if my skin were hers and we were one brown body. She didn't seem to mind my curious fingers touching and soaping every curve and mystery of her body. There were no boundaries, no place I could not explore. After our bath we lay on the sofa in our clean white pajamas, listening to the radio until we fell asleep. I loved sleeping with her warm belly pressed into my back, one arm across my waist. Sometimes she would hold my hand as we slept.

On weekends me and Mama played Ocean. Around bedtime she would get dressed in beautiful clothes and go out dancing. She left me alone with instructions to stay on the sofa, warning me that if I got off, even to go to the bathroom, I might drown in the ocean. She gave me toast left over from breakfast which I tossed bit by bit to the sharks in the dangerous waters all around my island so they wouldn't nibble on my toes when I slept. I remember a pink lamp with a pink bulb burning and the radio turned down low. A few drops of scotch and lots of pink punch swirled in a chipped blue china cup burned sweetly in my throat. I drifted further out to sea than I imagined I could swim. The sharks began to circle as my eyelids dropped and the horizon across the ocean grew hazy. The sound of small waves rocked me like arms into the deepest part of sleep. Usually I began dreaming right after Mama left.

I look like my mother. My hair is dyed blonde, my eyes are narrow, shaped like almonds and lined in black ink. My lips are rich with soft, pink kisses. Her hair. Her eyes. Her lips. I even have my mother's breasts. Her thick, delicious nipples. In my favorite, secret dream I dress in her clothes, tight-waisted, sparkly, pink dresses, and dance in a circle of light. I dance until my feet become so light that I float across the dance floor, up toward the ceiling of moving stars, then fly out of my window into other oceans.

Mama was always there when I woke up. One time she woke me in the middle of the night crying. She told me that a special friend of hers, a hospital doctor, was being sent overseas and because Mama wasn't his wife—he had one already—she couldn't go. Because Mama was sad, I was sad. Her tears were mine. When Mama was crying, it seemed as if the whole world were crying.

Before long, right out of the blue, Mama began to change. I was scared and confused. After school I wanted to tell her about my new classmates in second grade: the Korean girl who put her hands to her face and cried quietly all day; the red-haired, blue-eyed boy from Arkansas who talked like he had rocks in his mouth; the dark-skinned, wide-eyed girl named Meera with clouds of jet-black hair she let me touch at recess and whose mother was an Indian from India. I had a new friend, new books, and a new teacher, but Mama wasn't interested in any of it. She seemed to be sleepwalking through our lives. More and more I was in charge. She let me do everything. In the afternoons I led us home. Her movements became slower, she walked as if strong hands gripped her ankles. Her eyes were dull and her voice weak. Sometimes she wouldn't speak to me, but would mouth our word for the day while I untied her shoes and kneaded feeling back into her toes. I unhooked the stockings from their garters, rolling the silk carefully down her exhausted legs. She would fall asleep, and I would fill a small blue pan with warm water and soak her feet, massaging them gently. I would unbutton her white uniform and hang it in the closet. The wig she had started wearing was curly and dark. I would slide it off her head and place it on its stand. I would take a comb and scratch the dandruff from her scalp, oiling it with bergamot while she dozed, wondering why her hair had begun to fall out. It was dry and coarse and no longer blonde. I would watch her, slumped into the sofa in her pink satin slip, watching the rise and fall of her breasts. Curling up in her lap, I would smooth the satin over the rise of her breasts with both my hands pressing the shape of her body from shoulders to waist, over and over again. Her eyes stayed closed, her breathing raw and hollow. Sometimes Mama would sleep for whole days when she wasn't working. When she woke up she wanted water. Cool water.

Mama had an answer for everything even when she didn't know.

"Where is my father?" I would ask her in the lazy pink light before we fell asleep at night.

"In Mexico, painting the sky blue." She drew pictures with her answers.

"Is he handsome?" I asked, secretly hoping for more.

"Very handsome. You have your father's hands," she'd say, kissing my fingers, each one.

Her voice was twilight, and the stories she told me about him sounded like fairy tales that found their way into my dreams. Did

I remember them or did I dream them? She never spoke of him outside of these times between waking and dreaming.

I would close my eyes to listen, seeing every detail, my imagination filling in all the blank spaces.

"How did you meet him? Tell me everything about him," I demanded. Mama closed her eyes and drifted beyond my reach. She tossed me bits of stories to nibble on. I devoured the nights, the days of her memories, growing fat from their richness. The details of her stories changed over time. The season, the city, the natural disaster that took place the day they met, the color of his eyes.

"I was happy then," she would begin each time. "I was so happy then."

One legend began: "It was springtime, in California. A light breeze was blowing off the ocean. I had just come on duty when he walked into the emergency room. A cut from his head was bleeding. He had fallen off a ladder. There was pale blue paint all over his face and arms. I thought he had fallen from the sky, he was so beautiful, like an angel. His eyes were so black, I was afraid I would be hypnotized by them. I was taking his blood pressure when the room started to slip sideways. The earth shook me like a nervous child, and I fell into his wide, blue arms. My mind was racing so fast I could see through him. I could see you. Me being earth and him being sky, I knew we would have an angel child. And we did. I wanted to name you Angelita, Walks with Angels, but he said no, so we called you Mariah after his mother."

Other times the story went: "It was winter in New York. It was so cold the day I met your father, my eyelashes froze, and he melted them with his breath."

Sometimes in her memory, they discovered each other on a windswept Caribbean beach: "Your father was at the top of a tall ladder the first time I saw him. A strong wind blew him right into my arms. When we first met, he painted pictures of me every day. Orange bodies with yellow faces, purple arms and red hair. He drank raspberry beer and rubbed my feet with mint leaves. When I met your father there was a strong wind in my hair twisting my mind like a hurricane."

In my mother's stories my father was always handsome and always, always there was pale blue paint all over his face and arms. I grew to love him too.

At school, me and my friends Meera and David, the blue-eyed boy from Arkansas, played Army during recess. We invented wars and fought against invisible armies of dragons and sea creatures. We always won by the time recess was over and what I liked most was that we were always on the same side.

Mama's beautiful blue script was replaced by shaky, uncertain block letters written in pencil or with a broken red crayon. The words on the slips of paper began to change. *Vieja . . . lluvia . . . vé vé . . . lagrimas . . . mohosas . . .* x's and o's. Once she filled a small square of paper with z's and q's. Sometimes the paper was wet with her tears. Her writing became hard to read, the lines, no longer separated or curved, going nowhere. She seemed hurt and nervous, as if she were afraid of everything. One morning she forgot to give me a word altogether. When I reminded her she pulled a torn scrap of paper from the pocket of her uniform. Her fingers were trembling and couldn't hold the pencil I gave her, so she pressed the paper to her lips twice, then crushed it into my hand. At lunchtime, after eating the slice of dry bread and bruised banana in my lunch bag, I unfolded the paper Mama gave me and pressed it to my lips. I closed my eyes and tried to feel the warmth of her paper kisses.

One time Mama took me to the hospital where she worked. I waited out in the emergency room. One of the nurses gave me a lollipop and asked me if I could do any of the new dances. I said, "No, but I can sing." I stood up on a chair and opened my mouth. I don't know why Billie Holiday came out. "God Bless the Child" haunted the air. Sometimes Mama sang it when she was sad. The nurses and some of the sick people clapped when I was done. Mama's doctor friend was there; he said it sounded like there was an angel in my throat. I explained to him that I put clouds there for safekeeping. He said I was just like my mother. I liked him even though he was the one my mama always seemed to be crying about. I let him kiss me because Mama said it was all right. Up close he smelled sweet, like a woman not my mother.

It was April by the time we left Kansas. I was sure I'd miss ice cream floats at the commissary, swinging into the sky, and my friends Meera and David, but I was hoping what I missed most would come back, the sound of Mama laughing. The day we left, Mama picked me up from school just after lunch. She was wearing a tiger-print scarf tied under her chin, her eyes hidden by large dark glasses. She wore a capped sleeved navy blue dress that showed off her figure. White buttons shaped like little boats floated down the front of the dress to the hem just below her knee. The dress was so tight across the front I could see flashes of her pink satin slip between the buttons when she breathed. She wore dark stockings with runs in them, and scuffed black high-heeled pumps. A hard green suitcase, her red sweater and her box-shaped fake alligator purse were in one hand, my hand was in the other. We were going to take the train to Georgia. She put five kisses in my pocket.

Buildings, gates, and sidewalks rolled behind us. I only looked back once as we were leaving the base on a big green bus. I waved good-bye as if my friends could see me. The huge flag we pledged allegiance to every morning was flapping in the wind halfway down the pole in an enormous blue sky. I saw two soldiers salute each other in front of the library. If we hadn't been leaving it would've been a perfect day. Mama said somebody important had died. She was crying so hard I thought she knew this Martin Luther King, Jr., personally.

"Mama, why we leaving here?" I asked as we boarded the train at the station.

"We ain't leaving, we going someplace else," she said sadly.

"Why, Mama?" I whined.

After a long silence she said, " I like to travel."

Mama let me sit by the window. Small towns and big cities spread out before us. I saw a sign that read: YOU ARE LEAVING THE SUNFLOWER STATE. One station after the other. Babies cried and newspapers rattled open and shut. The train's rhythm rocked me to sleep and shook me awake. The tall, bony conductor whose broom-colored hair stuck out from under his gray hat like stiff toothpicks smiled at Mama with crooked teeth and winked at her. Mama gave him her ticket without even looking up. People got on and off the train. They hugged good-bye and kissed hello outside my window. The new conductor's smooth brown face leaned in close and he whispered to Mama that we'd crossed into Mississippi. We had to change our seats twice. Mama said the view was better, but I didn't like riding backward or sitting next to the toilet. I wondered who would be waiting for us at the end of our ride. I kept looking out the window until all I could see was me, and Mama's reflection sipping ladylike from a big, brown medicine bottle she kept in her purse.

When our train rolled into Georgia, Mama woke me up. WEL-COME TO THE PEACH STATE. Tall green trees and red dirt. Rusty piles of metal in unmarked fields of car graveyards. Coke machines sat on the front porches of little wooden houses that looked about to fall down. Mama looked scared. She started talking as if she was trying to convince me of something. She left spaces wide enough for me to ask questions, as if I knew enough to ask the right ones. Her voice changed. She sounded dif-ferent, almost like a little girl. She sounded as if she believed half of what she was telling me. She offered her words to me like sweet poison.

"I'm gonna take you to visit your great aunties. Aunt Faith and Aunt Merleen. You be nice. You be nice, you hear? Do what they tell you." She licked her pointing finger and used it to brush down my eyebrows. "They're strict, but they're good people. I used to stay with them when I was little. They like things clean."

I squinted as she picked sleep out of the corners of my eyes.

"I would stay with my aunties when my mama had to go work on Saturday nights and sometimes when she'd go down to Florida to pick fruit I'd stay with them all summer. They was some kinda nice. They're ladies . . . and they know how to cook." Mama

stopped talking and looked out the window like she was remembering and seeing at the same time all their niceness. Her eyes were hungry—maybe she was looking forward to a plateful of something good.

"Maybe they'll teach you how to cook a red velvet cake or a blackberry cobbler. I haven't had a cobbler since . . . oh, I don't know when. They sure do know how to cook. Oh, and Aunt Faith, she play the piano. Maybe she'll teach you how. She only plays classical music, though, and church songs."

Mama's smoky voice whispered pieces of a song, "*The cares of the world may leave us crying . . . . Life will be sweeter some day . . .*" Her voice trailed off into a hum. Even when I couldn't hear it anymore, I could still see the song swaying in her body.

"They got a big fine house, them two. They'll be nice to you. You'll see. They'll be nice." Mama got busy taking my hand in hers and rubbing it against her face. I wondered why they had to be so nice to me.

"Mama, why you crying?" I got scared and pressed my hands to her face and neck to soak up her tears.

"I'm happy. We're almost home," she said, gently putting my hands back in my lap. She stopped talking. Her face didn't look happy, it cast a stony gaze on the landscape outside the window.

Gradually, small broken houses leaning so close they seemed to be listening to one another rolled beside us. The train crawled into the town where my mother grew up. The train station was just a raised platform by the side of the road. Nobody was there to meet us. Mama went over to a yellow taxi and asked the driver if he could give us a ride. The man said something to Mama that made her jump away from the cab as if she had been bit by a snake. Mama called him an "ignorant cracker." She was mad, but she wouldn't tell me why. Another woman with long red hair and pretty white teeth got in the cab and they drove away in a cloud of dust. Mama took off her high heeled shoe and threw it at the cab, then she sat on the curb and started to cry.

"It's okay, Mama. We can take another train somewhere else," I said, sitting down next to her.

"No, baby, we at the end of the line," she said, limping after her shoe.

Mama took my hand and we followed the train tracks for a long time until we started seeing people. Friendly faces, all smiles, some waved, some hollered out a "Good morning." I asked Mama if she knew all these people and she said, "No, folks just friendly down south." I started waving and saying good morning to people I didn't even know. We passed a red brick school building with a flag waving out front, a grocery store, a liquor store, and some long wooden houses Mama said were shotgun houses. Finally we came to where we seemed to be going. Mama stood looking at the big white house in front of us, then she spit on her handkerchief and wiped my face. She brushed my hair back with her hand. When she was satisfied she adjusted her scarf and we walked past the tall, black gate.

Coming up the neat brick walk lined with flowers, we saw the lace curtains move away from the window and fall back again. Mama walked quickly up the steps dragging me along.

"Aunt Faith, Aunt Merleen, this is my little girl, Mariah. She's seven years old and already she can sing like an angel," Mama announced loudly to the closed door. "Sing, baby," she said to me.

Mama was anxiously squeezing my hand. It hurt a little, but I didn't say anything. I kept my eyes low, on the dusty points of Mama's shoes. I had a bad feeling in the bottom of my stomach. Before I could open my mouth, I heard the door open and looked up to see two old women looking back at us.

Through the screen Aunt Merleen looked me over like I was a spoiled ham, then turned and went deep inside the house. The other one, Aunt Faith, seemed afraid to let us cross the threshold into the big white house with the ocean-blue porch ceiling and tall shuttered windows.

"We haven't seen you in quite some time, Coral," the soft, round one said accusingly.

"You been to see your mother?" the tall, stormy one demanded from inside the darkness.

"Not yet," Mama answered timidly. There was a long, sweaty

silence. Mama dabbed at her neck with the ends of her scarf and fussed with my collar. We stood there, shifting from foot to foot, waiting for a sign of welcome.

"Sure is hot!" Mama said at last.

Aunt Faith said something to the tall one behind her, then opened the screen door reluctantly to let us pass. It was cool and dark inside. I held on to Mama's dress like I did in a crowd so we wouldn't be separated. We followed Aunt Faith into a large room with heavy drapes on the window. We sat on an uncomfortable high-backed sofa covered in an itchy wool fabric while Aunt Faith sat across from us in a matching chair.

"I need to talk to you, Aunt Faith. I'm in trouble."

Aunt Merleen came into the room and stood by the large black piano.

"Coral, seems like you always in some kind of trouble. Didn't you leave here under a dark cloud?" Aunt Merleen's rough voice filled the room.

I sat on Mama's lap and tried to unbutton her dress so that I could find some comfort against her pillows of softness, but she pushed me away.

"The child look too big for that." The rough voice clouded my ears.

Under their scrutiny I felt shame for the first time. I began to shrink to the size of a baby that would fit into the palm of my mother's hand. Mama folded my hands in my lap and buttoned her dress in the wrong hole. Then Mama took off her scarf and gave it to me. She cupped my face in her hands and kissed me on the lips. She held me too tight, then stood up and stepped away from me, looking at me as if she were trying to take a picture. Her eyes were sad and wet. She started crying out loud, then left the room with Aunt Faith's hand on her shoulder. Me and Aunt Merleen stared at each other until I backed down and started looking at the pattern in the carpet, counting the flowers along the border under my feet.

"Can you talk?" she shouted, as if I were deaf.

"Yes," I whispered.

"Yes, what?"

"Yes, I can talk." I dared to look into her rough and wrinkled face, the light-colored eyes, the wide flat nose and small tight mouth.

"Yes, ma'am. Didn't your mother teach you any manners?" she asked accusingly.

I turned my eyes back to the maze of flowers blooming on the carpet inches below my feet. I tried to think of words to defend my mother. I pressed my hands against my middle and tried to push the pain out of my stomach. Suddenly I heard a door slam and the sound of Mama's high heels running down the front porch steps. I slid off the couch scratching the palms of my hands on the bumpy fabric and ran to the door, but it was shut, locked tight. The hard green suitcase was all that was left of Mama.

"Where's my mama?" I asked the closed door, panic bubbling in my chest.

"She had to go somewhere. She'll be back. She'd like you to stay with us for a while. We want you to stay," Aunt Faith whispered to my back. Her voice was the only one I heard. I wanted to cry, but I didn't. I went back to sit on the sofa and pretended me and Mama were playing Ocean.

> *My father is in Mexico painting the sky blue, but I am lost in a forest of dark trees. Trees so tall and dark the sky is not visible. The trees begin to sing to me in Spanish. I sing too, even though I don't know the words. I see a light in front of me and walk toward it. After walking for what seems like days I come to a place where two witches are sitting around a fire. They tell me that they have been waiting for me, that they are going to chop me up into little pieces and boil me into a soup to feed their dead children. One of the witches holds me by my arms while the other one plucks out my eyes. I scream but no sound comes out of my mouth.*

When I fell off the sofa, I found myself drowning in the ocean of thick red flowers.

The Book of the Dead

By Edwidge Danticat

Edwidge Danticat (1969–) left Haiti at the age of 12 to join her parents in Brooklyn, New York. In 1995, she was nominated for a National Book Award for her short story collection, *Krik! Krak!* Danticat has also published two novels, *Breath, Eyes Memory* (an Oprah Book Club selection) and *The Farming of Bones;* an anthology of Haitian writing, *The Butterfly's Way;* and *After the Dance,* a tour of carnival in Haiti. In her short story "The Book of the Dead," a daughter comes to terms with her father's veiled past.

My father is gone. I am slouched in a cast-aluminum chair across from two men, one the manager of the hotel where we're staying and the other a policeman. They are waiting for me to explain what has become of him, my father.

The manager—"Mr. Flavio Salinas," the plaque on his office door reads—has the most striking pair of chartreuse eyes I have ever seen on a man with an island-Spanish lilt to his voice.

The officer is a baby-faced, short white Floridian with a pot belly.

"Where are you and your daddy from, Ms. Bienaime?" he asks.

I answer "Haiti," even though I was born and raised in East Flatbush, Brooklyn, and have never visited my parents' birthplace. I do this because it is one more thing I have longed to have in common with my parents.

The officer plows forward. "You down here in Lakeland from Haiti?"

"We live in New York. We were on our way to Tampa."

I find Manager Salinas's office gaudy. The walls are covered with orange-and-green wallpaper, briefly interrupted by a giant gold-leaf-bordered print of a Victorian cottage that somehow resembles the building we're in. Patting his light-green tie, he whispers reassuringly, "Officer Bo and I will do the best we can to help you find your father."

We start out with a brief description: "Sixty-four, five feet eight inches, two hundred and twenty pounds, moon-faced, with thinning salt-and-pepper hair. Velvet-brown eyes—"

"Velvet-brown?" says Officer Bo.

"Deep brown—same color as his complexion."

My father has had partial frontal dentures for ten years, since he fell off his and my mother's bed when his prison nightmares began. I mention that, too. Just the dentures, not the nightmares. I also bring up the claw-shaped marks that run from his left ear down along his cheek to the corner of his mouth—the only visible reminder of the year he spent at Fort Dimanche, the Port-au-Prince prison ironically named after the Lord's Day.

"Does your daddy have any kind of mental illness, senility?" asks Officer Bo.

"No."

"Do you have any pictures of your daddy?"

I feel like less of a daughter because I'm not carrying a photograph in my wallet. I had hoped to take some pictures of him on our trip. At one of the rest stops I bought a disposable camera and pointed it at my father. No, no, he had protested, covering his face with both hands like a little boy protecting his cheeks from a slap. He did not want any more pictures taken of him for the rest of his life. He was feeling too ugly.

"That's too bad," says Officer Bo. "Does he speak English, your daddy? He can ask for directions, et cetera?"

"Yes."

"Is there anything that might make your father run away from you—particularly here in Lakeland?" Manager Saunas interjects. "Did you two have a fight?"

I had never tried to tell my father's story in words before now, but my first sculpture of him was the reason for our trip: a two-foot-high mahogany figure of my father, naked, crouching on the floor, his back arched like the curve of a crescent moon, his downcast eyes fixed on his short stubby fingers and the wide palms of his hands. It was hardly revolutionary, minimalist at best, but it was my favorite of all my attempted representations of him. It was the way I had imagined him in prison.

The last time I had seen my father? The previous night, before falling asleep. When we pulled into the pebbled driveway, densely lined with palm and banana trees, it was almost midnight. All the restaurants in the area were closed. There was nothing to do but shower and go to bed.

"It is like a paradise here," my father said when he saw the room. It had the same orange-and-green wallpaper as Salinas's office, and the plush green carpet matched the walls. "Look, Annie," he said, "it is like grass under our feet." He was always searching for a glimpse of paradise, my father.

He picked the bed closest to the bathroom, removed the top of his gray jogging suit, and unpacked his toiletries. Soon after, I heard him humming, as he always did, in the shower.

After he got into bed, I took a bath, pulled my hair back in a ponytail, and checked on the sculpture—just felt it a little bit through the bubble padding and carton wrapping to make sure it wasn't broken. Then I slipped under the covers, closed my eyes, and tried to sleep.

I pictured the client to whom I was delivering the sculpture: Gabrielle Fonteneau, a young woman about my age, an actress on a nationally syndicated television series. My friend Jonas, the principal at the East Flatbush elementary school where I teach drawing to fifth graders, had shown her a picture of my "Father" sculpture, and, the way Jonas told it, Gabrielle Fonteneau had fallen in love with it and wished to offer it as a gift to her father on his birthday.

Since this was my first big sale, I wanted to make sure that the piece got there safely. Besides, I needed a weekend away, and both my mother and I figured that my father, who watched a lot of television, both in his barbershop and at home, would enjoy meeting Gabrielle, too. But when I woke up the next morning my father was gone.

I showered, put on my driving jeans and a T-shirt, and waited. I watched a half hour of midmorning local news, smoked three mentholated cigarettes even though we were in a nonsmoking room, and waited some more. By noon, four hours had gone by. And it was only then that I noticed that the car was still there but the sculpture was gone.

I decided to start looking for my father: in the east garden, the west garden, the dining room, the exercise room, and in the few guest rooms cracked open while the maid changed the sheets; in the little convenience store at the Amoco gas station nearby; even in the Salvation Army thrift shop that from a distance seemed to blend into the interstate. All that waiting and looking actually took six hours, and I felt guilty for having held back so long before going to the front desk to ask, "Have you seen my father?"

I feel Officer Bo's fingers gently stroking my wrist. Up close he smells like fried eggs and gasoline, like breakfast at the Amoco. "I'll put the word out with the other boys," he says. "Salinas here will be in his office. Why don't you go back to your room in case he shows up there?"

I return to the room and lie in the unmade bed, jumping up when I hear the click from the electronic key in the door. It's only the housekeeper. I turn down the late-afternoon cleaning and call my mother at the beauty salon where she perms, presses, and braids hair, next door to my father's barbershop. But she isn't there. So I call my parents' house and leave the hotel number on their machine. "Please call me as soon as you can, Manman. It's about Papi."

Once, when I was twelve, I overheard my mother telling a young woman who was about to get married how she and my father had first met on the sidewalk in front of Fort Dimanche the evening that my father was released from jail. (At a dance, my father had fought with a soldier out of uniform who had him arrested and thrown in prison for a year.) That night, my mother was returning home from a sewing class when he stumbled out of the prison gates and collapsed into her arms, his face still bleeding from his last beating. They married and left for New York a year later. "We were like two seeds planted in a rock," my mother had told the young woman, "but somehow when our daughter, Annie, came we took root."

My mother soon calls me back, her voice staccato with worry:
"Where is Papi?"
"I lost him."
"How you lost him?"
"He got up before I did and disappeared."
"How long he been gone?"
"Eight hours," I say, almost not believing myself that it's been that long. My mother is clicking her tongue and humming. I can see her sitting at the kitchen table, her eyes closed, her fingers sliding up and down her flesh-colored stockinged legs.
"You call police?"
"Yes."
"What they say?"
"To wait, that he'll come back."
My mother is thumping her fingers against the phone's mouthpiece, which is giving me a slight ache in my right ear.
"Tell me where you are," she says. "Two more hours and he's not there, call me, I come."
I dial Gabrielle Fonteneau's cellular-phone number. When she answers, her voice sounds just as it does on television, but more silken and seductive without the sitcom laugh track.
"To think," my father once said while watching her show, "Haitian-born actresses on American television."
"And one of them wants to buy my stuff," I'd added.
When she speaks, Gabrielle Fonteneau sounds as if she's in a place with cicadas, waterfalls, palm trees, and citronella candles to

keep the mosquitoes away. I realize that I, too, am in such a place, but I can't appreciate it.

"So nice of you to come all this way to deliver the sculpture," she says. "Jonas tell you why I like it so much? My papa was a journalist in Port-au-Prince. In 1975, he wrote a story criticizing the dictatorship, and he was arrested and put in jail."

"Fort Dimanche?"

"No, another one," she says. "Caserne. Papa kept track of days there by scraping lines with his fingernails on the walls of his cell. One of the guards didn't like this, so he pulled out all his fingernails with pliers."

I think of the photo spread I saw in the *Haitian Times* of Gabrielle Fonteneau and her parents in their living room in Tampa. Her father was described as a lawyer, his daughter's manager; her mother a court stenographer. There was no hint in that photograph of what had once happened to the father. Perhaps people don't see anything in my father's face, either, in spite of his scars.

"We celebrate his birthday on the day he was released from prison," she says. "It's the hands I love so much in your sculpture. They're so strong."

I am drifting away from Gabrielle Fonteneau when I hear her say, "So when will you get here? You have instructions from Jonas, right? Maybe we can make you lunch. My mother makes great *lanbi*."

"I'll be there at twelve tomorrow," I say. "My father is with me. We are making a little weekend vacation of this."

My father loves museums. When he isn't working in his barbershop, he's often at the Brooklyn Museum. The ancient Egyptian rooms are his favorites.

"The Egyptians, they was like us," he likes to say. The Egyptians worshipped their gods in many forms and were often ruled by foreigners. The pharaohs were like the dictators he had fled. But what he admires most about the Egyptians is the way they mourned.

"Yes, they grieve," he'll say. He marvels at the mummification that went on for weeks, resulting in bodies that survived thousands of years.

My whole adult life, I have struggled to find the proper manner of sculpting my father, a man who learned about art by standing with me most of the Saturday mornings of my childhood, mesmerized by the golden masks, the shawabtis, and Osiris, ruler of the underworld.

When my father finally appears in the hotel-room doorway, I am awed by him. Smiling, he looks like a much younger man, further bronzed after a long day at the beach.

"Annie, let your father talk to you." He walks over to my bed, bends down to unlace his sneakers. "*On ti koze,* a little chat."

"Where were you? Where is the sculpture, Papi?" I feel my eyes twitching, a nervous reaction I inherited from my mother.

"That's why we need to chat," he says. "I have objections with your statue."

He pulls off his sneakers and rubs his feet with both hands.

"I don't want you to sell that statue," he says. Then he picks up the phone and calls my mother.

"I know she called you," he says to her in Creole. "Her head is so hot. She panics so easily: I was just out walking, thinking."

I hear my mother lovingly scolding him and telling him not to leave me again. When he hangs up the phone, he picks up his sneakers and puts them back on.

"Where is the sculpture?" My eyes are twitching so hard now that I can barely see.

"Let us go," he says. "I will take you to it."

As my father maneuvers the car out of the parking lot, I tell myself he might be ill, mentally ill, even though I have never detected anything wrong beyond his prison nightmares. I am trying to piece it together, this sudden yet familiar picture of a parent's vulnerability. When I was ten years old and my father had the chicken pox, I overheard him say to a friend on the phone, "The doctor tells me that at my age chicken pox can kill a man." This was the first time I realized that my father could die. I looked up the word "kill" in every dictionary and encyclopedia at school, trying to comprehend what it meant, that my father could be eradicated from my life.

My father stops the car on the side of the highway near a manmade lake, one of those artificial creations of the modern tropical city, with curved stone benches surrounding stagnant water. There is little light to see by except a half-moon. He heads toward one of the benches, and I sit down next to him, letting my hands dangle between my legs.

"Is this where the sculpture is?" I ask.

"In the water," he says.

"O.K.," I say. "But please know this about yourself. You are an especially harsh critic."

My father tries to smother a smile.

"Why?" I ask.

He scratches his chin. Anger is a wasted emotion, I've always thought. My parents got angry at unfair politics in New York or Port-au-Prince, but they never got angry at my grades—at all the B's I got in everything but art classes—or at my not eating vegetables or occasionally vomiting my daily spoonful of cod-liver oil. Ordinary anger, I thought, was a weakness. But now I am angry. I want to hit my father, beat the craziness out of his head.

"Annie," he says. "When I first saw your statue, I wanted to be buried with it, to take it with me into the other world."

"Like the ancient Egyptians," I say.

He smiles, grateful, I think, that I still recall his passions.

"Annie," he asks, "do you remember when I read to you from *The Book of the Dead?*"

"Are you dying?" I say to my father. "Because I can only forgive you for this if you are. You can't take this back."

He is silent for a moment too long.

I think I hear crickets, though I cannot imagine where they might be. There is the highway, the cars racing by, the half-moon, the lake dug up from the depths of the ground, the allee of royal palms beyond. And there is me and my father.

"You remember the judgment of the dead," my father says,

"when the heart of a person is put on a scale. If it is heavy, then this person cannot enter the other world."

It is a testament to my upbringing that I am not yelling at him.

"I don't deserve a statue," he says, even while looking like one: the Madonna of Humility, for example, contemplating her losses in the dust.

"Annie, your father was the hunter," he says. "He was not the prey."

"What are you saying?" I ask.

"We have a proverb," he says. "'One day for the hunter, one day for the prey.' Your father was the hunter. He was not the prey." Each word is hard won as it leaves my father's mouth, balanced like those hearts on the Egyptian scale.

"Annie, when I saw your mother the first time, I was not just out of prison. I was a guard in the prison. One of the prisoners I was questioning had scratched me with a piece of tin. I went out to the street in a rage, blood all over my face. I was about to go back and do something bad, very bad. But instead comes your mother. I smash into her, and she asks me what I am doing there. I told her I was just let go from prison and she held my face and cried in my hair."

"And the nightmares, what are they?"

"Of what I, your father, did to others."

"Does Manman know?"

"I told her, Annie, before we married."

I am the one who drives back to the hotel. In the car, he says, "Annie, I am still your father, still your mother's husband. I would not do these things now."

When we get back to the hotel room, I leave a message for Officer Bo, and another for Manager Salinas, telling them that I have found my father. He has slipped into the bathroom, and now he runs the shower at full force. When it seems that he is never coming out, I call my mother at home in Brooklyn.

"How do you love him?" I whisper into the phone.

My mother is tapping her fingers against the mouthpiece.

"I don't know, Annie," she whispers back, as though there is a chance that she might also be overheard by him. "I feel only that you and me, we saved him. When I met him, it made him stop hurting the people. This is how I see it. He was a seed thrown into a rock, and you and me, Annie, we helped push a flower out of a rock."

When I get up the next morning, my father is already dressed. He is sitting on the edge of his bed with his back to me, his head bowed, his face buried in his hands. If I were sculpting him, I would make him a praying mantis, crouching motionless, seeming to pray while waiting to strike.

With his back still turned, my father says, "Will you call those people and tell them you have it no more, the statue?"

"We were invited to lunch there. I believe we should go."

He raises his shoulders and shrugs. It is up to me.

The drive to Gabrielle Fonteneau's house seems longer than the twenty-four hours it took to drive from New York: the ocean, the palms along the road, the highway so imposingly neat. My father fills in the silence in the car by saying, "So now you know, Annie, why your mother and me, we have never returned home."

The Fonteneaus' house is made of bricks of white coral, on a cul-de-sac with a row of banyans separating the two sides of the street.

Silently, we get out of the car and follow a concrete path to the front door. Before we can knock, an older woman walks out. Like Gabrielle, she has stunning midnight-black eyes and skin the color of sorrel, with spiralling curls brushing the sides of her face. When Gabrielle's father joins her, I realize where Gabrielle Fonteneau gets her height. He is more than six feet tall.

Mr. Fonteneau extends his hands, first to my father and then to me. They're large, twice the size of my father's. The fingernails have grown back, thick, densely dark, as though the past had nestled itself there in black ink.

We move slowly through the living room, which has a cathedral ceiling and walls covered with Haitian paintings—Obin, Hyppolite,

Tiga, Duval-Carrié. Out on the back terrace, which towers over a nursery of orchids and red dracaenas, a table is set for lunch.

Mr. Fonteneau asks my father where his family is from in Haiti, and my father lies. In the past, I thought he always said a different province because he had lived in all those places, but I realize now that he says this to keep anyone from tracing him, even though twenty-six years and eighty more pounds shield him from the threat of immediate recognition.

When Gabrielle Fonteneau makes her entrance, in an off-the-shoulder ruby dress, my father and I stand up.

"Gabrielle," she says, when she shakes hands with my father, who blurts out spontaneously, "You are one of the flowers of Haiti."

Gabrielle Fonteneau tilts her head coyly.

"We eat now," Mrs. Fonteneau announces, leading me and my father to a bathroom to wash up before the meal. Standing before a pink seashell-shaped sink, my father and I dip our hands under the faucet flow.

"Annie," my father says, "we always thought, your mother and me, that children could raise their parents higher. Look at what this girl has done for her parents."

During the meal of conch, plantains, and mushroom rice, Mr. Fonteneau tries to draw my father into conversation. He asks when my father was last in Haiti.

"Twenty-six years," my father replies.

"No going back for you?" asks Mrs. Fonteneau.

"I have not had the opportunity," my father says.

"We go back every year to a beautiful place overlooking the ocean in the mountains in Jacmel," says Mrs. Fonteneau.

"Have you ever been to Jacmel?" Gabrielle Fonteneau asks me. I shake my head no.

"We are fortunate," Mrs. Fonteneau says, "that we have another place to go where we can say our rain is sweeter, our dust is lighter, our beach is prettier."

"So now we are tasting rain and weighing dust," Mr. Fonteneau says, and laughs.

"There is nothing like drinking the sweet juice from a green coconut you fetched yourself from your own tree, or sinking your hand in sand from the beach in your own country," Mrs. Fonteneau says.

"When did you ever climb a coconut tree?" Mr. Fonteneau says, teasing his wife.

I am imagining what my father's nightmares might be. Maybe he dreams of dipping his hands in the sand on a beach in his own country and finds that what he comes up with is a fist full of blood.

After lunch, my father asks if he can have a closer look at the Fonteneaus' back-yard garden. While he's taking the tour, I confess to Gabrielle Fonteneau that I don't have the sculpture.

"My father threw it away," I say.

Gabrielle Fonteneau frowns.

"I don't know," she says. "Was there even a sculpture at all? I trust Jonas, but maybe you fooled him, too. Is this some scam, to get into our home?"

"There was a sculpture," I say. "Jonas will tell you that. My father just didn't like it, so he threw it away."

She raises her perfectly arched eyebrows, perhaps out of concern for my father's sanity or my own.

"I'm really disappointed," she says. "I wanted it for a reason. My father goes home when he looks at a piece of art. He goes home deep inside himself. For a long time he used to hide his fingers from people. It's like he was making a fist all the time. I wanted to give him this thing so that he knows we understand what happened to him."

"I am truly sorry," I say.

Over her shoulders, I see her parents guiding my father through rows of lemongrass. I want to promise her that I will make her another sculpture, one especially modelled on her father. But I don't know when I will be able to work on anything again. I have lost my subject, the father I loved as well as pitied.

In the garden, I watch my father snap a white orchid from its stem and hold it out toward Mrs. Fonteneau, who accepts it with a nod of thanks.

"I don't understand," Gabrielle Fonteneau says. "You did all this for nothing."

I wave to my father to signal that we should perhaps leave now, and he comes toward me, the Fonteneaus trailing slowly behind him.

With each step he rubs the scars on the side of his face.

Perhaps the last person my father harmed had dreamed this moment into my father's future—his daughter seeing those marks, like chunks of warm plaster still clinging to a cast, and questioning him about them, giving him a chance to either lie or tell the truth. After all, we have the proverb, as my father would say: "Those who give the blows may try to forget, but those who carry the scars must remember."

Show Business

By Martha Southgate

Martha Southgate (1960–) won the Coretta Scott King Genesis Award for her first novel, *Another Way to Dance,* which was also named an American Library Association's Best Book of 1996. Her second novel, *The Fall of Rome,* was published in 2002. The Cleveland, Ohio, native holds a B.A. from Smith College and an M.F.A. from Goddard College, and her work has appeared in such publications as *Essence, O: The Oprah Magazine,* and the *New York Times Magazine.* In this short story, she examines how a mother's show business aspirations imprint her daughter.

Every night, I dream of actors. Kevin Costner. Denzel Washington. Daniel Day-Lewis. Richard Gere. When I wake up it's as though they've been with me, their well-cut hair gleaming slightly in the light, those special sincere looks they have aimed precisely at me. I can feel their hands on my forehead, trying to soothe me. They always say all the right things. When they close their eyes, you can see their eyelashes resting on their cheeks—movie stars these days always have long eyelashes, the kind I wish I had. I wonder sometimes if it's a rule of the profession.

My mother was an actress. She had skin the color of honey and the longest eyelashes I ever saw. She was in a lot of movies in the early 1970s just before I was born. Things with titles like *Coffy* and *Black Gold* and *Cleopatra Jones.* She wasn't like Pam Grier or anything though. Her credits read more like this: Girl in diner. Murder victim #1. Screaming Girl. Junkie in Park. When we lived up in

Harlem and she was working at the hospital, sometimes she would pull me out of bed late at night, her eyes shining, and sit me down in front of the television to watch some movie with a lot of guys with big afros and big guns. They would run, jump, shoot—they all wore leather and bright-colored, wide legged pants made of unnatural fibers. They said "That's baaad" a lot as cool synthesized music perked behind them. Then at some point, my mother would say, "See, see, there I am, behind that guy, laying on the ground. That's me." Or she'd say, "That's me in that booth." Then Richard Roundtree or Pam Grier or Fred Williamson would spray the room with gunfire and my mother would slump over the table, her mouth open and her eyes closed. Blood would seep slowly out from under her enormous afro. I'd turn to watch her as she looked at the screen. Her eyes shone and she smiled as she watched the gory death of her younger self. She made me believe that acting was a useful way to spend one's life even if it meant spending time spitting up Karo corn syrup mixed with food coloring onto a cheap Formica table.

My mother never said, but I knew, that I had ended her acting career. Sometimes I liked to think that my father might be Richard Roundtree, striding through the streets of Harlem, a complicated man, a black private dick who was a sex machine to all the chicks. But I suspected, though she never talked about him much, that my father was just a bit player like her. Thug #1. Or Man in Restaurant. I can imagine them, in those endless hours on set, slowly starting to talk to each other, my mother looking up shy but somehow direct, the low bass rumble of my father's voice as he asked her name, then finally asked her out. My mother always believed in the power of movies to change everything. She knew one day that someone would pick her out of the background and say, "That's the girl. I've got to have her!" and she would be whisked off to stardom and extra-high platforms and someone to do her hair and makeup for her. Maybe she thought my father would be the man to do that. Or maybe she thought they'd both be noticed at the same time, as a team. I don't know. He was long gone by the time I was born anyway.

We lived on a Harlem street that sparkled with glass, green and clear and shattered. In the summer, it was quite pretty, though it meant having to be careful where you stepped and never putting a foot out the door without shoes on. My mother told me once, with great pride, that part of *Cleopatra Jones* had been filmed there and that was why she'd named me Tamara, after the beautiful Tamara Dobson, the ex-model who played Cleo. When I was little, I loved my street, the crisp calls echoed between the buildings, the smells of incense and hot dogs in the air, the always-interesting garbage piled on the curb. But the more we went to the movies, the more I came to feel like something wasn't quite right. Nobody in the movies lived on a street like ours. Even in my mother's movies, streets like ours looked strange and unfamiliar, rearranged and cleaned up somehow. And only people who killed each other and fought all the time seemed to live there. All the nice people lived in cleaner, quieter places.

My mother and I went to a lot of movies. After school, I would let myself in with the key I wore around my neck and sit in the house with a glass of milk and some slightly stale Chips Ahoy cookies. I would do my homework with the TV on in the background for company. After what seemed like an eternity but was probably only a couple of hours, my mother would burst into the house, exclaiming, usually, about the weather, how hot or cold or nice it was outside. She'd come over to the table and kiss me briskly on top of my head. "Done with your homework?" she'd say. I always nodded yes, even if I wasn't. "Well, how about pizza and a movie then?" she'd say. I'd run and get the *Daily News* movie clock and we'd pick something. She liked things that were like the movies she used to be in, movies with a lot of action and violence and movement. I liked quieter things; I had a special fondness for WASP-y dramas like *Ordinary People*. The lost look in Timothy Hutton's eyes moved me in some way I could never account for. My mother and I took turns, one day something for her, the next something for me. If we especially liked a movie, we'd go back and see it again the next day.

We often went to one of the same four theaters, so the box

office guys got to know us. They'd sit up out of their slumped positions when they saw my mother coming, holding my hand. My hair was always perfectly combed in two neat braids with pink bows and I wore corduroys and a sweater, usually with lace at the collar. My mother wanted me to wear skirts—"They're more ladylike," she would say—but that was one of the few things I ever refused her. She retaliated by always making sure there was lace somewhere on my clothing or that it was a girlish pastel. She would be wearing something like a bright pink suit with a peplum, her hair smoothed with gel into a perfect chignon. She would always chat with the men in the booths a little—see which movie was most popular, argue the merits of Harrison Ford vs. William Hurt. Oddly, the men seemed to like her banter and encourage it, even if there were other people waiting. They might shepherd past the rest of the crowd waiting for movie tickets with barely a look, but they knew somebody had arrived when my mother showed up. They always seemed pleased to honor her presence with a few friendly words.

She kept reading *Variety* and *Backstage*. She liked to keep up. Always I remember them laid on the arm of the pilling, olive-green sofa or piled up in our trash at the end of the week, an unruly hint of glamour mixed in with the potato peelings and copies of the News and the PD51 and *The Amsterdam News*. I liked to look at the ads, especially around Oscar time when the studios touted this actor or that for an award. "For your consideration," they always said. And there would be a face, calm with repose or strained with intensity, looking for Oscar glory. I gazed at the photographs for hours, occasionally stroking a favorite actor's cheek, gently, with one finger. One time, I got up out of bed to get a drink of water and came upon my mother on the sofa, her *Variety* open in her lap, staring down at an Oscar ad. The living room was only half lit but I could still see, in the bend of her neck, the sorrow that lay upon her like a robe. She hadn't heard me come in and I went back to bed without my water. I lay there for a long time before I was able to fall asleep.

The day of the Oscars was always a holiday for us. My mother called in sick and let me take the day off from school. We would see everything that was nominated in the weeks beforehand. Some years that was tough; I had nightmares about *Raging Bull* for weeks afterwards. Even after hours of getting up and holding me while I screamed in terror, Robert DeNiro's bloody face before me, my mother never changed the rule that we had to see all the major nominees. I never asked her to.

We made a special trip to the grocery store the weekend before and got all the kind of stuff we could never afford to have. Steak and instant mashed potatoes and expensive Häagen-Dazs ice cream for dessert. I was even spared vegetables on this night of all nights. We'd spend hours carefully cutting out pictures of the nominees and pasting them up around the house. My mother insisted that we both dress up for the occasion. That was one night she'd get me into a dress easily. I had a black velvet with a lace collar that I saved only for Christmas, Easter and the Oscars. And on Oscar night, she'd let me wear sheer pantyhose instead of tights, something I wasn't permitted the rest of the time—she said sheer hose were tacky on little girls. We would have a formal dinner with lit candles on the table at around 7. I tucked my napkin into my collar so I wouldn't mess up my dress. Over dinner, we'd talk about who might win and what they might be wearing. We always tried to remember who had won various awards the year before but we never could.

Once the show started, my mother had something to say about each actresses's outfit, either sucking her teeth in outrage or nodding approvingly. She especially liked actresses who weren't afraid to show off their bodies and wore a lot of spangles. "That girl really knows how to work it," she'd say in a satisfied, soothed tone after an especially nice outfit came by. We listened intently to each speech, only going to the bathroom or running to get Cokes during the commercials and the Jean Hersholt award. What I loved most was the spectacle of it all, sitting next to my mother on the sofa, feeling the softness of her arm next to my cheek. I loved watching the stars arrive ludicrously overdressed in the sunny middle of the southern California day, the breathlessness of the announcer as each actor walked up the red carpet.

The year Louis Gossett won Best Supporting Actor for *An Officer and a Gentleman*, I thought my mother would have a heart attack, she was so happy. She kissed the television as he gave his acceptance speech. "It's about time one of us won this thing," she screamed. "Go on, boy!" It was the most out of control I ever saw her. As though he was somehow aware of her response, he looked shy and overwhelmed thousands of miles away, trapped on a tiny screen.

Things began to change in the weeks after that. Sometimes after dinner, she would sit on the sofa, gazing absently at the wall and picking at her thumbnail. She didn't seem to notice I was there unless I spoke or dropped something. I felt like we were standing on the edge of a cliff, holding hands, looking nervously into the space below. When we went to the movies, she began to lean a little forward, all through the film, as though she wanted to somehow live inside it, be speaking those lines, adding her own voice to each part. I began to see what she must have been like on the set when she was younger, the way she must have laid her head down on the table with a special little fillip that any director with a brain would have seen. She was special. She was different. I could see it. Why couldn't they?

She started to talk more about those days too. Always before, she dragged me up out of bed to watch the movies but was oddly perfunctory when I asked her what it was like to be in them. "Oh, it was fun," she'd say, her eyes distant and a little longing. "The hours were long and the food was awful but you got so you never really cared about all that. It was fun, really." I knew there was more to it than that, but I could never get her to say what that was.

Now though, she wouldn't shut up. Without prompting, she told me about how Fred Williamson once told her she was the prettiest woman on set; how she had to sit, motionless, for hours for her death scene in *Black Gold*—"It was about 100 degrees in there too. They had to keep putting more makeup on me and changing the blood but I never moved once they yelled 'rolling.'

Everybody else kept ruining takes by fidgeting and stuff. Not me. I was the best dead person in there. Everybody knew it. It was just a matter of time until I started getting better parts. Everybody knew that too." Her eyes filled with tears as she said this last. She quickly pressed her lips together and didn't say anything more.

I was pleased beyond words when she started to tell me these things. Even her tears seemed right, though they frightened me a little. We both knew what had been lost. It was worth mourning.

We went on like this until she saw the notice about the audition. It was a half-lit day, one of those spring days that is full of promise but not truly warm. I was sitting in a weak shaft of light at the kitchen table with my milk and cookies, looking like I was struggling with an especially intractable division problem but really wondering what movie we would see that night. She came in, clutching her *Backstage*, and breathlessly shrugged out of her raincoat. "Here," she said, plopping the paper down in front of me, "Look at this."

I looked up at her for a moment, then scanned the paper, confused. "I don't see, Ma. What am I looking for?"

"This." She stabbed at the paper with her coral-nailed finger.

There was an ad that read, "DOWN BROADWAY. Now casting SAG and non-SAG actors for DOWN BROADWAY, a new film from Columbia Pictures. To be shot in New York this summer. Various ethnicities needed. Females 20-30. Males 25-35. Bring a picture that you can leave with the casting directors." There was an address downtown, farther downtown than I'd ever been before. I looked up at my mother again. Her eyes glowed and her cheeks were flushed.

"You want to do this, Ma?"

"Yeah. Yeah, I do. I've been thinking it over. I've been sitting up at that damn hospital for the last 10 years, reading these magazines, letting it all go by me. I'm gonna be 34 soon. If I'm ever gonna do it, I've got to do it now. Once you hit 35, you're finished in this business."

I knew that. She'd told me before. 35 glowed in my mind as the end of a woman's life. My mother only had one year left. She had to act now. We both did. My heart started beating very fast, so fast it seemed she ought to be able to hear it. All those nights on the sofa, she'd been plotting our chance. We were on our way. I knew it. But as I looked at the ad again, a sudden horrible thought came to me. "Ma, they say they want females 20 to 30. You're too old."

Her eyes turned to glossy black marble. They only took on that look when I'd made her furious, like when I spilled apple juice all over her best dress when I was five. She looked at me, unwavering and said, "I look better than half these young girls out here. It won't be a problem." She walked out of the room without another word. I couldn't breathe. The air felt dangerous suddenly. I wanted to run after her but I knew I didn't dare.

I sat frozen at the table for about half an hour, rapidly eating Chips Ahoy and not tasting them. Finally, she emerged from her bedroom, her face composed, no apology there. "Things are changing for us, baby," she said, "Somebody like me might have a chance now. I knew it when Lou won. I have to take this shot. You want to come with me to the library to look for a speech?" I jumped up so fast that I almost knocked over my chair.

At the library, my mother's face was intent and rigorously beautiful as she pored over the titles. She murmured the opening lines of various monologues to herself, as if testing them out on her tongue before making a commitment. I sat close to her—she smelled of library dust and her own sharp, musky scent mixed with the cologne she always bought at the drugstore—"I would never leave the house without perfume," she would say. "It's all in the presentation."

She finally decided on a short monologue from *A Streetcar Named Desire*. She told me she'd seen the movie when she was 13 and never forgotten it. This was new too. She never told me what her life was like when she was a kid. I couldn't even really imagine her ever being my size. "Oh, that Marlon Brando," she said. "He was so fine you just wanted to weep. And Vivien Leigh was so beautiful. It was really something." She closed the book with a decided snap. "This is the one," she said. On the way home, she told me the story of Stanley and Blanche and Stella (though I found out later that she left out the rape at the end). I'd never even heard of New Orleans before, but as she wove the story for me, I could hear the chirp of foreign bayou crickets and feel the hot breeze as streetcars clacked by and people called lazily to one another. The characters were all white but she loved the story so much, she thought she could make it work anyway. "A good actress can do anything. Never forget that, baby," she said as we walked home through the darkening streets. She started practicing that night and never really stopped until after the audition. Her lips were moving all the time, murmuring the lines softly to herself. Her voice seemed to fill the apartment, a soft hum against the angular sounds of the street.

The day of the audition, my mother called my school. "Tamara has a bit of a cold today. She won't be in," she said. Her voice sounded odd, a little trembly, as though they would somehow know she was lying and angrily demand that I show up. That tone was never there when she called me in sick for the Oscars—then she sounded like an imp, a kid running a stick along a fence, enjoying some grand prank she's just made and daring you to challenge her about it. Her voice was sharp as she called me into the bedroom to help her choose which outfit to wear.

She had bought two—neither of which, I now realize, she could possibly afford. She must have been paying them off on her credit card for months afterwards. She shimmied into a tight black velvet number that emphasized her long legs, then asked me to compare it to a bright yellow mini that made her skin look like dark tea. She looked beautiful in both but she looked beautiful in everything to me. I used to sit in my room and look into the mirror for hours, searching my face for some sign that I would look like her when I grew up, the curve of a cheekbone, the width of my smile. But I never found any evidence. Maybe I favored my father.

Anyway, after going back and forth for a while, we decided on the yellow mini. "It makes me look younger," she finally said, and indeed, the bright color gave a girlish cast to her features, made you think of sunny days and a car driving by with the radio blasting so loud that you lost your breath for a moment. She put her hair up extra carefully and took what seemed like hours over her makeup. She leaned over to put a dash of lipstick on my lips, something she always did when I watched her put on her makeup. "There you go, punkin. Now you look glamorous," she said. She always said that when she put lipstick on me but this time, her eyes drifted back to her own face in the mirror even before she finished speaking.

The half-warmth of early spring was gone and it was getting almost hot out, the air a surprise to the skin. It smelled of sunlight and the peculiar acidic funk that emanated up from the gratings on the street. We didn't talk much on the way to the subway. My mother's lips moved quietly, still reciting her monologue.

She remained distracted until we got on the train. Once we got settled, we found we were across from a dark-skinned woman with five kids. She kept cursing at them and lightly slapping them alternately as they squirmed around on the seats. Their clothes were dirty and their hair stood on end, grayish. Occasionally one of them would let out a wail, his mouth a round O, tears leaving trails in the dust on his cheeks. My mother looked daggers at the woman as we got off but the woman didn't even look up. We walked in silence for a while. "Tamara," she finally said, "if you ever have kids, don't you ever treat them like that. Don't you ever go out looking like that. There's just no excuse for it. Water is free and soap is cheap." I nodded somberly.

She was quiet a few more minutes. She didn't say anything but I knew she was thinking about her monologue. Suddenly, she spoke. "Listen, baby, I need you to come in real quiet after I go in and sit in the back, real quiet while I read. People don't bring their kids to auditions. It might look kind of funny." She stopped. We were almost there now.

I didn't know what to say. I had a sudden memory of a time when one of the big girls had hit me in the stomach on the playground. "I can't sit up with you?" I said. "No, baby. But you'll still be able to see me and everything. It'll be fine."

"Then why'd you bring me then? Why didn't you just let me go to school?" My voice was rising to a wail.

Her voice hardened in response. "Tamara Ruby Edwards, I do not have time for this nonsense now. You can come in behind me and wait in the back or you can wait out here on the street or you can take the train home. I really don't care. But you can't sit with me."

The sun went behind a cloud. My mother stood by the door, her hand on the jamb, the expression in her eyes unreadable. I knew I was licked. "Okay. Okay. But I wish you'd just told me. I thought I was gonna sit with you."

She leaned forward suddenly and kissed me on the forehead. "I'm going in now. Wish me luck," she whispered.

"Break a leg," I said, automatically. She had told me about the old tradition almost as soon as I could understand words. She always said it to me before tests at school.

And then she was gone. I waited outside for a few minutes, watching people hurry by, trying to look like I belonged in the middle of this rush. They were all white. They were all wearing suits. I didn't see one single man without a tie. No other children, no glass on the street. Everyone was taller than me, seemed to have a place they were going, a place they belonged. I didn't have a choice but to go watch my mother audition. I went into the audition hall.

When my mother went up to read, I had been sitting, unnoticed, in the dark for a long time. I suppose now it wasn't as long as it seemed but while I waited for her, it felt like time had stopped altogether. Woman after woman came up to read, some cried, some were funny, some sang but none of them were my mother. I squirmed in my seat, feeling the old patchy wool of the seats scratch against the back of my neck. Ahead of me in the audience, two tall, thin white men sat, making notes on a clipboard and occasionally inclining their heads towards one another to speak. "Angela Edwards?" one of them finally called out. My mother came on stage.

She shifted from foot to foot for a few seconds then began to read her carefully prepared piece. I still remember her words: "I don't want realism. I want magic! Yes, yes, magic! I try to give that to people. . ." That's all they let her read. "Thank you, Miss Edwards. We'll let you know." A voice disembodied in the dark. My mother stood, hesitating for a moment. Her lips parted as if she would say something else; she stepped forward a bit, so her face began to be in shadow. Then she nodded, murmured "Thank you," and walked off the stage. She stood by my side again in what seemed like seconds. I couldn't understand what had happened. She stood at the end of the aisle, impatiently. "Ma, Ma, why wouldn't they let you finish? You practiced so much."

"Hush, now, Tam. Come on." The two men had turned at the sound of my voice. I heard one of them say to the other, "A kid. Can you believe it?"

"Come on, Tam." My mother's voice was imperious. Ordinarily I'd have responded to it without question. But I wanted to be in the audience at the Oscars, to get a new velvet dress and open my mouth with my mother in surprise and delight as Goldie Hawn called her name. I wanted to see her as she was in those movies she woke me up for, young and serious and beautiful. I didn't want to walk back out onto the pavement and see her in the sunlight. I didn't want to walk back over shattered glass to our tiny apartment. This was our only chance. "But Ma, it wasn't fair. They didn't even let you finish. Make them let you finish."

"Is there a problem?" A voice came from the front of the theater.

"No. No problem. I'm leaving. I'm sorry." She grabbed my arm roughly and dragged me up the aisle. I kept looking back. I was crying loudly now. Another woman stood in the circle of light that my mother had just left.

Outside, my mother and I leaned up against the brick wall of the building, composing ourselves. I could tell my mother was mad enough to hit me but she never did that. She made and unmade fists for a few minutes. I snuffled and hitched, wiping at my eyes with the back of my hand. Finally, I could speak. "Ma, why didn't you make them let you do more? You were the best one."

She closed her eyes and breathed deeply. "That's just not how it works, Tam. They take who they want."

"That's not fair. They didn't even give you a chance."

"Well, that's just how it works," she said. "I can't do anything about it."

"It's not fair."

She handed me a Kleenex out of her purse. The sun had come back out but it was weaker. I felt cold but that didn't seem like anything I could do anything about. "I guess it's not," she said. "Come on, Tam. Let's go home."

My mother has never stopped dressing her best, but she finally let her subscriptions to *Variety* and *Backstage* run out. She still works at the hospital, smiling and welcoming nervous patients, having lunch with her two friends, Anna and Ruth. They never go to the movies. They just wait until things come out on video and rent them.

I finally saw *A Streetcar Named Desire* when I was 17. I rent it a couple of times a year, soothed by the voices and the power of Marlon Brando's presence. I never rent the movies my mother was in, though. Even though blaxploitation is all the rage now, I can't stand to watch those movies. Everything in them, the music, the actors, even the hair, seems so garish and full of misplaced hope. I'm always afraid I'll see my mother in the background, her eyes reflecting someone else's light, one hand pressed to her shot and falsely bleeding heart.

A Son in Shadow

By Fred D'Aguiar

Fred D'Aguiar (1960–), born in England and raised in Guyana and London, now teaches English at the University of Miami. His three novels and four books of poetry evoke themes of immigrant longing and the cruelties of slavery. *The Longest Memory,* his haunting depiction of the life and death of an escaped slave in antebellum Virginia, won the Whitbread First Novel Award. In the modern-day story that follows, D'Aguiar's young male protagonist obsessively deconstructs the details of his parents' courtship to find clues to the father he never knew.

I know nothing about how they meet. She is a schoolgirl. He is at work, probably a government clerk in a building near her school. At the hour when school and office are out for lunch their lives intersect at sandwich counters, soft-drink stands, traffic lights, market squares. Their eyes meet or their bodies collide at one of these food queues. He says something suggestive, complimentary. She suppresses a smile or traps one beneath her hands. He takes this as encouragement (as if any reaction of hers would have been read as anything else) and keeps on talking and following her and probably misses lunch that day. All the while she walks and eats and drinks and soaks up his praise, his sweet body-talk, his erotic chatter and sexy pitter-patter, his idle boasts and ample toasts to his life, his dreams about their future, the world their oyster together.

Am I going too fast on my father's behalf? Should there have been an immediate and cutting rebuttal from her and several days before another meeting? Does he leave work early to catch her at the end of the school day and follow her home just to see where she lives and to extend the boundaries of their courtship? Throwing it from day to night, from school to home, from childhood play to serious adult intent? Georgetown's two-lane streets with trenches on either side mean a mostly single-file walk, she in front probably looking over her shoulder when he says something worthy of a glance, or a cut-eye look if his suggestion about her body or what he will do with it if given half a chance exceed the decorum of the day—which is what, in mid-Fifties Guyana? From my grandmother it's, "Don't talk to a man unless you think you're a big woman. Man will bring you trouble. Man want just one thing from you. Don't listen to he. Don't get ruined for he. A young lady must cork her ears and keep her eye straight in front of she when these men start to flock around. The gentleman among them will find his way to her front door. The gentleman will make contact with the parents first. Woo them first before muttering one thing to the young lady. Man who go directly to young ladies only want to ruin them. Don't want to make them into respectable young women—just whores. Mark my words." My grandfather simply thinks that his little girl is not ready for the attentions of any man, that none of them is good enough for his little girl, and so the man who comes to his front door had better have a good pretext for disturbing his reverie. He had better know something about merchant seamen and the character of the sea, and about silence—how to keep it so that it signifies authority and dignity, so when you speak you are heard and your words, every one of them, are rivets. That man would have to be a genius to get past my grandfather, a genius or a gentleman. And since my father is neither, it's out of the question that he'll even use the front door of worship. His route will have to be the yard and the street of ruination.

So he stands in full view of her house at dusk. It takes a few nights before her parents realize he is there for their daughter. Then one day her father comes out and tells him to take his dog behavior to someone else's front door, and the young man quickly turns on his heel and walks away. Another time her mother opens the upstairs window and curses him, and he laughs and saunters off as if her words were a broom gently ushering him out of her yard. But he returns the next night and the next, and the daughter can't believe his determination. She is embarrassed that her body has been a magnet for trouble, that she is the cause of the uproar, then angry with him for his keen regard of her at the expense of her dignity, not to mention his. Neighbors tease her about him. They take pity on the boy, offer him drinks, some ice-cold mauby, a bite to eat, a dhalpouri, all of which he declines at first, then dutifully accepts. One neighbor even offers him a chair, and on one night of pestilential showers an umbrella, since he does not budge from his spot while all around him people dash for shelter, abandoning a night of liming (loitering) and gaffing (talking) to the persistence and chatter of the rain. Not my father. He stands his ground with only the back of his right hand up to his brow to shelter his eyes zeroed in on her house. She steals a glance at him after days of seeming to ignore the idea of him, though his presence burns brightly inside her heart. She can't believe his vigilance is for her. She stops to stare in the mirror and for the first time sees her full lips, long straight nose, shoulder-length brunette hair, and dark green eyes with their slight oval shape. Her high cheekbones. Her ears close to her skull. She runs her fingers lightly over these places as if to touch is to believe. Her lips tingle. Her hair shines. Her eyes smile. And she knows from this young man's perseverance that she is beautiful, desirable. She abandons herself to chores, and suppresses a smile and a song. She walks past windows as much as possible to feed the young man's hungry eyes with a morsel of that which he has venerated to the point of indignity. She rewards his eyes by doing unnecessary half-turns at the upstairs window. A flash of clavicle, a hand slowly putting her hair off her face and setting it down behind her ears, and then a smile, a demure glance, her head inclined a little, her eyes raised, her eyelids batted a few times—she performs for him though she feels silly and self-conscious. What else is there for a girl to do? Things befitting a lady that she picked up from the cinema. Not the sauciness of a tramp.

Her mother pulls her by one of those beautiful close-skulled ears from the window and curses her as if she were a ten-cent whore, then throws open the window and hurtles a long list of insults at this tall, silent, rude, good-for-nothing streak of impertinence darkening her street. The father folds his paper and gets up, but by the time he gets to the window the young man is gone.

My mother cries into the basin of dishes. She rubs a saucer so hard that it comes apart in her hands. She is lucky not to cut herself. She will have to answer to her mother for that breakage. In the past it meant at least a few slaps and many minutes of curses for bringing only trouble into her mother's house. Tonight her mother is even angrier. Her father has turned his fury against her for rearing a daughter who is a fool for men. Her mother finds her in the kitchen holding the two pieces of the saucer together and then apart—as if her dread and sheer desire for reparation would magically weld them whole. Her tears fall like drops of solder on that divided saucer. Her mother grabs her hands and strikes her and curses her into her face so that my mother may as well have been standing over a steaming, spluttering pot on the stove. She drops the two pieces of saucer and they become six pieces. Her mother looks down and strides over the mess with threats about what will happen if her feet find a splinter. She cries but finds every piece, and to be sure to get the splinters too she runs her palms along the floor, this way and that, and with her nails she prizes out whatever her hand picks up. She cries herself to sleep.

The next night he is back at his station, and her mother and father, their voices, their words, their blows sound a little farther off, fall a little lighter. His presence, the bare-faced courage of it, becomes a suit of armor for her to don against her mother's and father's attacks. She flies through her chores. She manages under her mother's watchful eye to show both sides of her clavicle, even a little of the definition down the middle of her chest—that small trench her inflated chest digs, which catches the light and takes the breath away, that line drawn from the throat to the upper-most rib exuding warmth and tension, drawing the eyes twenty-five yards away with its radiance in the half-light of dusk, promising more than it can possibly contain, than the eye can hold, and triggering a normal heart into palpitations, a normal breath into shallowness and rapidity.

"Miss Isiah, howdy! How come you house so clean on the west side and not so clean on the east? It lopsided! Dirt have a preference in your house? Or is that saga boy hanging around the west side of your house a dirt repellent?" The gossip must have been rampant in the surrounding yards, yards seemingly designed deliberately so people could see into one another's homes and catch anything spilling out of them—quarrels, courtships, cooking pots, music—and sometimes a clash of houses, a reaction against the claustrophobia of the yard, but not enough yards, not enough room to procure a necessary privacy in order to maintain a badly sought-after dignity—clean, well dressed, head high in the air on Sundays—impossible if the night before there is a fight and everyone hears you beg not to be hit anymore, or else such a stream of obscenities gushes from your mouth that the sealed red lips of Sunday morning just don't cut it.

My father maintains his vigil. Granny threatens to save the contents of her chamber pot from the night before and empty it on his head. Could she have thrown it from her living room window to his shaded spot by the street? Luckily she never tries. She may well be telling him that he doesn't deserve even that amount of attention. If there is any creature lower than a gutter rat—one too low to merit even her worst display of disdain—then he is it. How does my father take that? As a qualification he can do without? How much of that kind of water is he able to let run off his back? Poor man. He has to be in love. He has to be wearing his own suit of armor. Lashed to his mast like Odysseus, he hears the most taunting, terrible things, but what saves him, what restores him, are the ropes, the armor of his love for my mother. Others without this charm would have withered away, but my father smiles and shrugs at the barrage of looks, insults, gestures, silence, loneliness.

Watch his body there under that breadfruit or sapodilla tree; the shine of his status as sentry and his conviction are twin headlights that blind her parents. They redouble their efforts to get rid of his particular glare, then are divided by the sense of his inevitability in their daughter's life. My grandmother stops shouting at him while my grandfather still raises his cane and causes the young man to walk away briskly. My grandmother then opens the windows on the west side, ostensibly to let in the sea breeze but really to exhibit in all those window frames a new and friendly demeanor. My grandfather shouts at her that he can smell the rank intent of that black boy, rotten as a fish market, blowing into his living room and spoiling his thoughts.

But the windows stay open. And my mother at them. With the love Morse of her clavicles and her cleavage as she grows bolder. Smiling, then waving. And no hand in sight to box her or grip her by the ear and draw her away from there. Until one night she boldly leaves the house and goes to him and they talk for five minutes rapidly as if words are about to run out in the Southern Hemisphere.

My father's parents wonder what has become of their Gordon.

"The boy only intend to visit town."

"Town swallow him up."

"No, one woman turn he head, stick it in a butter churn and swill it."

"He lost to us now."

"True."

They say this to each other but hardly speak to him except to make pronouncements on the size of foreign lands.

"Guyana small?"

"What's the boy talking about?"

"Why, England and Scotland combined are the size of Guyana."

"How much room does a man need?"

"That woman take he common sense in a mortar and pound it with a pestle."

The two voices are one voice.

Opportunity is here now. The English are letting go of the reins, a whole new land is about to be fashioned. And he is planning to leave! What kind of woman has done this to our boy? The boy is lost. Talking to him is like harnessing a stubborn donkey. This isn't love but voodoo, obeah, juju, some concoction in a drink, some spell thrown in his locus. A little salt over the shoulder, an iodine shower, a rabbit foot on a string, a duck's bill or snake head dried and deposited into the left trouser pocket, a precious stone, lapis lazuli, amethyst, or anything on the middle finger, a good old reliable crucifix around the neck, made of silver, not gold, and at least one ounce in weight and two inches in diameter. A psalm in papyrus folded in a shirt pocket next to the heart. A blessing from a priest, a breathing of nothing but incense with a towel over the head. A bout of fasting, one night without sleep, a dreamless night, and a dreamless, sleepless, youngest son restored to them. He wants to stay around the house, he shows them why he loves his mummy and poppy and the bounteous land. There is no plan to flee. There is no city woman with his heart in her hand. And his brain is not ablaze in his pants. His head is not an empty, airless room.

They have one cardboard suitcase each, apart from her purse and his envelope tied with a string that contains their passports and tickets, birth certificates, and, for him, a document that he is indeed a clerk with X amount of experience at such-and-such a government office, signed "supervisor"—a worthless piece of shit, of course, in the eyes of any British employer. But for the time being, these little things are emblematic of the towering, staggering optimism that propels them out of Georgetown, Guyana, over the sea to London, England.

So what do they do? My mother is a shy woman. My father, in the two photos I've seen of him, is equally reserved. Not given to experimentation. The big risk has been taken—that of leaving everything they know for all that is alien to them. My mother knows next to nothing about sex, except perhaps a bit about kissing. My father may have experimented a little, as boys tend to do, but he, too, when faced with the female body, confronts unfamiliar territory. Each burns for the other, enough to pull up roots and take off into the unknown. Yet I want to believe that they improvise around the idea of her purity and respect it until their marriage night. That they keep intact some of the moral system they come from even as they dismantle and ignore every other stricture placed on them by Guyanese society: honor your father and mother; fear a just and loving God; pledge allegiance to the flag; lust is the devil's oxygen. All that circles in their veins.

Over the twelve days at sea they examine what they have left and what they are heading toward. At sea they are in between lives: one life is over but the other has not yet begun. The talking they do on that ship without any duties to perform at all! My mother tells how her father, despite his routine as a merchant seaman, finds time to memorize whole poems by the Victorians: Tennyson, Longfellow, Browning, Jean Ingelow, Arnold, and Hopkins. The sea is his workplace, yet he makes time to do this marvelous thing. She tells how when he comes back to land he gathers them all in the living room and performs "The Charge of the Light Brigade" or "Maud" or "My Last Duchess" or "Fra Lippo Lippi" or "The High Tide on the Coast of Lincolnshire" or "Dover Beach" or "The Kingfisher" or "The Wreck of the Deutschland." He recites these poems to his Creole-thinking children, who sit there and marvel at the English they are hearing, not that of the policeman or the teacher or the priest, but even more difficult to decipher, full of twists and impossible turns that throw you off the bicycle of your Creole reasoning into the sand. If any of them interrupts my grandfather he stops in midflow, tells them off in Creole, and resumes his poem where he left off. When particularly miffed by the disturbance he starts the poem from the beginning again. Does my grandfather recite these verses before or after he gets drunk, swears at the top of his voice, and chases my grandmother around the house with his broad leather belt?

But when my parents are out at sea, they have only the King James Bible in their possession. What they plan and rehearse is every aspect of their new life.

"Children. I want children."

"Me too. Plenty of them."

"I can work between births."

"Yes, both of us. Until we have enough money for a house. Then you can stay home with the kids."

"A nanny. Someone to watch the kids while we work. What kind of house?"

"Three bedrooms. A garden at the front, small, and back, large. A car—a Morris Minor. With all that room in the back for the children and real indicators and a wood finish." Neither has a notebook or dreamed of keeping one. They do not write their thoughts, they utter them. If something is committed to memory, there has to be a quotidian reason for it, apart from bits of the Bible and a few calypsos. My grandfather's labor of love, his settling down with a copy of Palgrave's *Golden Treasury* and memorizing lines that bear no practical relationship to his life, must seem bizarre to his children. Yet by doing so he demonstrates his love of words, their music, the sense of their sound, their approximation to the heartbeat and breath, their holding out of an alternative world to the one surrounding him, their confirmation of a past and another's life and thoughts, their luxury of composition, deliberation, their balancing and rebalancing of a skewered life. I imagine my mother benefits from this exposure in some oblique way—that the Victorians stick to her mental makeup whether she cares for them or not, that a little of them comes off on me in the wash of my gestation in her.

There is an old black-and-white photo (isn't there always?) and fragments of stories about his comings and goings, his carryings-on, as the West Indian speak goes, his mischief. "Look pan that smooth face, them two big, dark eye them, don't they win trust quick-time? Is hard to tie the man with them eye in him head to any woman and she pickney them. He face clean-shaven like he never shave. He curly black hair, dougla-look, but trim neat-neat. The man got topside." His hair, thick and wavy because of the "dougla" mix of East Indian and black, exaggerates an already high forehead. Automatically we credit such an appearance, in the Caribbean and elsewhere, with intelligence—"topside." And a

European nose, not broad, with a high bridge (good breeding, though the nostrils flare a bit—sign of a quick temper!). And lips that invite kisses. "They full-full and pout like a kiss with the sound of a kiss way behind, long after that kiss come and gone." He is six feet tall and thin but not skinny, that brand of thin that women refer to as elegant, since the result is long fingers and economic gestures. Notice I say economic and not cheap. A man of few words. A watcher. "But when he relax in company he know and trust, then he the center of wit and idle philosophizing. He shoot back a few rums, neat no chaser, with anyone, and hold his own with men more inclined to gin and tonic. He know when to mind he Ps and Qs and when to gaff in the most lewd Georgetown, rumshop talk with the boys. What chance a sixteen-year-old closeted lady got against such a man, I ask you?"

But most of the puzzle is missing. So I start to draw links from one fragment to the next. He begins to belong—fleetingly, at first—in my life. As a man in poor light seen crossing a road mercifully free of traffic, its tar-macadam steamy with a recent downpour. As a tall, lank body glimpsed ducking under the awning of a shop front and disappearing inside and never emerging no matter how long I wait across the street, watching the door with its reflecting plate glass and listening for the little jingle of the bell that announces the arrival and departure of customers.

Or I cross Blackheath Hill entranced by the urgent belief that my father is in one of the cars speeding up and down it. Blackheath Hill curves a little with a steep gradient—less than one in six in places. It's more of a ski slope than a hill. Cars and trucks, motorbikes and cyclists all come down the road as if in a race for a finish line. Going up it is no different. Vehicles race to the top as if with the fear that their engines might cut off and they will slide back down. I want to be seen by my father. I have to be close to his car so that he does not miss me. I measure the traffic and watch myself get halfway, then, after a pause to allow a couple of cars to pass on their way up, a brisk walk, if I time it right, to allow the rest of the traffic to catch up with me, to see the kid who seems to be in no particular hurry to get out of their way looking at them. I step onto the sidewalk and cherish the breeze of the nearest vehicle at my back—Father, this is your son you have just missed. Isn't he big? Pull over and call his name. Take him in your arms. Admonish him. Remind him that cars can kill and his little body would not survive a hit at these high speeds. Tell him to look for his father under less dangerous circumstances.

I am searching the only way I know how, by rumination, contemplation, conjecture, supposition. I try to fill the gaps, try to piece together the father I never knew. I imagine everything where there is little or nothing to go on. And yet, in going back, in raking up bits and pieces of a shattered and erased existence, I know that I am courting rejection from a source hitherto silent and beyond me. I am conjuring up a father safely out of reach and taking the risk that the lips I help to move, the lungs I force to breathe, will simply say "No." No to everything I ask of them, even the merest crumb of recognition.

"Father." The noun rings hollowly when I say it, my head is empty of any meaning the word might have. I shout it in a dark cave but none of the expected bats come flapping out. Just weaker and weaker divisions of my call. "Father." It is my incantation to bring him back from the grave to the responsibility of his name. But how, when I only know his wife, my mother, and her sudden, moody silence whenever he crops up in conversation?

You ever have anyone sweet-talk you? Fill your ears with their kind of wax, rub that wax with their tongue all over your body with more promises than the promised land itself contains, fill your head with their sweet drone, their buzz that shuts out your parents, friends, your own mind from its own house? That's your father, the bumblebee, paying attention to me.

My sixteenth birthday was a month behind. He was nearly twenty. A big man in my eyes. What did he want with me? A smooth tongue in my ears. Mostly, though, he watched me, my house, my backside when he followed me home from school. His eyes gleamed in the early evening, the whites of his eyes. He stood so still by the side of the road outside my house that he might have been a lamppost, planted there, shining just for me.

My father cursed him, my mother joined in, my sisters laughed at his silence, his stillness. They all said he had to be the most stupid man in Georgetown, a dunce, a bat in need of a perch, out in the sun too long, sun fry his brain, cat take his tongue, his head empty like a calabash, his tongue cut out, he look like a beggar. They felt sorry for him standing there like a paling, his face a yard long, his tongue a slab of useless plywood in his mouth. "Look what Ingrid gone and bring to the house, shame, dumbness, blackness follow she here to we house to paint shame all over it and us. Go away, black boy, take your dumb misery somewhere else, crawl back to your pen in the country, leave we sister alone, she got more beauty than sense to listen to a fool like you, to let you follow her, to encourage you by not cursing the day you was born and the two people who got together to born you and your people and the whole sorry village you crawl out of to come and plant yourself here in front of we house on William Street, a decent street, in Kitty, in we capital."

I should have thanked my sisters; instead I begged them to leave him alone. Ignore him and he'll go away. My father left the house to get hold of the boy by the scruff of his neck and boot his back-side out of Kitty, but he ran off when my father appeared in the door frame. With the light of the house behind him and casting a long, dark shadow, he must have looked twice his size and in no mood to bargain. Your father sprinted away, melting into the darkness. I watched for his return by checking that the windows I'd bolted earlier really were bolted, convincing myself that I had overlooked one of them, using my hands to feel the latch as I searched the street for him. But he was gone for the night. My knight. Shining eyes for armor.

My mother cursed him from the living room window, flung it open and pointed at him and with her tongue reduced him to a pile of rubble and scattered that rubble over a wide area then picked her way through the strewn wreckage to make sure her destruction was complete: "Country boy, what you want with my daughter? What make you think you man enough for her? What you got between your legs that give you the right to plant yourself in front of my house? What kind of blight you is? You fungus!"

As she cursed him and he retreated from the house sheepishly, she watched her husband for approval. These were mild curses for her, dutiful curses, a warm-up. When she really got going her face reddened and her left arm carved up the air in front of her as if it were the meat of her opponent being dissected into bite-size bits. That's how I knew she was searching for a way to help me but hadn't yet found it. Not as long as my father was at home. Soon he would be at sea, away for weeks, and things would be different.

That is, if my onlooker, my remote watcher, my far-off admirer wasn't scared off forever. And what if he was? Then he didn't deserve me in the first place. If he couldn't take a few curses he wasn't good for anything. If I wasn't worth taking a few curses for . . . well, I didn't want a man who didn't think I was worth taking a few curses for! I loved him for coming back night after night when all he got from me was a glance at the window. Sometimes less than a glance. Just me passing across the window frame as I dashed from chore to chore under four baleful eyes.

It seemed like he was saving all his breath and words for when he could be alone with me. Then he turned on the bumblebee of himself and I was the hapless flower of his attentions. He told me about my skin that it was silk, that all the colors of the rainbow put together still didn't come close to my beautiful skin. That my face, my eyes, my mouth, my nose, the tip of my nose, my ears, my fingertips, each was a precious jewel, precious stone. He likened the rest of me to things I had read about but had never seen, had dreamed about but had never dreamed I would see: dandelions, apples, snow, spring in England's shires, the white cliffs of Dover. In his eyes my body, me, was everything I dreamed of becoming.

That was your father before any of you were a twinkle in his eye. More accurately, that was my lover and then my husband. Your father was a different man altogether. Suddenly a stranger occupied my bed. His tongue now turned to wood. All the laughter of my sisters, the halfhearted curses of my mother, my father's promise of blue misery, all came true in this strange man, this father, this latter-day husband and lover.

I saw the change in him. My hands were full with you children. He went out of reach. He cradled you as if he didn't know which side was up, which down. He held you at arm's length to avoid the tar and feathers of you babies. Soon I earned the same treatment, but if you children were tar and feathers I was refuse. His face creased when he came near me. What had become of my silk skin? My precious features disappeared into my face, earning neither praise nor blame—just his silence, his wooden tongue, and that bad-smell look of his. I kept quiet for as long as I could. I watched him retreat from all of us, hoping he'd reel himself back in since the line between us was strong and I thought unbreakable; but no. I had to shout to get him to hear me. I shouted like my mother standing at the upstairs window to some rude stranger in the street twenty-five yards away. I sounded like my father filling the door frame. My jeering sisters insinuated their way into my voice. And your father simply kept walking away.

Believe me, I pulled my hair and beat the ground with my hands and feet to get at him in my head and in the ground he walked on that I worshiped. Hadn't he delivered England to me and all the seasons of England, all England's shires and the fog he'd left out of his serenades, no doubt just to keep some surprise in store for me? The first morning I opened the door that autumn and shouted, "Fire!" when I saw all that smoke, thinking the whole street on fire, all the streets, London burning, and slammed the door and ran into his arms and his laughter, and he took me out into it in my nightdress, he in his pajamas, and all the time I followed him, not ashamed to be seen outside in my thin, flimsy nylon (if anyone could see through that blanket) because he was in his pajamas, the blue, striped ones, and his voice, his sweet drone, told me it was fine, this smoke without fire was fine, "This is fog."

He walked away and everything started to be erased by that fog. That smoke without fire crossed the ocean into my past and obliterated Kitty, Georgetown, the house on William Street, everything he had touched, every place I had known him in. I swallowed that fog. It poured into my ears, nose, eyes, mouth. He was gone. I got a chest pain and breathlessness that made me panic. There wasn't just me. There were you children. I had to breathe for you children. The pain in my chest that was your father had to be plucked out, otherwise I too would be lost to you all, and to myself.

The first time I see him is the last time I see him. I can't wait to get to the front of the queue to have him all to myself. When I get there my eyes travel up and down his body. From those few gray hairs that decorate his temples and his forehead and his nose to the cuffs at his ankles and sparkling black shoes. He wears a black suit, a double-breasted number with three brass buttons on the cuff of each sleeve. He lies on his back with his hands clasped over his flat stomach. There is too much powder on his face. Let's get out of this mournful place, Dad. We have a lot of catching up to do. He has the rare look—of holding his breath, of not breathing, in between inhaling and exhaling—that exquisitely beautiful corpses capture. For a moment after I invite him to leave with me, I expect his chest to inflate, his lids to open, and those clasped hands to unfold and pull him upright into a sitting position as if he really were just napping because he has dressed way too early for the ball.

There are myths about this sort of thing. Father enslaves son. Son hates father, bides his time, waits for the strong father to weaken. Son pounces one day, pounces hard and definite, and the father is overwhelmed, broken, destroyed with hardly any resistance, except that of surprise and then resignation. Son washes his hands but finds he is washing hands that are not bloodstained, not marked or blemished in any way. He is simply scrubbing hands that no longer belong to him—they are his father's hands, attached to his arms, his shoulders, his body. He has removed a shadow all the more to see unencumbered the father in himself. There is the widow he has made of his mother. He cannot love her as his father might. While his father lived he thought he could. The moment his father expired he knew his mother would remain unloved.

———

I alight too soon from a number 53 bus on Blackheath Hill, dis-
embark while the bus is moving, and stumble, trip from two legs
onto all fours, hands like feet, transforming, sprouting more
limbs, becoming a spider and breaking my fall. That same fall is
now a tumble, a dozen somersaults that end with me standing
upright and quite still on two legs with the other limbs dangling.
Onlookers, who fully expected disaster, applaud. I walk back up
the hill to the block of council flats as a man might, upright, on
two legs. My other limbs dangle, swing as if they are two hands.
Some days I will be out of breath, I will gasp and exhale, and the
cloud before me will not be my winter's breath but the silken
strands of a web, or worse, fire. Other days I might look at a bed
of geraniums planted on the council estate and turn all their
numberless petals into stone. A diamond, held between my thumb
and index finger, crumbles in this mood, in this light, like the
powdery wings of a butterfly.

I stare out of an apartment on the twenty-fourth floor of a tower
block overlooking the nut-brown Thames. That wasp on the
window-pane nibbling up and down the glass for a pore to exit
through, back into the air and heat, tries to sting what it can feel
but cannot see. My father is the window. I am the wasp. Sometimes
a helping hand comes along and lifts the window, and the wasp
slides out. Other times a shadow descends, there is a displacement
of air, and it is the last thing the wasp knows. Which of those times
is this? I want to know. I don't want to know. I am not nibbling
nor trying to sting. I am kissing, repeatedly, rapidly, the feature-
less face of my father. It feels like summer light. It reflects a
garden. Whose is that interfering hand? Why that interrupting
shadow? My child's hand. My child's shadow. My son or my
father? My son and my father. Two sons, two fathers. Yet three
people. We walk behind a father's name, shoulder a father's
memory. Wear another's walk, another's gait. Wait for what has
happened to their bodies, the same scars, maladies, aches, to surface in ours.

I want to shed my skin. Walk away from my shadow. Leave my name in a place I cannot return to. To be nameless, bodiless. To swim to Wallace Stevens's Key West, which is shoreless, horizon-less. Blackheath Hill becomes Auden's Bristol Street, an occasion for wonder and lament. Blackheath at 5:45 a.m. on a foggy winter morning becomes Peckham Rye. There are no trees on Black-heath, but angels hang in the air if only Blake were there to see them. On the twenty-fourth floor towering above the Thames, water, not land, surrounds me. Everything seems to rise out of that water. Look up at ambling clouds and the tower betrays its drift out to sea.

On Earth

By Jacqueline Woodson

Jacqueline Woodson (1963–) was born in Columbus, Ohio, and grew up in Greenville, South Carolina, and Brooklyn, New York. A former drama therapist for homeless children in New York City, she has won numerous awards for her novels and children's books, including The Kenyon Review Award for Literary Excellence in Fiction. In "On Earth" she evokes a girl's longing for the mother left behind when she and her siblings are sent to their grandmother in the rural South.

It is July when the letter comes from my mother. The letter is part of Jehovah's plan, we know but still, it silences us.

Although I miss you all terribly, the letter says, *I am not ready for you to come home.*

We sit at my grandmother's feet on the front porch stairs while yellow jackets and butterflies circle around us and the porch swing whines and creaks with her rocking. My sister Layana is fifteen and has taken on a faraway look this summer. She is walking the wide road, Layana is. The one that can only lead to destruction. She prays with her eyes open. Her head unbowed. When my grandmother reads the part about my mother needing more time, Lay turns and stares off into the distance, her eyes closing into slits. We have been at my grandmother's house since March when Layana found my mother huddled and crying on the floor of our apartment in New York City. A nervous disorder, the doctors said. Complicated by a hormonal imbalance.

"She went crazy," Layana said. "Simple as that."

It is almost a blur now—my mother huddled in the corner speaking a language that wasn't a language, whispering words that weren't words, the ambulance screaming down our street, my friends running to our front stoop and asking in whispers "What happened?" Then the four of us in a room somewhere, bright fluorescent lights above us and a woman asking questions about our next of kin. A day later, my grandmother was standing in the doorway saying, "You all will have to come stay with me for a while." And me and the twins running into her arms, but Layana holding back, looking everywhere but at the four of us.

March seems like a long time ago.

Layana blinks, then rubs her eyes and frowns. She has pulled her thick hair back into a braid and sits chewing the end of it. Layana is the beautiful one, people say. She is tall and narrow with Mama's dark eyes and thick lashes. Last summer, when we were visiting our grandmother and the relatives came, they turned Lay this way and that, saying, "Let me look at you." "Girl, you are surely Carletta's child. Got all her pretty, didn't you?" "Gonna break hearts if you ain't already." But now when the relatives come, Layana leaves. You look right, you see their cars pulling in. You look left, you see Layana taking off down the road, her thin linen dress blowing slow in the breeze, her thick black braid bouncing soft between her shoulder blades.

"Maybe I got all her crazy too," Layana whispers at night. "Some nights I ask Jehovah to take it all away. You're lucky, Carlene. You probably didn't inherit anything from her." And it's true. I am not pretty like Layana. My nose is too narrow and my cheekbones jut up out of my face too fiercely. My eyes and hair are the same brown as my skin so that when you stand looking at me, it's hard to tell where skin stops and hair begins. Even my name, although it sounds like my mother's, has nothing to do with her. I was named for the way I was born, inside the back of my father's Mustang—a black convertible he got into two years later and kept on driving.

Now Layana glares down the road as my grandmother reads our mother's letter.

The doctors say I need more time alone.

The road is red dirt and curves at the end of our property onto a wider, paved one. That paved road keeps going, getting wider and wider until you're finally in Charleston, South Carolina. Charleston's our big city, but my grandmother tells us Anderson is growing, says soon this town will be a big city town like Charleston. My grandmother's southern accent is heavy. She has lived in Anderson all of her life. When we ride the bus, she herds us all four to the very back. "It's what I know," she says when Layana reminds her that the laws changed a long time ago. "It's a law that stayed in my bones."

Like God.

"The first time I walked into a Kingdom Hall," our grandmother tells us. "I knew I was home."

"How," Layana asks. "You going to tell us God came down into the Hall and called your name."

"He didn't have to," she says, ignoring Layana's sarcasm. "I had already called his. Jehovah, I said. Jehovah God."

"How old was Mama," I ask again because I've heard this story and asked this question so many times.

"Twelve," my brother Clay says. "Twelve twelve twelve."

"Did she called Jehovah's name, too?"

Layana glares at me, but I just go on resting my head on my knees waiting for an answer.

"Has she *ever*?" Layana says.

"When she was a child, she believed like ya'll do," our grandmother says.

I look up at the sky. It is blue and nearly cloudless. Jehovah is up in that blue. Sitting on a throne looking down at us. Looking right straight through to our marrow.

At night, Layana makes me practice. "Say 'I think so'," she whispers. "Don't say 'I reckon.' Say 'You' not 'Ya'll.' You want to lose all your city?" And I shake my head because my city is the only thing I have left. And the silver ring my mother gave me for my twelfth birthday. But as my grandmother reads, I feel my city slipping away from me. The cracks in the sidewalk in front of our building are fading. The double-Dutch games and running to the corner store for potato chips and cream soda are almost gone. My mother leaning out the window to call us in for dinner is all whispery and blurred. New York is becoming a dream I used to have.

Way off I can hear my sometime friends Cora and Lubell singing Miss Lucy had a baby. My big brothers are playing with the cuffs of their pants. They're both thirteen, born a minute apart and identical. Clay has a mole above his right eye and Scott has one right where his thumb meets the rest of his hand. Otherwise, if you're not related to them, it's hard to tell who's who. Clay is quiet and Scott is the one who can sing.

I swallow and stare towards the sun, not right at it because I know that will make me go blind but sort of sideways and at the edges of it where orange and red meet the darkening sky. Soon the sun will drop down and disappear and it will be night. My mother has done this. Dropped down and disappeared. I twirl the silver ring. There are blackbirds etched into it, circling. My mother is a blackbird. And we're her four hatchlings. Without wings.

Give the kids hugs for me and tell them how much I love them. Tell them, Jehovah's Will, they'll be home by September. Tell Carlene not to worry. I know how she worries.

"I'm not worrying," I say, watching my grandmother fold the letter over and over itself. Watching my mother disappear.

"Your face is all bunched up," Scott says. "Look at your eyebrows. They're all knitted up."

Clay looks at me and frowns.

"I'm not worrying," I say again.

Armageddon is what will claim the ones that don't believe in Jehovah. Fire falling from the sky, floods, famine and plagues. If you try to hide in the water, poisonous snakes will be there to bite you. If you hide beneath your bed, God's hand will pull you from your hiding place and strike you dead. There is no place you can go on Earth and be saved. No place but into the heart of

God. I stand up straight inside His heart, say my prayers, don't curse or disrespect anyone. I walk a narrow path. The hardest kind to walk. Believe in Jehovah's Will, my grandmother says, and everything will work out in the end. I bite my bottom lip hard, close my eyes and try to believe I will see my mother again.

My grandmother tells us to stand up, and we do, one behind the other with Layana last so she can hug us for Mama. When she gets to Layana, she hugs extra long and hard but Layana puts her arms out, keeping our grandmother's hug from our mother at a distance.

My grandmother sighs. "You all go on and get ready now. A letter from your mama don't mean we got to be late for the Meeting." She sits on the porch rocking, staring off down the road. And rocking.

Scott holds the screen door open until we are all inside. "She can keep New York," he whispers to us. "Anderson got schools and stuff."

"Anderson got a girl named Lori," Clay says, punching Scott in the arm. "Got you with your lips on hers all evening."

Scott punches him back. "I ain't studying no Lori."

"You more than studying her."

"You keep kissing on country girls and talking like that, you're going to lose your city," I say. But Scott and Clay just look at me.

"You worry too much," Clay says.

I try not to think about my mother's letter as I pull a flowered dress over my head. I listen to the porch swing. When it stops, I hear the faint sound of paper and wonder if my grandmother is unfolding the letter or balling it up to throw away. Until this day, the only leaving I know is through death. My grandfather's death years and years ago. I know tears for the dying and a body being put into the ground. I know my grandfather's soft brown hands folded across his chest and his face, contorted in pain for months, at rest. I know how a disease sometimes wins in the end. Takes a person away.

Some mornings when I'm sitting with Cora and Lubell on the front porch stairs, Cora asks what's it like to not have a mama around and I shrug and say I miss the smell of her, that's all. But that's everything. And Cora and Lubell frown and shake their heads at me. They think I'm a strange city girl, exotic as the pictures they've seen of Birds of Paradise but nothing they'd ever want to be or get too near. "You're all brown," they say when they want to be mean. "Head to toe brown like swamp-water." And then days go by without us speaking.

The house is hushed and solemn. My grandmother has put a record on—Witness songs. We have always been Jehovah's Witnesses. It will be the religion of my own children if I ever have any. If the world doesn't end before I am married. My mother is no longer a Witness. Two years ago she was ex-communicated because she was dating a man who was not in the Truth—our religion. The true one. A worldly man, the elders said. A man who smoked and drank and spent the night at our house sometimes. His name was Luther and he taught me how to play chess and cornrow my own hair. At night I lay in bed imagining the day they'd marry—Luther in a black tux, my mother in a blue dress and me following down the aisle behind them sprinkling white rose petals. But it didn't happen.

"Tell them," my grandmother warned my mother. "Tell the elders about him." But my mother refused to. So that fall, when my grandmother made the trip to New York to return us to our mother, she visited our congregation and had a talk with the elders.

Don't come to New York again, my mother said.

And my grandmother didn't.

Until last March.

My mother doesn't call. She is afraid of my grandmother's voice. Afraid of the damage one voice can do.

Technically, we are not allowed to speak to our mother. It is against the religion. But it is against the Ten Commandments not to honor her. Honor Thy Father and Thy Mother, the Commandments tell us. Jehovah's Witnesses are the chosen people. Cora and Lubell will be destroyed when God sees fit to put an end to this system of things. My mother will be destroyed. *Our Father who art in Heaven. Please see fit to spare her.* But the Witnesses will be part of a

New World, God's second Garden of Eden. The elders refer to it as Paradise on Earth. Even the dead ones, my grandmother promises, will be resurrected.

Every Monday we sit in my grandmother's living room for Bible study. And Thursday night we go to the Kingdom Hall for Ministry School. We will all go into the ministry once we are done with high school. When Layana says she might want to go to college, my grandmother tells her not to be a fool, and Layana presses her lips closed with the words still swimming around behind them. In New York, we had our Bible studies with an elder from our congregation there. When he arrived, he and my mother didn't speak. *Get your Bibles,* our mother would say as she retreated upstairs. Soon, we could hear music wafting down; soft, sad music that my mother always listened to.

To be welcomed back into the religion, my mother was supposed to sit in on every Meeting with us—Bible studies, Ministry School and our Sunday Watchtower Study. But she didn't. If she had, she would not have been allowed to speak to anyone nor would anyone have been allowed to speak to her. *I wouldn't be able to stand it,* she said. *Walking into that Meeting and having everyone turn away from me.*

"But you'll never be a Witness again, Mama," I pleaded the first time my mother turned to retreat upstairs. "And you'll be destroyed in Armageddon."

Don't worry, Carlene. Jehovah has a plan for us all.

As I watched my mother disappear up those stairs, as I watched her beautiful back sway heavenward, up into the dying light of evening coming in through the sky window, I knew she was slipping away from God even as she walked toward him. I knew she was slipping away from me. Even as she called my name.

"What is Jehovah God's plan?" the elder asked while Mama's music played upstairs.

"There will come an end to this system of things," I said. "Death and suffering will be no more. Nor will wrongdoing." As my mother's music took a seat on one side of me. And God on the other.

The elder smiled and nodded. Pleased.

We know right from wrong. We know we are special, God's chosen people. When the color-guards at school raise the flag, we leave the room. We pledge allegiance only to God. We do not celebrate birthdays or Christmas because these are worldly ways and although we are in this world, the elders tell us, we are not of it. I will never curse or drink. I will never dance or play Spin the Bottle. I will never learn the hand movements of worldly games like Miss Lucy Had a Baby and Miss Mary Mack. My brothers will never go to war. One day, we are promised, we will have happiness and life everlasting—one day.

It is almost evening when we leave the house, Layana and me in dresses, our hair unbraided, brushed and oiled, Clay and Scott in shirts and ties. Our grandmother behind us wearing a soft blue dress and navy beads. As we climb into her car and drive to our meeting, Layana sits in the front seat beside our grandmother and sighs. Even after all these years, the car still smells of my grandfather's pipe, the one he was never allowed to smoke in the house, smells of the tobacco that is against our religion. But the elders didn't know he smoked. No one ever told them. I stare at the back of my grandmother's head, at the gray curls pulled to the top of her head, at the straight neck and shoulders. She is proud of her holiness. Proud of the good Witnesses she and her grandchildren have become. There is no room on the narrow road for smoking or worldly men. There is so much room at its edges for hypocrisy.

Layana rolls the window down and sticks her head out. Three years from now, she will be gone, down that road and off into the foggy light of morning, her suitcase banging against her leg, her acceptance letter to Swarthmore folded up inside her knapsack. And for months, I will wake to find her gone and cry.

Beside me, Clay and Scott play scissors, paper, rock. Scott singing the words softly over and over again: "Scissors, paper, rock, scissors, paper, rock, scissors, paper, rock . . ." They will stay here in Anderson always, going from door to door every Saturday morning to say, "Hi, I'm one of Jehovah's Witnesses and I'm here to bring you some good news today." And they will pray for the people who slam the door in their faces and preach to the ones who will listen.

I press my head against the window and watch pines and oak trees move slowly by me. We will not see our mother again. The letters will be fewer and fewer until there are no more. And her voice on the phone saying, *Soon, baby, soon,* will come out of nowhere a year later, stay on for a few months then slowly grow unfamiliar. Less promising.

Charleston is not far by bus. It is bigger than Anderson and as alive as New York at night. In a café, years later, I will look up and see a woman who reminds me of my mother and stand quickly, knocking my coffee over. "Ma?" I will call and the woman will turn, look at me. And for a moment our eyes will register something. *You found me!* our eyes will say. *After all these years!* But then the light will change and the woman will become who she always was, a stranger who is not my mother. And the stranger will turn slowly, pay her check. And leave.

And somewhere inside of me Jehovah God will settle, a part of my blood and bones. But my fear of Armageddon and my belief in life everlasting will grow as faint as my mother's voice, as far away as the promise of her. Familiar and foreign as a stranger's face.

"Scissors, paper, rock," Scott sings.

My grandmother's back is straight.

Layanna leans her head further out the window.

Her hair is wild like Mama's.

It blows and blows and blows.

Three Sonnets for Mister Kent

By Kendel Hippolyte

St. Lucian poet and playwright **Kendel Hippolyte** (1952–) works in traditional forms like the sonnet and in free verse influenced by rap and reggae. Awarded the St. Lucia Medal of Merit (Gold) for Contribution to the Arts, he has published four poetry volumes, including *Birthright,* in which "Three Sonnets for Mister Kent" appears. "The sonnets came out of a sense of gratitude to my father," Hippolyte explains. "I didn't plan to write a tribute, but I just felt the thanks rising in me."

Delirium Tremens

Towards the end he got the d.t's. He would see
a smiling girl in a white first communion dress
waving at him. He'd smile back, point her out to me
and i stopped arguing because she, more than i, could bless
even a little, those last days when my presence
only made heavier a weight of guilt and love
that he was tired of. He turned to her, his innocence,
he turned to her—with joy, the way he would have
turned to me, his son, if i had known enough
to see, past a son's need, what he was giving:
his rebel walk, trampling all boundaries, and his child's laugh
bursting like fireworks, igniting from a flame of living.
i grew too fast. i never met, in me, the child
he later raised from his own need, who waved and smiled.

'So Jah Sey'

Dread song. 'Not one of my seed' the words said
(and it hurt every time i heard Bob sing)
'shall sit on your sidewalk and beg your bread.'
No, Pa, i'd think, never. My eyes would sting.
And yet it could have happened. Easily.
i burned to live a different kind of life;
more wild, more free—in fact, the kind that he
had lived, even with children and a wife.
My simmering rage would boil sometimes, would spurt
hot scalding words on him. i'd almost leave.
But i knew he'd turn beggar. And that hurt.
Why? Pride? The thought that when he died i'd grieve?
No. But somehow he had become my son,
my seed. And i, a tree now, couldn't run.

Mister Kent

My father left me the city's derelicts.
At thirty-one, it was a strange legacy:
whores on their last flare, bums, alcoholics,
the smell of rum-and-cigarette, poverty.
An acrid smell that i could recognise.
But there was something else as well.
They had a burning. It inflamed their eyes.
Their look could scorch your world to hell.

And yet they called me Mister Kent.
And the muted warm way they said
it breathed a bright blaze from that patronym,
illumining for me what his life meant
and why, although in one sense he is dead,
in a new light i have inherited him.

The Shifting Self

The Drill

By Breena Clarke

Breena Clarke (1951–) grew up in Washington, D.C., was educated at Webster College and Howard University, and now lives in New Jersey. Her first novel, *River Cross My Heart,* about a family dealing with the loss of a child, was an Oprah Book Club selection. In her short story, "The Drill," Clarke illuminates the heart of a mother who, terrified of the dangers that might befall a Black teenage boy, must nevertheless allow her son's bid for independence.

Take the bus out Forty-second Street—the crosstown bus, the M42—and get off at Seventh Avenue. Then take the Number One train. Get off at 157th Street. Don't get off at 168th Street. Okay? When you're riding the Number One and you get off at 168th Street, you have to ride the elevator and the elevator is nasty. Also, there are too many homeless people on the platform at 168th Street. Anything can happen in that station. Don't get off at 168th Street. Take the Number One at Times Square and get off at 157th Street. Okay? I'll wait in the station at 157th Street. But if you don't see me, don't wait for me. Start walking up on the east side of the street, and I'll walk down on the east side and I'll see you. So walk on the east side of the street."

She starts off a good ten minutes earlier than the earliest time he could have gotten to the station at 157th Street unless they got let out early. It's the middle of winter and has been dark for hours. She turns over in her mind the color of the cap he wore that morning and recalls what color the coat was. As if she needed clues to recognize him! She is absolutely certain that blindfolded and unable to hear or touch him, she'd be able to distinguish her son in a stadium full of fourteen-year-olds. She knows him in every cell of her body. But when you *love* someone, you memorize their clothes.

It's ten p.m. and she wishes she were reclining in front of the TV. She is playing and replaying in her head the tape of his itinerary from the deck of the docked aircraft carrier *Intrepid*, through the midtown streets, north on the subway, to the subway station where she'll meet him. "He can do it. I mean, there's no reason to think he'll get lost or anything."

They'd struck a bargain. He wanted so badly to be independent and out after dark that he agreed to all her prerequisites. If she would agree not to go over there with him—after the first time—and stand around waiting for him to be finished and walk him home, he promised to follow the one and only agreed-upon itinerary and not make any unauthorized stops. She agreed he should have money for a slice and a Coke or a hot dog and a Coke and some candy probably. He agreed to travel quickly and prudently in the company of his new friend, Derrick. He would sit in the subway car with the conductor in it—only.

His smile when she was finally won over was triumphant. He exchanged a victory glance with his stepfather over her head as if they'd been together on a strategy against her. They thought she didn't catch it, but she could smell the testosterone in the air. She detected a difference in the house lately. Those two sharing a certain odor of complicity. Their hormones lined up against hers.

She is letting the kite out a little farther every day. She's giving it more string, exposing it to the wind, but holding her end tighter and tighter. The city closes in around kids nowadays, and walking through the streets is like passing through a gauntlet. Her husband thinks it's queer the way she leaps into the gutter to put her arms out like a crossing guard when the three of them approach a street corner. "Look at all these people," he says sarcastically. "Most of them born and raised in New York City, and somehow they've survived as pedestrians without your help." This is not amusing to someone who regularly tests her own reflexes to be sure she's alert enough to charge in front of a raging bull of a car, driven by Lucifer's own taxi driver, careening directly toward her child.

Her letting him go by himself to the cadet practice way across town, his walking in a part of the city that's dark, his having to move through the gaudy neon swirl of Times Square, his traveling by himself on the subway at a dicey hour—this is all new.

He's had to memorize four different combinations for four different locks this year: his locker for coat and books, his locker for gym stuff, his swimming locker at the Y, and the lock for the chain on his bike. She bought him a bicycle, but they both know he better not take his hand off it unless he puts on the fifty-dollar lock with the money-back guarantee. When he had to replace a defective part on the bicycle, she put on jeans and a sweatshirt and rode with him and the bike on the subway. They're both glad he prefers his skateboard. It's easier to defend and cheaper to replace.

He's not a street child, but he's got pluck. He's not a fighter, but he's scrappy. He's tall, brown, with a sweet face, and she ruminates about what the cops will think if he reaches into his pocket for his gloves.

His wanting to join the cadet drill team is all tied up with the new friend, Derrick. They want to solidify their friendship with uniforms and syncopated walking. She disapproves of mumbling, but likes this boy who mumbles shyly and respectfully. He's got home training.

"Better to exit up this stairway than that because you'll be facing the right direction. Best to stand directly under the streetlamp so the bus driver will see you. Remember how we decided that standing well back from the edge of the platform is the best protection against an insane person pushing you onto the tracks in front of an arriving train? Keep your eyes and ears open, your mouth shut. Don't spend the transportation money on junk snacks and then try to get away with using your school pass after seven p.m. Don't jump the turnstile no matter what except in a case of being utterly stranded and having exhausted all other alternatives, including pleading with the token clerk."

Per the agreement, on the first night of the cadet program she went with him. She traced the route and discussed the idiosyncrasies in detail. She rolled her head from left to right and back again, surveying the street ahead—a walking defense mechanism picked up in the city. You let your eyes sweep the street broadly as far in front of you as possible. This way, you see certain crazies and drunks and friends you're not in the mood for before they see you. Leaving the *Intrepid,* standing with the two boys in the full bloom of a streetlamp, she was quietly annoyed with Derrick's people for not sending someone to accompany him. "He lives in the Bronx, for chrissake!" Suddenly she was not sure if she wasn't overreacting to the perceived dangers. "Don't smother the boy." Even her father chimed in. Acutely sensitive to the Daniel Patrick Moynihan school of thought on pathological black female emasculators, she checks herself. "No, they should've come. These boys are still too young to scrabble around New York at ten o'clock at night."

They mounted the bus finally and the driver was cheerful. She fought the impulse to ask him if he always drove this route and if it always rounded the corner at exactly this time. When the bus crossed 42nd between Eighth Avenue and Seventh, the boys stared out the window into the nine-hundred-watt sex and sadism marquees. She saw some woman's tits and name lying across her son's cheek and *Terminator* and *Friday the Thirteenth* flickering across his blinking eyes. She really wanted to tell him not to look out the window, but realized how stupid it would sound.

Most often she believes forewarned is forearmed, but once or twice she has surrendered to an overwhelming desire to pretend that some things don't happen if you don't ever see them happening. One time she surveyed the street ahead of them as they walked together and caught sight of a man pulling down his disgusting pants and bending over and tooting his ass over a pile of garbage right on the corner of 50th Street and Eighth Avenue. She reached around and put her hand over the boy's eyes. It was a simple reflex, but he pouted a long while because he knew he'd missed seeing something interesting.

Tonight she walks down the east side of the street but sweeps the whole thoroughfare with her eyes, in case he didn't do what he was supposed to do. One of the pillars of maternal wisdom: after you've drilled into the child's head what he must do, you try to imagine what will happen if he does exactly the opposite. You've got to be prepared.

She waits at the turnstiles. She can see the platform. There is only one way to exit the station. If he's sitting in the car with the conductor, he'll be in the middle of the train. As each train enters the station, she looks at the middle first, then fans out to scout the front and back. Three trains come through and he doesn't arrive. She is sick of looking at the token clerk and annoyed that he is looking at her. She walks back toward the stairs. He's the kind of bullet-headed clerk who thinks the Transit Authority is paying him to scout fashion models rather than sell tokens. Out of his line of vision, she reads the subway map, traces grimy tiles with an index finger, and wipes her finger with a tissue.

He is not on the next train. She's getting angry and mutters to herself. She's getting scared. "Walk to the bus stop, ride across Forty-second Street, get off at Seventh Avenue, catch the uptown Number One, sit in the car with the conductor, get off at 157th Street. Simple."

Her stomach is not quiet. One hundred and thirty-eight pounds. The last time he went to the doctor's that's what he weighed, one hundred and thirty-eight pounds. I think that's accurate. Five feet eight inches tall. Half an inch taller than she. She can feel the brush of the bird's wing—the bird who brushes his wing against the mountaintop and in an eternity will have worn it to a pebble. This tiny bird of worry who brushes his wing against the soul of a mother and thus shortens her life by minutes, hours, days.

A throng of people come out of the next train and he is not among them. She sits disconsolately on the crummy station steps next to a plaque about the Jumel Mansion and silently begs who-ever is listening to give her a break. "Let him be on the next train. Please!" All the while knowing that personal prayers don't alter events already in motion.

A train pulls in. She leaps to attention at the turnstile, leans over, looks anxious. She searches the windows. He bounds out of the middle of the train, poised for fussing but begging with his eyes for her to be calm. "They let us out late and the bus took forever." His voice is trembling. Words dam up behind her front teeth. She takes his hand silently and climbs the stairs behind the exiting crowd. At street level, he tactfully disengages his hand to show her the badges that have to be sewn on the sleeve of a white shirt. She stands looking at the knit cap he wears fashionably above his naked ears. Worried about the cold, she pulls it down. They walk home.

Dear Aunt Nanadine

By Alexis De Veaux

Harlem-born **Alexis De Veaux** (1948–), is a poet, short-story writer, essayist, biographer, playwright, children's author, and lecturer. She is chair of the Department of Women's Studies at the State University of New York at Buffalo and has just completed a biography of the late poet-activist, Audre Lorde. Her books include *Don't Explain*, a biography of Billie Holiday, *Spirit Talk*, a poetry collection, and *An Enchanted Hair Tale*, an award-winning children's book. In "Dear Aunt Nanadine," she reframes the message given to so many little girls: that dark skin can never be quite beautiful.

Dear Aunt Nanadine,

As much as I love to write, I've never written you a letter. And "What do we need with letters?" you say. "We live in the same city, a bridge and a subway apart." Well, yesterday I took from the back of my closet that red three-piece suit you gave me. "Too fat to wear it now," you said, pushing it in a Macy's bag. "Take it."

So this letter is to say I used to admire you in that red suit; how it colored your light handsome beauty. And made you look so rich, so pockets full of freedom and loose change. Red, you instructed me, was a color *I* should *never ever* wear. I was absolutely "too dark." "Whose little black child are you?" you'd tease. "Who knows who you belong to?" Did you know then that your teasing mirrored my own apprehension? *Who did I belong to?* Who does a dark-skinned child belong to in a family where lighter skin is predominant, in a society where dark can't mean anything positive? It's not supposed to. Who do you belong to and who do you trust?

Should I have not trusted you then when I was eight years old? Not listened when you advised me at ten that not only reds but certain bright pinks, yellows, blues and oranges were also off limits to me? And to other girls my color, like Cheryl Lynn Bruce, who grew up on the South Side of Chicago (grew up to become an actress). Cheryl was ten, and dark, and recalls: "I remember going to my grandmother's house one day (she taught piano). I put on a red outfit—red coat, red dress, red shoes, red everything. I was fascinated with the color red. And off I went to my grandmother's house. Well, my grandmother gasped when she saw me, and called my mother, and sent me back home. My mother opened the door, grabbed me inside and said, 'Take off all that red. You are too dark to wear all that red.'" I hadn't understood there was a construct that decided what colors a dark girl could wear. I was ten at the time. Red is such a vibrant color. It calls attention, and it was calling attention to my skin. After the red incident, I felt there was a search to find a color I could wear that would not draw attention to my color. Mother dressed me in navy blue a lot because it was a neutral color. I became very conscious of how colors affected my skin.

Quite frankly, Aunt Nanadine, I was a little surprised when you gave me the suit. On the train, I wondered if you still thought I was "too dark." Was I lighter to you now? More acceptable? Had your feelings changed after some twenty years? At home, I stuck the suit in the closet of my writing room. I never wore it. It waited among my piles of complete and incomplete ideas, filed away, an unfinished draft of an old story. One day I would get back to it. But I could not sincerely thank you. And the next month, rummaging through some old notebooks, I came across this fragment of story: *I am a little girl. I am in the third grade. I come home from school. I run all the way today. My favorite dress—the navy one with tiny white polka dots—is torn at the sleeve and neck, with buttons missing and Lord, it's so dirty. There are dried tears on my face. My hair stands all over my head. I am pissed-as-shit. I know my mother is going to kill me. I bust through the apartment door.*

"Girl, what happened to you?" she say.

"Had a fight."

"Fight 'bout what?"

"Livia and them keep calling me Blackie—"

"I send you outta here to go to school and learn something. Not to fight, miss."

"She started it. Callin' me Blackie and Lil Black Sambo."

"Well the next damn time she do, you tell her YOUR MOTHER say sticks 'n' stones might break your bones, but words will never harm you. Hear me?"

BULLSHIT, BLACKIE AIN'T MY NAME, I want to say. It hurts. It's painful. It's embarrassing, Momma. Livia is dark as me. Why everything Black got to be evil, everything dark got to be ugly? I say nothing. I learn the bravado of strike back. Incorporate the language of segregation: "inkspot," "your Momma come from Blackest Africa," "tar baby tar baby," "Black nigga." I say it in (great) anger to others on the block. This is a skill. It is a way to hurt another deeply. We all prac-tice it. In 1956, nobody wants to be a "Blackie" or a "darkie" or no other kind of African nothing. Africa to (most of) us is Tarzan 'n' Jane: uncivilized life on the "Dark Continent," half-naked cannibals on TV. Africa was something to be ashamed of. The closer we are to that which symbolizes it, the greater our poten-tial for shame.

Reading and rereading the story, I wondered if anyone, any Black person, ever dared to call you Blackie, Aunt Nanadine, you with your elegant, light skin. And what would you have done to them if they had? What would you have done if *your* grandmother anointed elbows and knees religiously every Sunday with Pond's Vanishing Creme, to keep away the ashiness of "dark"?

I am not ungrateful for all the things you did teach me about my color: how to use Nadinola bleaching cream as a foundation under makeup; to buy my stockings in a shade of off-black; how to assimilate and integrate to survive; to *fade in* as much as possible (however ridiculous, at times); to "act my age and not my color." All the ways you penetrated the interior of my feelings, where you and I lived, I believed then, in a separation of shades; where our different colors wedged between us like a yoke. Separated and politically bound us to the psychological and psychic brutality that was American slavery. *That still binds us to generations of self-hatred,* a hatred of our darkness. Hatred for the overwhelming, monumental, lynching pain attached to it.

"Color has made extremely deep scars in Black people," says Sandra Ross, a good friend. (You might have seen some of her work, Aunt Nanadine. She's a freelance lighting designer in theaters around the city.) "It has affected what we do with our lives, what we *think* we can do or accomplish. It has shaped our self-esteem and sense of personal and group power. In my family, color wasn't mentioned. We talked about Black and white, but we didn't talk about light and dark." The neighbors did, though indirectly: "She's pretty for a Black child, smart for a Black child," they would say.

Is it just circumstantial that we are blood kin, women, products of America, descendants of heroines and slaves, that we have shared family crises and skeletons, but never talked intimately or honestly about skin tones and color? That I have never said to you: I like my color. I want to be even darker, blacker, still.

"I'm glad I'm as dark as I am because there is a certain point beyond which I can't compromise, beyond which I can't assimilate," Cheryl Lynn said to me over the phone. "I like to wear a lot of colors and bells and stuff to remind me that *I am different. I am an African.* And all the stares I get on the street and in the subway, even from my own people, are a healthy sign because we all need to be reminded that Black *is* beautiful, inherently beautiful, and we can enhance that beauty or twist it into something grotesque when we hide it."

When we deny it. When I am wrong *just because I am darker than you.* When my color *and* my sex are considered heavy deficits in the outside world. When, like Sandra, I cannot see myself as attractive for a long time, because I am, society says, repugnant and exotic: with my large breasts, my period, my pussy. "Just a dark, nappy girl." And as such, I must never call attention to myself. Never want it.

And never deserve it; because a dark girl was also unfeminine, unworthy, ignorant. *Neither ambition nor achievement was expected of me.* I could be propositioned by Black men old enough to be my uncle. Rubbed against by a strange man in the subway on the way to school. I could be trespassed against in any number or variation of social ways, simply because, after all, I was only a Black girl. What a sad thing it was to learn that *a dark girl meant an ugly girl.* That my people had no standard for judging colored beauty. That within our race we judged ourselves by outside criteria. That there was no beauty underneath the nappy, unruly hair I was taught to fry and radically alter; no grace to my African buttocks squeezed into panty girdles at fifteen. Could I ask my mother if she thought I was beautiful? Could I demand to know if colored people had the *right* to be beautiful? If all the Sojourner Truth in me, all the Harriet Tubman, the Ida B. Wells-Barnett, all the Hatshepsut Queen of Egypt, all the dark, handsome history of my smell, talk, dreams, would not, indeed, one day rot inside the choking rope of

> *if you light you all right*
> *if you brown stick around*
> *if you Black git back*

Can you see how your red suit in my closet would make me see red? That to open the closet door daily was to open a Pandora's box of racism between us? Because we are in the closet too. A color closet we cannot get out of. It is too personal, too much a knife in a never healing wound. There is nowhere inside my color, inside your color, to be objective. No way to fade in. No way not to be dark. *And what color is dark? Who is dark? Compared to what, compared to whom? Is a dark woman in a darker skinned family light or dark? Is a light woman in a high light/mulatto family dark? Will we end the racism or shall we perpetuate it?*

"What do you think?" I say to Cheryl Lynn, taking notes. She replies: "I've seen so many ranges of color since I became conscious of my own color that sometimes it seems pointless to make any distinctions between dark and dark. I've seen navy-blue people and dusty-gray ones and some a sandy, translucent black. Is an eggplant person darker than a maroon person? What does it mean, beyond that?" Some of us are darker than others but, Aunt Nanadine, we are all dark peoples.

That's what the sixties taught me. In the red, black, green artifacts of my African heritage, I could *learn to love* the dark me that was the Civil Rights movement here in America. The dark me that was the independence movement in Africa. That was an outside shade of brown. When I went on those marches and stood on those demonstration lines and chanted against our oppression, *I felt Black.* And the natural Black was beautiful to express. And it was as beautiful to express my anger as it was to express my natural, nappy hair; to express my skin by painting it. I celebrated every ritual that celebrated my darkness: Kwanzaa, nose piercing, braids, nationalism. I wanted American saturated with the henna on my lips. I wanted color: I wore reds and yellows and greens in provocative African combinations. *I wanted the freedom to be dark;* I could not get dark enough. In the summer, I disappeared on the beaches for days at a time. "Stay out the sun," you warned me. "It's just making you dark and oversensitive." "There's nothing wrong with being dark," I defended myself. Remember?

I remember *believing,* in the sixties. Many others do too. Like Carole Byard: "When we chanted 'Black is beautiful,' we were very assertive because we were *involved* in turning history around," she reminisced. "But some of the young people are not as aggressive as we were at their age. For many of them, it seems as if the sixties never happened. They are culturally embarrassed. There seems to be more of a willingness to merge, and not to assert cultural identity, particularly if it relates to Africa. Maybe they feel less threatened than we did by involvement with white cultural things."

I remember believing I wanted to judge myself from then on against *my own* darkness. And the darkness of my history. The sixties gave me a solid foundation, a bridewealth of "Africanity." Taught me to carry cultural beauty in my hair, my clothes, the words in my mouth. Taught me that while there was a "cultural Blackness" (artifacts), there is a "genetic dark," an *inside dark*, I must learn to love. *Learn to love the dark and trust it* because there are schools, clinics, governments, families, freedom, art to build between us.

But the sixties were only a beginning. And while it released some of our racial tension, it did not free us from our own color prejudices. When our slogans and anger no longer served us, when government and social backlash tested our spirit in the seventies, and Black was defined by Madison Avenue instead, some of us forgot that *our struggle did not begin in the sixties* and would not end there. Some of us mistook the invisibility of our darkness as the end of it.

Maybe that's not the stance to take at all, Carole disagrees. "Maybe the way we went about it is just no longer necessary. Maybe that's the difference between this decade and the last ones. Maybe we who were active in the sixties are like generals from another war. Maybe it's a *different* war, with different equipment for fighting it. Maybe it's not all gone, just different."

Different, but the same. Whether in Brooklyn, Baton Rouge, or Baltimore. Whether in Africa, the Caribbean, or America; at the core of our struggle lies an ugly pattern of color consciousness between family, strangers, friends. It lies deceptively, and hides, beneath our global view, like a pain. Or a journal entry:

After dinner, Margo and I lay on her bed. Her quilt is a weave of cloth from the Ibo of Nigeria. We talk about her master's thesis topic: "The Impulse to Love in the Narratives of African American Slave Women." Margo is a light-skinned Black woman. Her 'fro is big, but not kinky. Margo has African facial features. She's attractive. I am much darker. I have a short kinky 'fro. I have African facial features. I'm attractive. I was born in Harlem. Margo was born in Mississippi. She attends a prestigious Ivy League school. We live in Boston. Margo is very, very intelligent. Her mind is mercurial. When Margo smokes reefer she is aggressive. She sees how tall she is, how tall I am not. Wrestles me on the bed: "Let's play," she says. Punches me: "Let's fight." "No," I say. "Stop." When Margo's nose gets clobbered she cries, turns red. "You Black bitch," she spits. "I didn't mean to call you that," she says later. "Forget it," I say. Margo is my friend. We were lovers once. I quit her after that.

Aunt Nanadine, it is the impulse to love that does not quit. To love my history sex skin. Not in spite of it but because of it. To *love myself*. As Carole says, "We must deal with the internal aspects of 'Black is beautiful.' Work on a stronger sense of self to make the whole group stronger by caring about our family histories, our health, our spirit, what kind of people we are. Our self-love. *If I love myself then I have to love you too.*"

And I have to love the visibility of mass protests that created the sixties, transformed lives forever, Africanized me. And still love it now, as it regroups underground; as today's fashions and the current national politics turn back the clock—turn our 'fros to Geri Curls and our cornrows to "extensions." "We have to evolve to a point of caring about contributing to the whole," Carole is quick to encourage. "It's a personal thing. Something each one of us has to do. In the sixties there was a lot of emphasis on mass health, mass healing, but now we have to strengthen the individual parts. We have to remember that the whole is equal to the sum of the parts."

Remember that in these ugly times, there *is* something to fall back on. Remember that it is the impulse to love that comes between the silence between aunt and niece. Comes in this letter saying I love you. Comes, as I write, struggling to internalize beauty, because *color is still a critical issue between our people.* We still discriminate against our own. The darker ones against the lighter ones. The light ones against the dark. Little kids on the street today still call each other Blackie as a way to hurt each other deeply. And yet we cannot afford that "luxury." Or any other "luxury" of segregation that diminishes our numbers. We cannot afford to believe that we have been defeated; that "Black is beautiful" is dead. That dark is ugly. I am not dead and I am not defeated. I am beautiful. Black is in my heart, blood, work; in the eyes of my dreads, in the amber/cowrie of my tongue.

So Aunt Nanadine, I have taken the red suit out of my closet. I am going to the cleaners with it. Then to the mailbox to drop this letter. Please get in touch with me. I'd like to know how you feel about all this. Perhaps I can come see you soon. Next week I will give a talk on "Writing as Activist Art." I will wear our red suit. Thank you for giving it to me. I have always loved it.

Take care.

Moving forward to freedom: Your niece, Alexis

Brooklyn, 1982

Who Shot Johnny?

By Debra Dickerson

In her memoir, *An American Story,* St. Louis native **Debra Dickerson** (1960–) examines the effects of poverty on African-American families like her own. An award-winning journalist with a Harvard Law degree, she has written for *U.S. News and World Report, Essence, New Republic, The Washington Post, New York Times Magazine,* and *Vibe,* among others. In this essay, she laments the lost potential of her teenaged nephew.

O n July 27, 1995, my 16-year-old nephew was shot and paralyzed.

Talking with friends in front of his home, Johnny saw a car he thought he recognized. He waved boisterously—his trademark—throwing both arms in the air in a full-bodied hip-hop Y. When he got no response, he and his friends sauntered down the walk to join a group loitering in front of an apartment building. The car followed. The driver got out, brandished a revolver and fired into the air. Everyone scattered. Then he took aim and shot my running nephew in the back.

Johnny never lost consciousness. He lay in the road, trying to understand what had happened to him, why he couldn't get up. Emotionlessly, he told the story again and again on demand, remaining apologetically firm against all requests that he divulge the missing details that would make sense of the shooting but obviously cast him in a bad light. Being Black, male and shot, he must, apparently, be involved with gangs or drugs. Probably both. Witnesses corroborate his version of the events.

Years have passed since that phone call in the night and my nightmarish headlong drive from Boston to Charlotte, North Carolina. After 20 hours behind the wheel, I arrived haggard enough to reduce my mother to fresh tears.

And at the hospital, this is what I found: my nephew reassuring well-wishers with an eerie sangfroid. I take the day shift in his hospital room; his mother and grandmother, a clerk and cafeteria worker, respectively, alternate spending nights there on a cot. They don their uniforms the next day, gaunt after hours spent listening to Johnny moan in his sleep. How often must his subconscious replay those events and curse its host for saying hello without permission, for being carefree and young while a would-be murderer hefted the weight of his uselessness and failure like Jacob Marley's chains? How often must he watch himself lying stubbornly immobile on the pavement of his nightmares while the sound of running feet syncopate his attacker's taunts?

I spend these days beating him at gin rummy and Scrabble, holding a basin while he coughs up phlegm, crying in the corridor while he catheterizes himself. There are children here much worse off than he. I should be grateful. The doctors can't, or won't, say whether he'll walk again.

I am at once repulsed and fascinated by the bullet, which remains lodged in his spine (having done all the damage it can do, the doctors say). The wound is undramatic—small, neat and perfectly centered, an impossibly pink pit surrounded by an otherwise undisturbed expanse of mahogany. Johnny has asked me several times to describe it but politely declines to look in the mirror I hold for him.

Here on the pediatric rehab ward, Johnny speaks little, never cries, never complains, works diligently to become independent. He does whatever he is told; if two hours remain until the next pain pill, he waits quietly, eyes bloodshot, hands gripping the bed rails. During the week of his intravenous feeding when he was tormented by the primal need to masticate, he never asked for food. He just listened while we counted down the days for him and planned his favorite meals. Now required to dress himself unassisted, he does so without demur, rolling himself back and forth valiantly on the bed and shivering afterward, exhausted. He ma'ams and sirs everyone politely. Before his "accident," a simple request to take out the trash could provoke a firestorm of teenage attitude. We, the women who have raised him, have changed as well: We've finally come to appreciate those boxer-baring, oversize pants we used to hate—it would be much more difficult to fit properly sized pants over his diaper.

He spends a lot of time tethered to rap music still loud enough to break my concentration as I read my many magazines. I hear him try to soundlessly mouth the obligatory *mothafuckers* overlaying the funereal dirge of the music tracks. I do not normally tolerate disrespectful music in my or my mother's presence, but if it distracts him now. . . .

"Johnny," I ask later, "do you still like gangster rap?"

During the long pause I hear him think loudly, *I'm paralyzed, Auntie, not stupid.* "I mostly just listen to hip-hop," he says evasively into his *Sports Illustrated.*

Miserable though it is, time passes quickly here. We always seem to be jerking awake in our chairs just in time for the next pill, his every-other-night bowel program, the doctors' rounds. Harvard feels a galaxy away—the world revolves around Family Members Living With Spinal Cord Injury class, Johnny's urine output and strategizing with my sister to find affordable, accessible housing. There is always another long-distance uncle in need of an update, another church member wanting to pray with us, or Johnny's little brother requiring some attention.

We Dickerson women are so constant a presence that the ward nurses and cleaning staff call us by name and join us for cafeteria meals and cigarette breaks. At Johnny's birthday pizza party, they crack jokes and make fun of one another's husbands (there are no men here). I pass slices around and try not to think 17 *with a bullet.*

Oddly, we feel little curiosity or specific anger toward the man who shot him. We have to remind ourselves to check in with the police. Even so, it feels pro forma, like sending in those $2 rebate forms that come with new pantyhose: You know your request will fall into a deep, dark hole somewhere, but still, it's your duty to try. We push for an arrest because we owe it to Johnny and to ourselves as citizens. We don't think about it otherwise—our low expectations are too ingrained. Harvard aunt notwithstanding, for people like Johnny, Marvin Gaye was right: Only three things are sure—taxes, death and trouble. At least it wasn't the second.

We rarely wonder about or discuss the brother who shot him because we already know everything about him. When the call came, my first thought was the same one I'd had when I'd heard about Rosa Parks's beating: A brother did it. A non-job-having, middle-of-the-day-malt-liquor-drinking, crotch-clutching, loud-talking brother with many neglected children born of many forgotten women. He lives in his mother's basement with furniture rented at an astronomical interest rate. He has a car phone, an $80 monthly cable bill and every possible phone feature, but no savings. He steals relatives' social-security numbers and assumes their identities to acquire large TV sets for which he will never pay. If he's brought to justice, he'll have a colorful criminal history and no coherent explanation to offer for this act. His family will raucously defend him and cry cover-up. Some liberal lawyer like me will help him plea bargain his way to yet another short stay in prison that will only add another layer to the brother's sociopathology and formless, mindless nihilism.

We know him. We've known and feared him all our lives. As a teenager, he called, "Hey, baby, gimme somma that boodie!" at us from car windows. Indignant at our lack of response, he followed up with, "Fuck you, then, 'ho!" He called me a "white-boy-lovin' nigger bitch oreo" for being in the gifted program and loving it. At 27, he got my 17-year-old sister pregnant with Johnny and lost interest without ever informing her that he was married. He snatched my widowed mother's purse as she waited in predawn darkness for the bus to work and then he broke into our house. He chased all the entrepreneurs from our neighborhood with his violent thievery; he's why we put bars on our windows. He kept us from sitting on our own front porch after dark and laid the foundation for our periodic bouts of self-hating anger and racial embarrassment. He made our neighborhood a ghetto. He is the poster fool behind the maddening community knowledge that there are still some Black mothers who raise their daughters but merely love their sons. He and his cancerous carbon copies eclipse the vast majority of us who are not sociopaths, and they render us invisible. He is the Siamese twin who has died but cannot be separated from his living, vibrant sibling. Which of us must attract more notice? We despise and disown this anomalous loser but, for many, he is Black America. We know him, we know that he is outside the fold, and we know that he will only get worse. What we didn't know is that, because of him, my little sister would one day be the latest hysterical Black mother wailing over a fallen child on TV.

Alone, lying in the road bleeding and paralyzed but hideously conscious, Johnny had helplessly watched his would-be murderer come to stand over him and offer this prophecy: "Betch'ou won't be doin' no mo' wavin', motha'fucker."

Fuck you, asshole. He's fine from the waist up. You just can't do anything right, can you?

Going Home

By Janus Adams

Janus Adams (1947–), the daughter of immigrants, writes extensively on African-American history and Civil Rights. Her most recent book is *Sister Days: 365 Inspired Moments in African-American Women's History*. Currently at work on a family memoir, Adams lives in New York. In this narrative, she returns for the first time to St. Kitts, the almost-mythical "home" that sustained her grandparents in America.

Recently, along with Grandma's passport, I discovered her American naturalization papers and a citizenship book in which family and friends signed congratulations on December 5, 1955. My Lord, what a morning! In Alabama that day, Rosa Parks was in court, facing jail for violating segregation's rule. Other Blacks rallied around her, sparking the 385-day Montgomery Bus Boycott that catapulted a young Dr. Martin Luther King, Jr. to world acclaim. And, in New York, my grandmother pledged allegiance to a flag that promised her freedoms still denied Blacks south of the Mason-Dixon line.

Among the messages in my grandmother's citizenship book was this from her eldest daughter: "Now you can go to Canada and home at last." *Home.* I remember hearing Grandma intone that word with a longing that left me in pain. After thirty-eight years in America, home for her—and our family—was still St. Kitts. I had come-of-age the immigrant's child, an inductee in the integration generation, foot soldier in the army of the

Lord, as we sang in the Movement. I'd known moments of celebration and separation, disconnection and alienation, and
after all that marching forward and sliding back, I was in sore
need of healing and renewal. And so, decades after Grandma
pledged allegiance to the American flag, worn out by my own
struggles in the promised land, I heeded her ancestral call and
headed to St. Kitts.

The flight is smooth. The landing perfect. The welcome gra-
cious. "You are home," my hosts beckon. The heat is so steamy,
I decide to acclimate slowly indoors. From my window, I can see
the Caribbean Sea. Over the next few days, I will visit places I
have heard of and seen, if only in my mind's eye, all my life.
The aptly-named Sandy Point. The sprite, yellow-gold monkeys
of Monkey Hill. The Moravian Church where my grandmother
and her twin were baptized. The bend at Cayon, to which my
grand uncle Hermie walked shoeless, asserting his religious
conversion to Seventh Day Adventism, to the chagrin of his
proper Church-of-England mother. Stories of family and faith
roll forth like the tides to mental sand. A century of immigrant
longing has made it so.

People I do not know have heard "the lady from the States—a
writer, she" is here. "Tis you, the one?" Yes I am. "Come to
church for the fair. I bring my best sugar cake for you." Like the
ancient parting of the waters, they have made a place for me at this
welcome table.

The historian in me cannot resist scouring records from the
early 1900s to find clues to why and how I have come to be here.
The history that stirred my grandparents to pick up roots and head
to America opens before me. The strikes, the suppression, the
workers' dissatisfactions, the plantation owner's disclaimers,
the government report of conditions so intolerable that to
improve them would be to risk still greater demands—give 'em an
inch, so to speak. I remember another uncle telling me how he
had led a plantation strike and fled for his life in the moonlight.

Overwhelmed by the wealth of it all, I choose random newspapers from a stack dated 1916. The archivist assures me there is nothing about Blacks in the papers from those days of staunch colonial rule. I can save my time. But, knowing how Grandma was counting the days that year until she could sail, I decide to read the news to feel something of her youthful sense of urgency, how she must have felt watching and waiting as the clock ticked fast on her dreams.

On Monday, May 29, 1916, in the *St. Kitts-Nevis Daily Bulletin,* I spy the name of the composer, Edward M. Margetson, whom I'd known as a child when he was organist at my family church. In a review of his concert, in fine print I see: "Mandolin Solo, Mr. H. Adams." Papa? Then, on April 18, 1916, this ad over my grandfather's name: "Notice: The Undersigned will sell at his Stall in the Public Market tomorrow, Wednesday, Green Back Turtle." My grandfather was a butcher? In the States, Papa, as we called my father's father, had had a dairy truck, bought two stores and owned "property," as West Indians say of real estate. And yes, I can still see his mandolin and its old black case lined in pale striped paper.

"I held his mandolin!" I tell the archivist. "I did!" She runs into the office to tell the other librarian. Everything has stopped. They're as thrilled as I am. Not every researcher makes such a fortuitous find. "So your grandfather was White?" she muses. "No, he was Black. Mr. Margetson too!" "He was Black and he owned a business! In 1916!" she exclaims, stunned. "But, my gawd. Can you beat that?"

No. No, I can't. Papa was a musician and a butcher. My grandfather owned a business when most Black Kittitians could barely own the shirt on their backs without White plantation owners finding cause for suspicion. In 1899, my great-grandmother owned her business, too, a land-and-carriage trade she'd inherited from her husband. Who were these people, this Black business class of a century ago? And who am I, this 1970s rebel who took to the streets in a rage my great-grandmother would have found unladylike, inappropriate and distasteful. If she hid my grand uncle's shoes to prevent his forsaking the Church of England to go to the wrong church on the wrong day, Saturday, what would she have had in store for me—with all my picketing and protesting and letting my hair out in public, unstraightened?

And yet her children, the younger generation of 1916, had come to the States, rebels in their own right, in search of a better life. Sacrificing everything, they had dared to come, because they could hold such dreams. The aspirations, if not the affirmations, of their elders had made possible and necessary their climb. They had contributed their dreams and pledged the lives of their children in the name of progress.

So busy and content in my quest, I do not make time for the beach until the last afternoon of my visit. The arch of my back set against the breeze at Frigate Bay, the waves pulling at my feet, I remember seeing my grandmother off on her first trip home to St. Kitts after forty-three years. Her eyes dimmed by cataracts, my grandmother could barely see when she departed New York. Not so the girl in her who landed in St. Kitts. For months she visited with old friends, daily bathing her sore eyes in the Caribbean Sea. When she returned to us in the spring, Grandma had changed. You could see it in her shoulders as she retrieved her hard-won passport at customs. Right-angled, erect, she returned to our embrace, reaching for us one by one. "I see you all now plain as day," she said.

In St. Kitts, at the neck of the bay, I look into the waters, clean as a mirror, and find my face. I, too, have come a distance of forty-three years—a journey from "desegregation baby" to finding "home." I, too, can see clearer than ever these ancestors of mine. Can they see me standing here, the child who carried forth their dreams, bearing calabash of mind and time? "What is in the root is in the branches," Grandma used to tell us. Let it be so.

My Daughter, Once Removed

By William Jelani Cobb

William Jelani Cobb (1969–) is assistant professor of history at Spelman College in Atlanta and the editor of *The Essential Harold Cruse: A Reader*. In the essay that follows, he writes of the step-daughter he lost to divorce.

I think about Aiesha in the mornings, first thing. I haven't spoken to her in a month, but all her messages are still saved on my answering machines. There is a T-shirt in the exact same spot she left it on her last visit three months ago. I still tell her that she is my favorite person. Aiesha is eight—spoiling for nine—and she's my daughter, once removed.

In my wide-eyed youth, I subscribed to wild notions like "love makes one a parent" and "twenty-three chromosomes don't make you daddy." I believed that fatherhood is created every morning at 6 a.m. when you creak out of your bed to crack eggs, rattle pans and allow yourself to be hustled into granting your kid ten more minutes of sleep. I believed that genes don't make the parent, but now I wonder what does a voided wedding vow make me?

If you listen to the running dialogue on talk radio, in barber-shops and pulpits, the American father has been dispatched, part of some planned obsolescence, done in by feminism and sperm banks. The old Dad model has been discontinued in favor of a newer sleeker, single-parent alternative. I don't subscribe to that theory, but I do think that we're in danger of becoming a society of temporary families. We're full of books and how-to guides that make it easier for people to survive the end of a marriage; but as a consequence, we run the risk of making divorce a cure-all for marital woe.

I know Aiesha because her mother Shana was my college girl-friend. I broke up with her and years later found myself wishing for her again. She was wild and beautiful, the opposite of my self-conscious, bookish way. Our relationship lasted less than six months but we stayed in touch. Five years later, when I moved to New York for graduate school, she was the first person I invited to my housewarming party. When we threw a surprise party for my mother's 50th birthday, I invited Shana and she showed up with a buoyant two year-old with impossibly round cheeks whose favorite word was "NO!" As in "You are adorable," "NO!"

Soon Shana and I were hanging out, back to our old routines. When I occasionally spent the night, I slept on the couch so that Aiesha wouldn't get the wrong idea. The first night we slept together again, Shana told me that she wasn't looking for another short-term relationship. I understood; neither was I. At some point, in the early days of that relationship, I realized that I loved Shana again and that Aiesha had already chosen me as her father. Shana and I married a year and a half later.

I think men secretly want to raise their daughters to be the kind of women who were out of their league when they were young. And so it was with Aiesha. But really, it was about the words, teaching her the words to old classics like "Sittin' on the Dock of the Bay," and "Ain't No Sunshine" and giggling through the part where Bill Withers sings "And I know, I know, I know, I know, I know . . ." Kids dig repetition. She turned out volumes of poems, plays, songs and stories that were duly typed up and emailed to all friends, coworkers and distant relatives as evidence of her bur-geoning literary genius.

There were signs, now that I think of it, that the marriage was headed south early on. I saw in gradual degrees that my wife was less and less interested in our relationship and knew that we were at the point where many men would've bailed. Instead, I worked harder. When the newspapers ranked Aiesha's school in the bottom half of those in the city, I reduced my grad school classes and worked part-time to send her to a private school. When Shana was stuck at work a few hours before her women's group meeting, I came home early and surprised her by cleaning the apartment and preparing the food. I was like an outfielder who knows that the ball is headed for the bleachers, but smashes face first into the wall trying to catch it anyway.

In my world, there was no such thing as a warning track. A marital cliche: You're in the kitchen, cooking dinner, when your spouse returns home from a hard day at the office and announces that it's over. Just like that. It's a scenario that any writing instructor worth his salt would trash, but that's really how it went down. The exact words were: "I don't love you the way a wife should love a husband and I would like for you to move out." Then silence. I stared at her blankly for about five minutes. I was broken for a long time. She had married me because I was the theoretical good catch, not out of a desire to build a lifelong connection. We had lasted five years.

When Shana told Aiesha that I was leaving, Aiesha asked, "Does this mean I don't have a father anymore?" There are the easy answers. Friends (mainly female) tell me, once a father, always a father. Experience tells me something different—that I could just as easily be evicted again, that Shana could remarry and leave me a parental third-string player. Experience tells me that ex-step-father does not exist as a census category. That I no longer qualify for a Father's Day card.

Looking at it now, I know that I deeply and profoundly love that little girl. I understand the weight of the bond between parent and child. I also know that I was trying to single-handedly undo the mythology directed at black men, that I wanted a family that would laugh past the bleak statistics and damning indices of black male irresponsibility. When I married Shana, Aiesha had not seen her biological father in over a year. She has not seen him since then.

I saw tragedy in her growing up as yet another fatherless black girl, another child whose father abandoned her in favor of emptier pursuits. I wanted to be like my old man, quietly heroic in raising my brother and sister and never once letting on that they were not his biological kin. I wanted to be a keeper.

These days, I know that the relationship is unwieldy, sagging under the weight of its own ambiguity. Christmas is a hard, bright day and I wake up that morning with my head heavy from the previous night's bender. Aiesha has left me a message saying that she has a gift for me and please come today so she can give it to me. Her mother and I have been apart for six months, and I don't know her as well as I did in June. In another six months, she'll be a different child altogether.

When I see her outside, riding her bike in the parking lot of her building, I think how she's grown tall and slender as a reed. I bought her a watch; yellow and red, but with no cartoon characters because Aiesha fancies herself a sophisticate. The note says "Dear Aiesha, My father once told me that keeping track of time is the first step to becoming an adult. I hope you think of me when you wear this." She gives me a gift card and written in her best eight-year-old scrawl it says "I love you." She's telling me the plot points to her latest story, the one she wants to publish when she's twelve. A moment later, she wants me to toss her into the air and pleads "one more time" until my deltoids are burning. She still remembers most of the words to "Ain't No Sunshine." Today, she is my daughter. Today.

The Feather

By April Reynolds

April Reynolds (1974–) was born in Dallas and now lives in New York. A graduate of Sarah Lawrence College, she won second place in the 1997 Zora Neal Hurston/Richard Wright Foundation, Virginia, writing contest for her forthcoming novel, *Red Ribbons and the Broken Memory Tree.* Her short story, "The Feather," follows a southern family grappling with a ticklish problem.

No one notices a thing until he can't stop laughing. Inappropriately, Jimmy Brazil's laughter had first shown up at his friend's second cousin's wake, then twice while the collection plate passed through the congregation and the latest chuckle appeared as Jimmy was fired for perpetual tardiness. Still, no one notices. Instead, the phenomena is seen as the slight insanity that infects every black family in Lafayette County, Arkansas. Most of the town understands Jimmy's behavior as harmless craziness pricking the otherwise dull country living.

The old compare his recent foolishness to others better known for acting out. "Jimmy ain't got nothing on Willie Boy. Member him? Pissing in white folks yards. Liked to got us all kilt." At the grocery store, mothers watch him in the dairy section laughing at the choice between whole and skim milk and cluck their tongues. "Them three little hellions he got, make anybody crack up. No help from that wife of his. She don't want to be nothing but cute." And the young wisely opine, "He ain't crazy. I heard a while back, Reverend got on him about not putting nothing in the collecting plate. Shit. You tell me. And I bet you ninety to nothing Janice put him up to that shit at the wake. You know how she is."

But at home Jimmy's family cowers underneath his uninvited giggles. Erupting at the dinner table, while he dresses for work, in the middle of the night, his laughter seems borne out of nothing. A month has passed since Jimmy's sudden affliction, and now in the evening his children hear him before he reaches the front door. Uncontrollable chortles gallop around the block to announce their father's daily arrival home. Jimmy's children, seven-year-old Joe-Joe, five-year-old Pen-Pen and baby Shawn brace against the kitchen table as they hear the front door's clapping report and their father's guffaw. "Sit down ya'll," their mother Janice tells them. She, too, braces against the stove, locking her knees together while she stirs the rice into mush. She hears her husband shuffle into the living room. "And be good."

Over the past thirty days, Janice has worried herself sick about Jimmy's condition. Despite what they say about her, Janice was surprised as anyone when her husband first began laughing during the wake for his friend's cousin. She remembers his barely concealed giggle snaking out of his mouth, growing into a chortle. When he had excused himself, Janice followed. Jimmy had walked in the parking lot beside the funeral home and bent over from the waist. "What's got you?" Janice asked, and began to laugh softly behind her hand, unwilling to admit she didn't know what was so funny. "Come on. Tell me." Her undecided laughter began to mimic his. Jimmy continued to laugh. If it was a joke, Janice wanted to know it. Minutes passed with nothing in the quiet morning except for the couple's burst of giggles. "Well?" She shook her head in embarrassment. Jimmy grabbed his knees and began rocking back and forth on his heels, the sound of his laughter climbing higher. And just as she began to whip herself into anger, he suddenly stopped. Pulling himself upright again, Jimmy gave his wife an apologetic smile, taking her hand to lead her back into the funeral parlor.

She had looked up at him as they approached the door. Her

husband. Their courtship of less than a year had turned into eight years of a marriage that, if not full of bliss, were at least blessed by decency. Jimmy didn't womanize or swear. Didn't hit her or the children. He even prayed nightly when she reminded him. Jimmy didn't sing, couldn't dance; he wasn't a talker, but Janice didn't want to be with somebody who ate up the conversation anyway. She was the star of the family. And if that wasn't decent, then she didn't know what was. For her part, Janice made sure her husband and children went to school and work with sack lunches and in clean clothes. Her well-fed, well-ironed children all went to church on Sundays and Wednesdays, and Janice made sure to have at least a dollar for the congregation's collection plate. Except for their poverty, the Brazils were the quintessential American family. Three children and a dog and cat that got along. Jimmy's one job took care of the entire family. Bills were paid on time without exception. Birthdays were small but celebrated; Janice was the only wife in her neighborhood who made real birthday cakes studded with unrecycled candles instead of a cupcakes.

Jimmy had held the funeral parlor door open and Janice walked through. During the rest of the wake, Jimmy made nary a peep. He had been so quiet, so solemn that afterwards Janice hadn't bothered to get an explanation. But when the next Sunday rolled around, just as the reverend spoke his customary words—"Now brothers and sisters, you know the church just don't run on love and goodwill"—Jimmy had let loose. Tilting his head back, he had let go a loud peal of laughter that echoed throughout the church. "Now I don't think helping the church run is a laughing matter, Brother Jimmy," the reverend had said. But Jimmy sputtered on, cackling louder, clutching his stomach as he laughed. Horrified, Janice had grabbed her husband underneath his arms, almost lifting him off the ground.

"Jimmy?" Janice hissed in his ear. "You, Jimmy. Come on." She pulled him into the aisle and for a moment they stumbled over each other's feet.

"Ma'am?" Pen-Pen said. Janice turned to her children. Despite the uncertainty on Pen-Pen's face, she seemed prepared for anything. Joe-Joe sat planted where she had left him, eyes closed, mouth agape, ready to burst into tears at any moment, and her little baby Shawn squirmed in the pew as if she had messed in her pants.

"Pen-Pen get Shawn and everybody's jacket," Janice whispered. She looked around and saw the parishioners' wide eyes. "And don't forget to bring Joe-Joe with you."

Once outside, Janice, breathless with anger, whirled on her husband. "Did you see Sister Cookie? She's going to walk a mile with this one." She had wanted to shake that silly grin off Jimmy's face. "Okay. Okay." Still laughing, Jimmy fell back onto the wall of church and slid to the ground. "Keep laughing." Janice paused, waiting for Jimmy to stop. "James Brazil don't you hear me talking to you? What's all this about? What's so funny?" But her husband had continued to laugh, though now he seemed worn out, his cackling slowed, punctuated by an occasional pant.

"Ma'am?" Pen-Pen said, holding her little sister.

"What Pen-Pen? What is it now?"

"Ma'am, I think Shawn gone poop."

"Okay. Okay." Janice walked over to her daughter. "Hand her here." Pen-Pen handed her sister to her mother. As Janice cradled her youngest, she felt the softness in Shawn's diaper. Oh, that's nice, she thought. Aloud she said, "And get the keys from daddy."

Pen-Pen slipped her small hand inside her father's jacket. Lord help me if he carrying on like this at work, Janice thought. Don't know what's liable to happen if he is. The ride back to the Brazil house was quiet and once home, Jimmy fell fully clothed into bed and slept till morning.

But his wife had spent the rest of that Sunday incensed and afraid to go out for groceries lest she run into somebody from the church. She wasn't raising nasty children and she was proud of that. But now it looked like she'd married a nasty man. Carrying on like that. In the church, no less. Didn't I give him a son first off? I got the two girls for me, but I gave him a son first and look at the shit he pulling. He could of waited till we got home. And he knows I have to go grocery shopping this evening. I bet Cookie done gone house to house by now.

Her children had stood huddled in various corners in the house, watching her pace. Janice had passed from the living room to the kitchen, from the kitchen to the children's room and back again. Before this, Jimmy was as kind as he was calm. She'd married him because he was so even-tempered. Eight years ago, that's what she had told her mother: "Oh, Momma. I don't know if I love him or not. But he just as kind and calm as can be. And I know for sure he gone take care of me. Plus he's tall. Maybe I can have some tall kids. All I got to manage is looking good and having babies. Ain't that what it's all about?"

"I'm telling you girl, something about that boy funny."

"Okay, what?"

"He ain't got no friends. That's the first thing."

"So. That just mean he'll come home at night."

"So? So, it just ain't right. And another thing. Ain't nobody that calm, that decent, that good all the time. You tell me you ain't never seen him mad, and I believe you. But, girl that's some kind of funny ways."

"Momma."

"You gone and marry him. But—"

"But what?"

"But nothing. You just gone and marry him. I'm telling you now, Janice. That Jimmy got some funny ways. And I hope to God I'm dead and cold when they come out."

Janice's mother had got her wish. By the time Jimmy giggled at the wake, Janice's mother had been dead for two years. And without her mother's advice to show her the way the next Sunday, Janice had gone to bed that night, praying for an entire congregation's amnesia and Jimmy's return to normalcy.

The next morning Jimmy rose from bed, wearing that same chagrined look that he gave Janice at the wake. But this time, she didn't believe it. Her Jimmy, who was slow to anger and slower still to speak, who, when asked for an opinion, often turned to Janice to give him words, couldn't be trusted. Who knew where they would be when he decided to act out again. The next two days she watched him closely. Jimmy would wake, shower and eat quietly and then head off to work. When Wednesday morning came, Jimmy woke up laughing, but Janice was prepared.

"Jimmy, you got to stop this now. You got to go to work, so you got to cut all this shit out." Jimmy said nothing. Snickering into his hand, he went into the bathroom. Janice heard the shower turn on. "You hear me James Brazil." Janice pressed her head against the closed bathroom door. "I hear you in there." Her husband's chuckles brimmed over the noise of the shower. "Shut up that shit before you wake the kids!" Janice screamed. And then she heard Shawn's piercing cry. "Look at you! See what you done did!" Janice ran from the bedroom into her children's room, sobbing.

The next few weeks had followed the same pattern. If Jimmy didn't wake up laughing, then it showed up during dinner. They all decided they wouldn't ask what was on their minds—"How come you laugh so much now?"—afraid he might say something they could not stand. Before, a few minutes of laughter had seemed to tide him over for a couple of days, but now the giggling appeared a dozen times during the day.

As Jimmy's condition grew more chaotic, Janice's anger melted into disgust. Most mornings she was sure to wake before her husband, make his breakfast of two eggs, fried bologna and toast, and take off to the furthest part of the backyard to hang and re-hang clothes on the line until Jimmy left for work. His children, on the other hand, kept as close as they could to their father. They, too, made a habit of waking before Jimmy, only to hover around their parents' bedroom door until their father walked through it ready for work.

Despite its unexpectedness, the children believed their father's laughter must have some notion of reason behind it. For a while, Joe-Joe tried out-laughing his father. First, he kept time with his father's scattered tempo, and then suddenly he slid a bit off beat, stopping abruptly in the hope that his father would stop too. Pen-Pen, who thought her father's laugh sounded like crying, would run her small hand back and forth across Jimmy's knee, trying to calm him. But nothing worked.

Like all children they assumed their father's recent behavior was inexplicably bound to them. And once they understood they couldn't trick their father back to normalcy, Jimmy's children became better than good. They headed for bed at eight o'clock with clean faces and brushed teeth without prompting. Joe-Joe swept the floors and took out the trash without being told. Pen-Pen picked up her toys when she was done with them. Everyone excused themselves before leaving the table, and no one spoke out of turn. But their good behavior went unrewarded.

They ruminated over the laughter's origin. Memories were brought up and then quickly dismissed. "Okay, member when Momma braked the cup? That's when. Daddy just start laughing. Member?" Joe-Joe had said. No, that was the sound of the television, they suddenly recalled and were forced to begin again. Any sound that reminded them of joy was considered, but more often than not, the laughter they remembered was their mother's. Once, they believed they nailed down the moment. Shawn's first walk. Ten steps, on her tip-toes, then their baby sister had lost her balance, almost falling over. Suddenly she righted herself and relief washed over her year-old face. They remembered their father's sudden bark of laughter, and how they had readily joined him. But so what, their young minds told them. Even at seven and five, Joe-Joe and Pen-Pen understood that knowing when it all started wouldn't make their father any better. His children took solace in the idea that as abruptly as the laughter had appeared, it could vanish, that one day they would wake up to their father's familiar face. They remembered his old laughter without sound, his smile without teeth and longed for it. Neither realized that irony had squatted over their small house in Lafayette, that laughter was tearing their family asunder.

And now Jimmy is home. They hear his footsteps travel the length of the living room. "Don't make me ask you to sit down twice, Joe-Joe," Janice says. Joe-Joe tries to shake out of his locked pose.

"You, too, Pen-Pen." Her son and daughter scamper to the table. "Jimmy, that you?" Janice says as Jimmy and his laughter appear in kitchen doorway. "Dinner's ready." She sounds so calm, she surprises herself. "I made pork chops." Her husband nods while a slow steady chuckle burps out of his mouth. He takes off his jacket and sits down at the table. "You have a good day at work?" Jimmy doesn't answer, but it doesn't matter since Janice only asks the question to hear some sound other than her husband's throaty laughter. "Hand your daddy them field peas."

"Yes, ma'am." Joe-Joe says, passing his father the bowl of peas.

"Yes, well. I hear Monroe and Wilde thinking of putting on some kind domino contest. Got a sign up sheet and everything at Bo Web's place." She pauses, as if waiting for her husband to respond. The children are uncertain as to what so say. Don't speak unless spoken to is an unbreakable rule. But their mother's one-sided conversation makes their stomach cramp. "And I heard from Bo Web's wife they got Sister Cookie in on it, too. So you know everybody 'tween here and Canfield know about it.

"My daddy used to play to play a mean hand of dominoes. Yes, he sure did. Monroe and Wilde would lose they shirt if daddy was still living." Janice pretends she isn't watching her husband. His hands jump and start as he struggles to get the peas on his plate, and he hasn't touched his pork chop. "It's suppose to be three days. Friday, Saturday and Sunday. Three days worth of dominoes." She whistles. "Lord if that don't beat all. Leave it to Monroe and Wilde to figure out a way to make money without working." Janice tries to laugh at her small joke, but nothing comes out. "Yes, well."

"Ma'am?"

"Yes, Pen-Pen?"

"Ma'am, can I get some more?" Pen-Pen says as she watches her father try to eat a spoonful of peas. His hands shake so badly, the peas fall back to the plate.

"Pen-Pen you ain't cleaned the plate you got."

"Yes ma'am," Pen-Pen says, happy she's side-tracked her mother's conversation. Now Janice makes sure to ask questions that her children can answer yes and no to. You make that bed? And Joe-Joe remembers to chew thoroughly and swallow before answering yes. Except for Jimmy's uninvited chortles, the rest of dinner is mundane. After seconds are offered and refused, Joe-Joe and Pen-Pen ask in unison to be excused. Janice watches them take off to their bedroom. *I got good kids, good kids,* Janice thinks while she quickly clears off the table. *Pen figured out how to save my pride without shaming me.* She heads outside to wash and hang clothes that are already clean.

She begins to avoid her weekly trip to the beauty shop unwilling to bear the sea of silence that greets her when she opens the door. Women suck their teeth when they see her and shake their heads. She would rather struggle at home with the straightening comb and curlers. The silence that surrounds her when she steps outside the house is worse than the cacophony she faces at home. She knows that as soon as she's out of earshot, they talk about her. Hadn't she done the same? Some poor family who had their lights turned off or couldn't keep up with the rent was beauty shop gossip for weeks. Yes, she knows exactly what they are saying, as if they had shouted it in her ear.

"Yeah, girl that's the one."

"That's her?"

"Walking like she ain't got a care in the world. Heard she drove that her poor husband of hers crazy as a peach orchard boar."

"Oh, stop it Cookie."

"It's the God heaven truth."

"You know that Johnson's boy?"

"You know I do."

"Told me the other day, he saw Jimmy at the grocery store laughing over a carton of milk."

"Girl, you stop."

"Don't tell me. First, tell me why he's doing the shopping. And second, what's so funny about a carton of milk?" Janice is sized up, quartered and judged as soon as she's in sight. But still, that's not what bothers her most. She treats those contemptible women who have nothing better to do than gossip about her with studied indifference. It's the men. The men who no longer look at her with admiration, but pity. It's the pity she can't stand.

The next morning Jimmy wakes, showers, walks into the living room and goes nowhere. Now Janice knows. He's been cutting up at work, too. And done messed around and lost his job. Now what? She doesn't realize she speaks aloud, "Now what, Jimmy?" He watches his wife pace in front of him. "Now what we spose to do? Why ain't you at work? You cutting up there, too? Mama always said you got funny ways. How we spose to eat and take care the children, if you ain't got no job?" Jimmy opens his mouth and giggles into his hand. "Oh, I guess you want me to work. Is that it? You mess around and lose you job, but you want your wife to get out there and get a job? Who gone take care of the kids while I'm working? You?" She crows false laughter. "You can't even get a spoon of peas in your mouth!" Jimmy's laughter climbs higher and higher during Janice's tirade. "Shut up! Shut up!" Janice leaps towards him, ready to strike. What's the point, she thinks. One more shout and I'll wake up the kids like last time. She stops pacing and walks out the front door. I just need a minute to get myself together, she thinks as she almost runs off the porch.

It takes more than a minute for Janice to calm down—it takes half the day. But when she finally returns, she feeds her hungry children and locks Jimmy in their bedroom. In the kitchen, she makes her morning coffee even though it is four o'clock, and then turns all of her concentration to the end of the month. The gas, light and rent are all due on the thirty-first and she has only twenty seven dollars saved up in her purse. Jimmy's got one more check coming, she thinks. At least the car is paid for. They can't take the car. All we need is fifty-three dollars. That's all. Janice sips her warm coffee. And I'm in good health. Been sick just two times my whole life. I can do just about damn near anything. Right? I got a good head on my shoulders.

And that's when Janice's doubt springs. Didn't her good head get into this mess? She shouldn't have married him, cause she ain't never loved him, but her good head said gone on and do it.

He was gone to take care of her and hers and all she'd have to worry about was her hairdo. Her plans for the next day unravel in her mind since she begins to trust herself less and less. She takes another sip of cold coffee. She can't trust herself; she can't trust her kids because they are too young and Jimmy isn't worth considering. Jesus, girl, what are you gone do now? If I had a just loved him a little bit, I could of had something to fall back on. But without that unreasonable love that marriages rely on, Janice's disgust blossoms.

She doesn't get dressed at all the next morning; her doubt gets the best of her. And in the following weeks the only thing she can manage is cooking, ground beef and onions with gravy and rice, the family's meal. She fails to notice that Jimmy eats less than half of what's on his plate or that his laughter, though quieter, is constant. Instead all of her time is spent thinking what jobs she can get. But the children see their father changing. Over dinner and lunch, Joe-Joe and Pen-Pen exchange looks. It's getting worse, they think. Jimmy doesn't wake up until after lunch, picks at the leftovers and giggles back into sleep. He is vanishing right before their eyes. His clothes begin to hang on him as if there is room for two. Despite their hoping, their father's laughter never collapses into tears, and as the weeks go by he ventures out of his room less and less. The children's morning camp outside his bedroom door is just habit. Pen-Pen knows now she won't be able to lead her father back into the way he was.

The end of the month comes and goes without one bill being paid. And Janice is on the move. She takes long walks and doesn't find her way back home until she believes Jimmy is asleep. Round and round the block, to the houses of high school friends, but Janice turns away from their front doors before she knocks. There is life beyond her family, her neighborhood and now because of Jimmy, she makes a point of finding out what it is. Today she finds a creek and a walking bridge she never knew was there, although Janice has lived in Lafayette County her whole life.

At home she begins to leave picnic fare on the dinner table. Hotdogs and potato salad are either made days before or in the middle if the night when no one is awake. Janice doesn't even try to be a half-hearted nurse. She doesn't bother to wake Jimmy up in the morning, or remind him to put on clean clothes. Her concern is to be dressed and out the door before her family wakes up in the mornings. The frustration of begging food down her husband's throat is left to her middle child. It's Pen-Pen who takes the ham and bologna sandwiches her mother leaves for them to her father. But he can't seem to get anything down. And while waiting on him as best she can, Pen-Pen tries to find language in her father's laughter. Small snickers means try to feed him; a quiet guffaw signifies a trip to the bathroom; a giggle means time for bed.

So it's Pen-Pen who finds the feather. One night as she undresses her father, she forgets to close her eyes out of respect and sees it. Something resembling a down feather the color of used kitchen water, sprouts west from the center of her father's back. It's just a feather, as small as Shawn's palm. "Daddy. Daddy?" She whispers, but Jimmy has already fallen asleep. Afraid of some outlandish scheme Joe-Joe might think of while their mother is away, she doesn't tell her brother, but she waits up for Janice, so excited that she doesn't have to fight sleep. Janice opens the front door at one o'clock. "It's a feather," Pen-Pen says as her mother walks through the door. Janice jumps at the sound of her daughter's voice.

"Pen-Pen what are you doing up this time of night?" The living room is dark, so Janice doesn't wipe the guilty look off her face.

"It's a feather, Mommy."

"What?" Janice pulls off her jacket, still a bit breathless from her daughter's nighttime appearance.

"Like on a baby bird. But maybe bigger." Pen-Pen is breathless, too. Excited, almost lightheaded, that soon everything will return to normal.

"Girl what are you talking about?" Janice picks her daughter's form out of the darkness sitting on the coffee table.

"Daddy, Daddy." Pen-Pen gulps in air. "Got a feather."

Janice slumps into the armchair and digs a cigarette out of her purse. During her long walks to nowhere she's developed the habit. "Girl, get off that coffee table."

"Mommy, go and see. Please. Please."

"Pen-Pen you think I got time for this mess. Here I am thinking you the one thing I can depend on." Janice scowls in the direction of her daughter and takes a drag of her cigarette.

"Please."

"In the morning."

And now there is anger, five-year-old anger that feels helpless. "No, Mommy! Now. Go see."

She wouldn't, Janice thinks. I got good kids. I don't care if I ain't been here. She just wouldn't lie. Janice takes a deep pull off her cigarette and walks to the porch to put it out. "Alright, Pen-Pen."

Her daughter flies to the back, screaming, "Joe wake up! Wake up!"

Janice, who hadn't been in her bedroom in more than a month, wrinkles her nose as she breaths in the room's staleness. "Keep the door open, Pen-Pen."

"Yes, ma'am." Janice peers over Jimmy's sleeping body. Jimmy is as his daughter left him—his shirt hitched up to his neck, the top button of his pants undone and shoes still on. Moonlight fills the room with a clear bluish light, and Janice sees it. A speckled gray feather the shape of an overgrown paisley grows out of her husband's back. It's shaft is the color of bone.

"Jesus."

"See, Mommy, see?"

"Sweet Jesus." She feels nothing but relief. She doesn't notice that her husband is a sack of bones. Nor does she blame herself for letting Jimmy's condition get as bad as it has gotten. The forced modesty that occurred with the birth of their children never went away. For years, Janice went to bed in her mother's nightgown, Jimmy in long loose pants and a T-shirt. Both wore socks. The only thing dangerous and naked in their bed were their hands. It never occurs to Janice that if she had slept with him this last month, she would've found the feather as soon as it appeared. She is tempted to call his boss, to tell him, "It's all right; it was just a feather. And we went on and pulled it out, so Jimmy can come on back to work, can't he?"

Joe-Joe has come in, baby Shawn trailing him. They all huddle around the bed. For the first time in a month, laughter spills out of a mouth other than Jimmy's. They look at the feather, a symptom so ghastly, its solution so simple.

Joe-Joe speaks first. "Just pull in out."

Pen-Pen touches her father's back gingerly, waking him and whispers, "Daddy, it ain't even that big." At her touch, Jimmy's chuckles fill the room. And yet they hesitate. Even Janice is not quite sure what do to, though she is thinking of asking Jimmy's boss for back pay. She finds she's reluctant to snatch out what could be. All wings start with feathers, don't they? So who knows? Who are we to pluck out what could be?

"Daddy it's just a feather. Like a pigeon." Pen-Pen tells him.

"Nah-uh. Like a dove." Joe-Joe says.

"I found it."

"So?"

"Shut up, you two."

"Momma ain't we gone pull it out?" Janice looks as her two children.

"Put on the light." Racing to the lamp switch, Joe-Joe turns it on. What Janice see takes her breath away. Under her breath, she counts Jimmy's ribs. Something has to be done. Sitting on the bed, she holds her husband's head in her hands. "Ya'll try to get it out. I'll hold on to your daddy."

If this is a sin, they all will be accountable, she thinks. Joe-Joe holds baby Shawn by the hand, and he and Pen-Pen grab the feather. "On three, all right?"

"One, two, *three*," and together they pull as hard as they can. Their father's skin lifts from the effort, but the feather doesn't budge.

"Momma, it won't come out."

Janice looks down at her children, dropping Jimmy's head back unto the pillow. Jimmy lies curled on his side but Janice pushes her husband over on his stomach. His laughter is abruptly muffled.

"Okay, I got it." But Pen-Pen and Joe-Joe won't let go. "You hear me? Let loose." She sighs. Unwilling to fight with her children, she begins to pull at the plume, digging her teeth into her bottom lip from the effort. "Come on," she whispers to herself, and as if it hears her, the feather lets go.

Janice and Joe-Joe jerk their hands away, but Pen-Pen holds on to the feather.

"Thank you," Jimmy says.

Despite all the laughing he has done, Jimmy's raspy voice sounds unused. Suddenly they realize their father hasn't said one word in more than two months. He sighs deeply. "You little scamp," he says to Pen-Pen. And smiles.

So now what? Janice almost tells Pen-Pen to burn the feather, but stops herself when she remembers that her five-year-old daughter shouldn't play with fire. But she can't bring herself to take it out of her child's hand.

"Ma'am, what should I—?" Pen-Pen asks as she walks closer to her mother, and Janice takes a step back as her daughter approaches.

"Take it to the window," she says, but then she catches herself. She can't tell Pen-Pen to throw it out the window, can she? Who knows who it might land on next?

"Put it out there, Momma?" Pen-Pen goes the window. "Joey, help me open it." Joe-Joe makes a wide circle around his sister, careful not to touch her or the feather.

"No," Janice says, but her children do not hear. All of Joe-Joe's attention is on Pen-Pen and the feather she holds. Still watching the feather, he fumbles with the rim of the window and raises it. "No, just a minute," Janice says. "Let me think." What if it finds its way back to her family? What then?

But Janice has taken too long to decide what to do. Her daughter's imagination flourishes and she thinks maybe the feather will grow into her hand the way it grew into her father's back. That she is will be compelled to laugh when nothing is funny. And this time they won't be able to get it out. Her small hand uncurls and the feather, sensing its freedom, spins lightly on Pen-Pen's palm. "Pen-Pen!" Janice shouts, but it's too late. The wind catches the plume, and the feather dances in the open window and then floats outside. Joe-Joe and Janice race to the window and lean out to watch the feather dip and swirl in the air. But Pen-Pen is unconcerned with the feather and its flight. After it leaves her hand, she walks back to the bed and watches Jimmy Brazil, father of three, go still.

A Taste of Eden

Sleeper's Wake

By Paule Marshall

Paule Marshall (1929–), the Brooklyn-born daughter of Barbadian parents, published her modern classic, *Brown Girl, Brownstones,* in 1959. She has written six novels since then and has received numerous awards, including an American Book Award and a MacArthur Fellowship. Marshall divides her time between teaching creative writing at New York University and writing at her home in Richmond, Virginia. In this excerpt from her 1983 novel, *Praisesong for the Widow,* a wife searches for the moment in her marriage after which nothing was the same.

It was an act of betrayal. But although she tried she couldn't help herself. The closing for the house in North White Plains had taken place, the actual move was only weeks away, when suddenly she found herself thinking not so much of the new life awaiting them but of the early years back on Halsey Street, of the small rituals and private pleasures that had lasted through the birth of Sis. And in the face of Jay's marathon effort and her own crowded wearying days, such thoughts seemed a betrayal. A sin against the long, twelve-year struggle. She felt like a secret tippler who, when everyone in the house was asleep, sneaked down to the liquor cabinet where the memories of that earlier period were a wine she could not resist. During those final weeks in Brooklyn they were a habit she indulged on the sly.

The thoughts usually waylaid her in bed at night, during the half hour or so when she would lie there waiting for her overtaxed body to relax enough for her to fall asleep.

Sometimes the most frivolous things from those vanished years on Halsey Street came to mind. One night, she caught herself reliving the ridiculous dances Jay used to stage just for the two of them in the living room whenever the mood struck him.

"What's your pleasure this evening, Miss Williams?"—calling her by her maiden name. "Will it be the Savoy, Rockland Palace or the Renny again?"

"Oh, I don't know," she would say, entering the fantasy with him. "Why don't we go on over to the Audubon for a change. I hear there's a dance there tonight. I'm kinda tired of those other places. And afterwards if we're hungry we can go back crosstown for chicken and waffles at Wells."

"Your wish, ma'am, is my command."

In minutes he would have the records stacked high on the turntable spindle and the three-way lamp in the room turned to low. Back at her side he would offer her his arm, and with his other hand clearing a way for them through the imaginary crowd in the make-believe ballroom he would lead her out to the center of the floor.

One by one the records would drop: "Flying Home," "Take the A-Train," "Stompin' at the Savoy," "Cottontail"—they would have to off-time to that one it was so fast. She was the better dancer, and sometimes partway through a number, he would spin her off to dance by herself, and standing aside watch her footwork and the twisting and snaking of her body with an amazed smile. Once, teasing her: "I hope you don't mind my saying it, Miss Williams, but when the white folks came up with the theory about all us darkies having rhythm, they must have had you in mind. Girl, you can out-jangle Bojangles and out-snake Snake Hips."

Those fanciful nights-out-on-the-town always ended with Avery Parrish's recording of "After Hours." This they played over and over again. Jay's arms around her waist, hers circling his neck, their bodies fused and swaying, they would slow-drag in the dimly lit room to the sound of Parrish's unabashedly sensuous, crystalline musings on the piano.

"You know something, old lady, you still feel like new"—whispering it in her ear.

There also had been the small rituals that had made Sundays a special day back then, truly their day. Some nights, lying awake beside
an exhausted Jay whose every muscle remained painfully tensed
even as he slept (she could feel them), her thoughts would turn to
that one priceless day off for them both.

Getting up early, Jay used to slip his clothes on over his
pajamas and leave her in bed to walk over to Broadway to buy the
papers, the coffee ring they always treated themselves to for
Sunday breakfast and a hard roll for Sis when she came along
and was teething.

That was the day when the phonograph in the living room
remained silent. But like spirits ascending, black voices rose all
morning from the secondhand Philco next to it. The South-
erneers, The Fisk Jubilee Choir, Wings Over Jordan (which was
her favorite of the groups), The Five Blind Boys of Atlanta,
Georgia . . .

Whenever the Five Blind Boys sang "Dry Bones," Jay would join
their complex harmonizing, forcing his modest baritone down to
a bass: ". . . knee bone connected to the leg bone/ leg bone connected to the ankle bone . . . Them bones, them bones, them-a
dry bones,'" he sang in a deep field-holler of a voice. "'Oh, hear
the word of the. L-O-R-D. . .!'"

Sis loved it.

Later on, when Jay recited from memory fragments of poems he
had learned as a boy, her eyes would all but take over her small
face. He had been taught the poets in the small segregated school
in Leona, Kansas, which he had attended as a boy. The schools up
north didn't teach colored children anything about the race,
about themselves, he used to complain.

". . . I bathed in the Euphrates when dawns were young. . ." he loved to
recite, standing in his pajamas in the middle of the living room,
while Avey, Sis in her lap, sat listening and eating coffee cake in
the armchair.

"'I built my hut by the Congo and it lulled me/to sleep. I looked upon the Nile and
raised the pyramids/above it . . .'"—with a raised hand he indicated their

great height, their grandeur. Then quietly: *"'. . . I've known rivers: /Ancient, dusky rivers./ My soul has grown deep like the rivers.'"*

He would go on then to offer them the other half-dozen or so poems he remembered from his boyhood.

"'Little brown baby wif spa'klin'/eyes . . . !'" He would burst out in dialect and, coming over, scoop Sis up in his arms. *"'Come to yo' pappy an' set on his knee . . ./Who's pappy's darlin' . . .'"* he'd ask her, *"'. . . an'/who's pappy's chile . . . ?'"* Then: *"'. . . Wisht you could allus know/ease an' cleah skies;/Wisht you could stay jes' a chile on my breas'—/Little broun baby wif spa'klin' eyes!'"*

Another of his favorites—one which Sis was also to recite some years later in a Sunday school program—was about the creation of the world. Striding up and down the living room he would perform the portions he remembered with all the appropriate gestures:

". . . He batted His eyes, and the lightnings flashed;
He clapped His hands, and the thunders rolled;
And the waters above the earth came down,
The cooling waters came down . . .
And God said, "That's good. . . !"

"The end," he would say finally. "That's it for today." And an enthralled Sis, who, it seemed, had forgotten even to breathe during the entire recital, would then take a deep and wondering breath.

". . . oh children think about the good times . . ."

Best of all had been the times when it was just the two of them, off to themselves in the narrow hallway bedroom, their limbs in a sweet tangle on the bed.

Lying awake nights her thoughts, her aching body, would secretly drink the heady wine of that memory.

Her pleasure had always been greatest those times when he had talked to her. Amid the touching and play at the beginning Jay sometimes talked, telling her, his mouth with the neat bush of hair against her ear, her cheek, and the feather-touch of his hand on her skin, what he thought of her skin, how the rich smooth feel of it had got all up inside him the first time they had met and he had taken her arm to lead her to the dance floor. Telling her also what he thought of her breasts as his hands and lips moved slowly over them—what they did to him—and her thighs, whose length and shapeliness excited him, he said, even when she was dressed and he couldn't see them. This when his hand, taking its time, had passed down the length of her body to caress them. And her behind was Gulla gold! Treasure that belonged to him alone. He wanted to kill the bastards who ran their thoughts over it as she walked down the street. He spoke then, his voice a whisper, of her trim, gently bringing his hand there to touch her in the way she had taught him; her lovely, still incredibly tight trim. It stayed on his mind. "How does Mr. B. put it in the song again? '. . . killed my mammy, and ran my pappy stone-blind . . .'? It's that powerful, Avey, that strong." He teased her about what he was going to do when she finally permitted him in, how he was going to carry on, tear up, go out of his mind. Jay! Talking that talk until he turned her into a wanton with her nightgown bunched up around her neck like an airy boa she had donned as a fetish to feed his pleasure, or abandoned altogether on the floor beside the bed.

There was his scandalous talk, and then, when she finally drew him into her, his abrupt, awestruck silence. His stillness. He would lie within her like a man who has suddenly found himself inside a temple of some kind, and hangs back, overcome by the magnificence of the place, and sensing around him the invisible forms of the deities who reside there: Erzulie with her jewels and gossamer veils, Yemoja to whom the rivers and seas are sacred; Oya, first wife of the thunder god and herself in charge of winds and rains . . . Jay might have felt himself surrounded by a pantheon of the most ancient deities who had made their temple the tunneled darkness of his wife's flesh. And he held back, trembling a little, not knowing quite how to conduct himself in their presence.

It was her turn then. Bringing her mouth to his ear and her limbs securely around him—in command now—she led him forward. Until under her touch and the words she whispered to him—

telling him what it felt like having him inside her, how he filled and completed her—his hesitancy fell away, and he was suddenly speaking again. But with his body this time. A more powerful voice. Another kind of poetry.

The end always took her by surprise. There would be the thick runaway beating of her heart (*"Just the beat, just the beat of my poor heart in the dark"*: Lil Green on the record they loved), the heat and her dissolving limbs. And then, without warning, a nerve somewhere in her body which had never before made itself felt would give a slight twitch, and growing stronger take over the work of the pulse at her wrists and temples and throat, and begin beating. But in a more forceful way. And in a swift chain reaction—all of it taking less than a second—the upheaval would spread to a host of other nerves and muscles, causing them to erupt also. Until pulsing together they brought to life the other heart at the base of her body.

And the miracle which was strictly a private matter, that had only to do with her, then took place. She slipped free of it all: the bed, the narrow hallway bedroom, the house, Halsey Street, her job, Jay, the children, and the child who might come of this embrace. She gave the slip to her ordinary, everyday self. And for a long pulsing moment she was pure self, being, the embodiment of pleasure, the child again riding the breakers at Coney Island in her father's arms, crowing in delight and terror. The wave she was riding crested, then dropped. But not abruptly. It was a long, slow, joyous fall which finally, when it had exhausted itself, left her beached in a sprawl of limbs on the bed, laughing wildly amid tears.

The sweetness of it!

One morning she awoke to find Jay—propped on his elbow on the pillow next to hers—gazing down at her with a smile that was both playful and amazed.

"I hope you know you carried on somethin' disgraceful last night, Miz Johnson, ma'am. *Almost had to turn on the lights and call the Law.*" He was misquoting a line from a Billy Daniels record.

She pushed him away in mock indignation, even as she fought back her laughter. "There you go getting your women mixed up again, Jay Johnson. I don't know a thing about that hussy you had in here with you last night."

Those private times in the bedroom! They had seemed inviolable. Yet, as with everything else they gradually fell victim to the strains, to the sense of the downward slide and to the punishing years that followed. Jay's touch increasingly became that of a man whose thoughts were elsewhere, and whose body, even while merged with hers, felt impatient to leave and join them.

Moreover, in place of the outrageous talk which she loved and needed, there was eventually only his anxious question at the beginning: "Did you remember to put in that thing . . .?" And at the end his wrenching cry, "Take it from me, Avey! Just take it from me!"

Love like a burden he wanted rid of. Like a leg-iron which slowed him in the course he had set for himself.

Sometimes, lying there with her body left abandoned far short of the crested wave, she wanted to shove him over to his side of the bed or to hit him with her fist as he fell into a dead sleep still clinging to her. But then she would think of his shoulders collapsed from the weight of the heavy sample cases when he came in from the futile search on a Monday and of the harried, bloodshot eyes that met hers whenever he glanced up briefly from the manual or textbook he was studying, and then not only would she hold him as tightly, she would want to take to the streets with an avenging sword. . . .

Not long after the move to North White Plains, Jay shaved off his mustache. A small thing, Avey quickly told herself as he emerged from the bathroom that morning with it gone; nothing to get upset about. Why then did the sight of that suddenly naked space above his lips fill her with such dismay, and even fear?

"Damn thing was getting to be a nuisance," was all he said by way of explanation. Then, irritably, as she continued to stare at him with the troubled, apprehensive look: "What're you looking like that for? It's just a little hair, for God's sake. You'll soon get used to me without it."

After a while it was as if he had always been clean-shaven. Nevertheless, at a deeper level, she remained unreconciled to the change, and as distressed and uneasy as she had been the first day. With the mustache no longer there it seemed that the last trace of everything that was distinctive and special about him had vanished also. Why she felt this she could not say.

Then, too—and this was what made her obscurely fearful—that thick bush above his mouth had served, she had always sensed, as a kind of protection, diverting attention from his intelligent gaze and the assertive, even arrogant flare to his nose. With it shaved off he had lost a necessary shield. He was as exposed and vulnerable suddenly as a prizefighter who had foolishly let drop his guard.

There was something even more disquieting which she slowly became aware of over the years. On occasion, glancing at him, she would surprise what almost looked like the vague, pale outline of another face superimposed on his, as in a double exposure. It was the most fleeting of impressions, something imagined rather than seen, and she always promptly dismissed it.

Nonetheless, there it was every so often, this strange pallid face, whose expression was even more severe and driven than Jay's, looming up for a subliminal moment over his familiar features.

Worse, during the same period, he began speaking in a way at times she found hard to recognize. The voice was clearly his, but the tone and, more important, the things he said were so unlike him they might have come from someone (perhaps the stranger she thought she spied now and again) who had slipped in when he wasn't looking and taken up residency behind his dark skin; someone who from the remarks he made viewed the world and his fellow man according to a harsh and joyless ethic:

"That's the trouble with half these Negroes you see out here. Always looking for the white man to give them something instead of getting out and doing for themselves . . ."

Saying this to people like Thomasina Moore and her husband, who were part of their new circle of friends.

Or: "Just look at 'em! Not a thing on their minds but cutting up and having a good time."

And again: "If it was left to me I'd close down every dancehall in Harlem and burn every drum! That's the only way these Negroes out here'll begin making any progress!"

Jay took to saying things like that. Or rather, it was Jerome Johnson who spoke. While continuing to call him Jay to his face, she gradually found herself referring to him as Jerome Johnson in her thoughts. She couldn't account for the change in any conscious way. Perhaps it was that other face she sometimes thought she detected hovering pale and shadowy over his. Or the unsparing, puritanical tone that had developed in his voice. Or the things he had taken to saying. Whatever it was, it eventually became impossible for her, even when she tried forcing herself, to think the name Jay. His full name, with its distant formal sound, became rooted in her mind during their last ten years together in the house in North White Plains. By the time of his death she could scarcely remember when he had been anyone other than Jerome Johnson in the privacy of her thoughts.

"*Do you know who you sound like?*" he had cried, starting up out of his sleep the night of his final stroke. "*Who you even look like?*" Still haunted up to the moment of his death by the memory of Halsey Street.

The day of his funeral when she was led forward, just her alone, to view the body for the last time, she had stood with her head bowed over the open top half of the coffin, giving the impression that she was gazing down at the face lying amid the wealth of shirred, cream-colored satin. But behind her widow's veil her eyes had been carefully averted. In the three days that the body had been on view she had not once fully looked at the face, afraid of what she might find there.

That final day she had simply stood, her gaze off to one side, waiting for the funeral director stationed next to her to lead her away after the proper interval. Then, just as she felt his slight pressure on her arm, signaling her that it was time, she had gathered together her courage and glanced down. And there it had been, as she had feared, staring up at her from Jerome Johnson's sealed face: that other face with the tight joyless look which she had surprised from time to time over the years. Jerome Johnson was dead, but it was still alive; in the midst of his immutable silence, the sound of its mirthless, triumphant laughter could be heard ringing through the high nave of the church.

Suddenly she had started forward, the upper half of her body lunging out until she was within inches of the laughing, thin-lipped, mouth. At the same instant, her gloved hand, hidden in the folds of the dress at her side, had closed into a fist, and as it started up the first note of a colossal cry could be heard forming in her throat. The man beside her, thinking she was giving way at last to her grief, had quickly restrained her. Then, holding her firmly around the shoulders, consoling her in his professional undertone, he had led her trembling and wild-eyed behind the thick veil back to her seat.

Afterwards everyone had congratulated her on how well she had held up in the face of her great loss.

Aunt Delia

By Valerie Wilson Wesley

Valerie Wilson Wesley (1950–), author of the Tamara Hayle mystery series and several novels and children's books, opened her first non-genre novel, 1999's *Ain't Nobody's Business if I Do*, with a narrative piece about a great-aunt who, who even from the grave could foresee her grand-niece Eva's future. In this excerpt, Aunt Delia, though dead, manages to convey that her powers are not lost to Eva.

Nobody but a fool crossed Aunt Delia, so Eva never did. When Eva was a girl before they moved up North, she had to fight her way through the smell of Vicks VapoRub that lingered in her great-aunt's small, damp house to take slices of her grandmother's bourbon-laced pecan pie. She would always dutifully dispose of her aunt's nail clippings as the old woman instructed, and kept one eye glued to the door when she kissed her wrinkled cheek.

Aunt Delia was a hoo-doo woman; she knew how to work some roots. She could make a person lie, scream or pine six weeks for a man she saw once in the A&P. She could make a snake dance, a cat bark, and when she was young, she'd made six of John Dixon's hens lay double-yolked eggs because he'd talked to her in sweet whispers out of both sides of his mouth.

She had something to do with Hannah Jones' bad luck too. Hannah, who walked with a switch that stopped grown men dead, stole Aunt Delia's best beau and wed him before he knew he was gone. She later had the first of three sets of twins six days after she turned thirty-six. Everybody knew it was Aunt Delia's doing because it involved the number six. Her spells always had to do with love, loss and a combination of the number six.

Her death at ninety-six didn't surprise Eva; what did was the arrival of the small black box with the words, *To Eva Lilton Hutchinson and her sweet man Hutch with all my love and devotion, Your Great Aunt D*, printed neatly in red across the top. When Eva opened it, all she found were a few dried twigs and the lingering smell of Vicks VapoRub. Aunt Delia always did like to have the last word.

Uncle Raymond

By Nelson Eubanks

Nelson Eubanks (1971–) is a graduate of the Masters in Fine Arts Program at Columbia University. Raised in New Jersey, he now lives in New York and is the author of the forthcoming collection of short stories, *The First Thing Smoking*. In "Uncle Raymond," Eubanks's fictional narrator is a keen observer of how an extended Michigan clan copes with a once-promising son.

He's got his new winter coat on with those headphones blasting real loud, blasting so loud we can all hear clear the words to all the songs, as he just sits there with his big brown body shlumped up at the kitchen table, his hazel eyes going googily at everything while grinning, sweating, laughing, yawning real wide with all his yellow teeth flashing as he giggles and drinks his beer and click, click, flicks through the TV channels and crosses and uncrosses his legs, to sit back in his stool, and jerk forward, and lean slowly back, and smile and fiddle with his walkman and laugh and frown and jerk, jerk, jiggle, sway, looking left, right, down, up, behind, out at the falling snow through the window to smile for a while at nothing I can make out from here. He's just sitting there flicking, drinking, sweating, smiling, frowning, grinning, jerking, easing, fiddling, crossing, uncrossing, looking here and there slowly and quickly at everything and nothing, red-drunk eyes, dazed like he's never seen it before and won't ever see it again, as his left hand rests calm across his big bulging belly with a drooping half-ashed cigarette in-between his uncut fingernails like a weed roach. Most everybody else sitting up there with him at my grandma's long kitchen-counter table tries to pay him no mind, but I see him. I watch him. They keep on talking loud around him trying to smile and laugh through him by way of good gossip, old stories and sweet lies. Then somebody'll nudge him, "Raymond," and he looks around and smiles and ashes his cigarette.

"Take that coat off," Grandma says.

Uncle Raymond is up there fidgeting in his brand new white high-top Christmas sneakers laced too tight and new blue Christmas coat with a furry hood like Eskimos wear, up there thinking folks are going to let him slide out again to get some more beer but company is coming. Family. Friends. And the liquor makes it worse.

"Take those headphones off and put that coat right back in the box where you found it," she says, but Raymond just looks out the window while burning through the channels.

From my Grandpa's big rose chair in the living room, alone, near the blinking tree, I just sit and watch. Eighteen and full of promise. They thought whatever it was they had done, whatever it is older people do to younger people to make them a certain right way had somehow come together in me. Had stuck and taken and now there were big hopes. Uncles and aunts would touch me and smile when I came around, a hand on the shoulder, an arm around the waist with lots of last minute dos and don'ts to tweak the many hours of work they'd put into me over the many long Flint summers to get me where I was going, an Ivy League school my mother had let them believe was paying me to play soccer for them, which, of course, wasn't all true.

Everybody's got an opinion but nobody knows for sure what went wrong with Raymond, which is to say nobody knows the exact when and how he started straddling worlds. Seems one day he just slipped this one altogether for some place else entirely. But what almost everybody who needs to know knows for certain is what my Uncle Otis, by way of Arkansas, likes to lean in and say come holiday times with a soft Little Rock drawl and candy-coated Crown

Royal Breath, "Rayyyyyymond's breaaaaaad ain't done," which is to say, Raymond is a little off, which is, of course, very true.

Holiday times when some friends and distant family folks who aren't familiar with things come to visit and Grandma and Grandpa get up out of ear shot and Raymond gets going grinning and jerking with his eyes going everywhere we Joyners quick to say with a wink and a smile, "Raymond ain't truly one of us," meaning he's adopted, which is mostly true too. It seems to put other folks at ease some. Somewhere down deep it seems to put all the rest of us family folk at ease too, for depending on who and what you believe, we all seem to think some horrible thing like that could never happen to the likes of us for coming from a different better sturdier stock of people.

Ever since my grandma fell that last time and broke her hip she doesn't move too good but uses a cane and never sits up at the kitchen counter with everybody any more but down in her low chair with wheels by the wall. From there she can still smile some- times, seeing almost everyone she helped raise, which means all of us. She has stories, good squirming hot-seat stories on everybody, which she lays out from time to time when someone gets on someone else a little too hard. She gets going telling and everyone goes quiet listening as her almond-shaped Egyptian eyes like mine get small then big as she travels back through the years, forgetting where she is, down in that low chair. Her face softens over the sto- ries of all of us as she gets going back, and further back when Ray- mond was young and going to do something great, making her wish for those times when Raymond could listen and smile right along with us, telling his own brand of great big ole gut-splitting lies he learned directly from years of listening and laughing while riding over to the north side with my Granddaddy in that beat-up faded blue Ford pick-up truck to fix somebody's busted toilet in some house Granddaddy owned over on Spencer Street of the north side of Flint. Before Raymond lost it, he used to be not just Grandma's favorite but Granddaddy's favorite too. His protégé.

From the low chair Grandma can get up and around the kitchen easier. My cousin Sidney put an old rotary phone right where she likes it, right there next to her down low on the wall with a long, long chord and one of those shoulder rests for when her friends call and get talking and she doesn't want to get up but wants to wheel slowly here and there about the kitchen, push the volume down on the TV when Raymond has it high and isn't listening or can't hear her asking or something. When we all get together that's where she sits, right there by the old phone but it's not the same. Grandma still doesn't want to believe it happened to her like this, not her hip, but Raymond, her baby, the way he is. And when it comes on her, you can see it coming from everywhere.

The smoked turkey, regular turkey, honeyed ham are cooking in the oven and big pots of greens and baked beans, gravy, pans of cornbread, cornbread stuffing, mac and cheese, sweet potatoes, rolls, are warming on top of the stove with steam oozing out of other pots all smelling of good things to come with the pound cake, apple pie, sweet potato pies, pumpkin pie, derby pie, sock-it-to-me cake, coconut cake, cheese cake and German chocolate cake cooling on a counter in the dining room. My aunts have been cooking for three days in four separate houses. It's snowing pretty hard outside, white on green, big flakes weighing down branches, evergreen leaves sagging towards the ground. Raymond is sitting still in his coat but zooming through the channels at the speed of light, grinning and laughing at something only he sees out in those trees. The younger cousins and women are moving quickly round the house and kitchen. Dishes, forks, knives are clinking and clanking out of the dishwater, against each other, as cabinets swing open and bang closed with the vacuum going on loud above everything but the TV. Like every year, the women are getting ready for the other friends, family, folks coming soon. It's going to be a big meal.

The men and my mother are sitting and talking and laughing up at the kitchen counter. Every now and then an aunt or someone will take a break and sit for a while with them, and let a story loose on somebody or something and laugh hard along with everyone else. This is how it's been every year for as long as

I can remember. Everybody falling and settling right into the same ways and grooves waiting right there for them from the last year's Christmas. Grandma is frowning at Raymond, wanting him to take off his coat and act different and right and not so sick, but the way how he was supposed to be.

Folks are feeling something, telling longer, louder lies and better stories above the TV and laughing hard and often, so Raymond's grinning and laughing almost seems in time and alright, but it's not. Grandma isn't having it. I can hear his headphones from here and when he laughs it's deep and hard and would stop anyone who didn't know the shape of things. All of it is getting Grandma real good so her eye is jumping and her mouth is bursting loaded nothings as she looks around at everyone moving here and there quickly, the way Raymond sometimes gets to looking around at everything and nothing. Her phone is ringing loud the way Sidney fixed it and she leans to get it and then stops and from the low chair starts in on him, soft to loud, "Raymond, Raymond, Raymonnnnn," as the old big black phone rings and rings but he doesn't hear any of that stuff from her anymore, but grins and stands up and sits back down and grabs one of his four cigarettes laying on the counter and then his lighter. Now leaning back with smoke coming out of his nostrils, rubbing the top of his hair so dandruff and brown things are falling over his shoulders. She's yelling, the phone ringing, everyone talking, his headphones blaring, the vacuum on loud, then off as she yells, "Raymond, Raymond, Raymonnn." He looks and looks away, out at the snow on the trees as the phone rings and the TV belches pieces of loud sound. He grins and kicks his wet white new no-name Christmas sneakers against the metal foot bar like he's gone outside already, as her phone rings, back and forth so there's a rhythmic basketball squeak, back and forth, with some tune he's hearing from far away and Grandma says, "Boy, what's so funny, turn that off, Raymond, turn them headphones off, Raymond! Raymond!" He stands up and I say loud above everything, "What are you listening to Raymond?"

"Bitches Brew," he says. "Bitches Brew." Without looking back at me. "Miles sucking all the juice out of them notes and Herbie Hancock settin' him up nice with them chords," he says, as all of his uncles and brothers go quiet, stop. Look.

The phone is ringing and the vacuum from somewhere in the back of the house sings low then louder then low again as someone on TV goes on too loud about weather in the Ohio Valley. Raymond sits and takes a drag and lets it come out of his nose.

"Daddy, I need a beer," he says. "It's not time," I hear my Granddaddy say, and Raymond stands. "Can anyone run me round to the gas station?" he says and sits and yawns. "Ain't time, and not open," cousin Benella says. The phone stops ringing. Grandma just watches him. Raymond jerks forward and grins and laughs. "I'm gonna go out soon," he says and gets up off the stool and rubs his hands and sits back down and grins at the snow while smoke comes out his mouth in rings, and my grandma says, "Not for any beer, Raymond. Why don't you take that coat off and help somebody. Someone needs help. Why don't you help Elton set the plates. Elton needs help."

"It's not time yet, Raymond," Granddaddy booms louder over Grandma.

"Ain't nobody gonna take you anywhere on Christmas, so you might as well take that coat off, Raymond," my cousin Betty says.

"Can't nobody run you over there, Raymond, with all these people coming, know you're not suppose to drink, so don't know why you're asking," my mother says loud, almost for show, touching Raymond's shoulder then pulling on the sleeve of the coat. Raymond grins at something. Shakes his shoulder to help my mother. One sleeve comes off and he sits back into his stool, blows smoke out the side of his mouth. My mother shakes her head. Raymond picks up the remote and leans back and crosses his legs and starts in on the channels fast as ever with one sleeve of his jacket brushing the floor so you can see the orange inside as he sometimes jerks.

My grandma watches him and starts up again. "Raymond! Raymond! Raymonnn!" Like nothing just happened. He's sweating.

He freezes. Eyes wide like he's heard something. Stands up. Starts quick down the hall towards his room with his jacket half on, one sleeve dragging and my grandma screaming after him and it's too much for the folks up there, and cousins, uncles, brothers, nephews are trying hard not to hear it the way Raymond doesn't hear it, trying to forget by talking louder and laughing harder so as to not have to see what Grandma sees, hoping it all might just up and fly away, and "Raymond, Raymonnnn!" She's half standing up, leaning on the arm of her chair for support, which means she means it. "And take that coat off, boy, and put it back in the box where you found it back under that tree," she yells, but Raymond is long gone, and everybody sitting is now getting up and looking down quiet, going to help somebody around the house, cause we all know what comes next when Grandma starts getting this way, feeling mad and sad about taking Raymond in, having him still around at her age, wondering, while knowing, why nobody will take him who can and should take him, everyone quietly knowing full well how hard it is for her to get around to make sure of him these days, knowing she won't be able to do it much longer.

"Maceo," she says, not so loud, "go and make Raymond a plate." She sits and reaches for the black phone. "And tell him to put that coat and shoes back away in his Christmas box and come back out here cause folks are coming soon want to see him." She knows I'll do it and not ask her why, and Raymond sometimes says a word to me from time to time and maybe she is hoping.

See, must be nearly forty folks between the Joyners, Hiltons and Browns all living close by each other in Flint. Least four families could stand to have Raymond. She knows it's not the money and she's right. She's got plenty saved special for when the time comes she's not around or when she can't do it anymore. She knows we all know this too. But the truth is nobody wants to go through it all over again, hear Grandma start asking her whys and why nots and find themselves the one having to say the reasons to her out loud again. Not at Christmas. But really, I guess, not ever.

Because Raymond lies and steals from Grandma's purse and

Granddaddy's wallet and picks the locked closet where the valuables get put away and nods off and falls asleep in chairs and beds with cigarettes still burning in-between his fingers and sometimes forgets to put his sticky nudie books away under the sink and leaves them right by the toilet where even my grandma can see them. And he says, "Yes, alright," and "Alright, yes," or nothing at all with his Walkman roarin' to anyone who says, "Don't do this," and "You gotta do that," and the one time my granddaddy went a little crazy himself and had a shovel and was really going to do something bad, banging on Raymond's locked door, Uncle Langston, who is the youngest of my mother's siblings besides Raymond, and who still lives in my grandma's basement, ran upstairs and talked Granddaddy out of the shovel, and then Grandma stopped talking to Granddaddy for a week, saying that's not what you do with someone who needs help. Cousin Benella, who's just about Raymond's age and actually might know, says quietly but often, "Raymond don't want to get no better. Happy just where he is. Ain't gonna let that fool burn me up. Stealing from me in my own house, please! Shouldda done somethin' while they had the chance to do somethin.'"

They say it wasn't always like that, Raymond crazy. I can still remember when he'd come out of it, *whap*. You never knew how long it'd last. That was long ago when I was barely eight and Raymond's face wasn't so soft and round and his gut didn't jut out over his belt buckle and he didn't drink quite how he drinks all the time nowadays.

He'd be watching the TV or be in his room or even during Christmas dinner gnawing on a turkey bone or something, burning non-stop through the stations with those headphones screaming Miles, fidgeting and grinning, looking at his thumb moving the remote button, and then up to the space where his cigarette smoke disappeared and *whap*, he'd just stop and look around clear. You could see it. His eyes. He'd look around all clear for a moment. Get up and go without a word to stand right in front of his B3 Hammond organ still waiting for him in the living room.

Pull his headphones down round his neck and move the sound down real low so not even he could hear. Sit down for a minute not doing anything. Turn the organ on. Close his eyes, listening to it purr as it warmed. Back straight, head cocked to the side as if hearing something coming from the sky. Eyes open and a smile and just like that, he'd start playing and playing and playing and playing with his eyes closed and head all the way back as his body rocked slow and swayed hard like Ray Charles, shoulders dancing, long basketball fingers jumping, floating, plunging, swinging up and down the white and black keys as his feet bounced and roared jazzy, bluesy, gospel bass lines down along the many wooden bass foot pedals, to turn round and look at us while slowly, slowly, sliding back into a church hymn he knew made my grandma smile and quickly, feet bouncing back into something bopping again for the rest of us.

"Watch him," my dad would say, "his feet, his feet playing the bass, watch him, watch him." And everybody in and out of my grandma's house would stop whatever it was they were doing and follow the music to stand all around the back of him to watch and sway and listen, enjoying the small time he was back here with us, the older folks thinking of when Raymond was young and gifted with prospects, back when he had promise and potential and was sane and always in this world, us young kids wanting to reach out and touch him to see if he were real, while wondering how in the world anybody, 'specially crazy Raymond, could play anything that sounded so good out of the big brown monster of an organ nobody else ever went near.

But that was long ago. Eleven years.

I knock on his door. Thin sounds of music coming from his headphones through the door, smoke from under it, smells of cigarette ash mixed with turkey, honeyed ham and gravy and laughing and talking wafting warm from the living room and kitchen down the hall.

"Raymond," I say but there's nothing. "Raymond," I say, "you alright, man? I got a plate a food here for you from Grandma." But there's only smoke from under his door, and the tin sound of some headphone's horn coming through softly. I try the door knob. "Everything taste terrible," I hear him say, and the knob won't turn. Locked.

"What happened?" I say, and I hear, "Terrible. Horrible right on the tongue." He says it real loud. "Okay," he says. "Wait," he says. "Wait." And then nothing but the horn from his head-phones, smells of smoke and ash from under his door.

"Grandma wants you to take that coat off and those shoes and put 'em back in your Christmas box," I say. "I'll help if you want. Whatta ya say, ya alright?" I press my ear to his locked door. "Ya, okay?" Listening for something, anything else.

"What ya listening to?" I say. But nothing.

I wait.

Nothing.

What will I tell her?

After a while I say, "Ya want me to leave this plate out here?" But he's gone, gone to that other place. Or maybe just out his window like I guess he sometimes must do. I take his plate to the bathroom window, bring it back clean to his door in case someone else comes to look and see.

My mother says she and my Aunt Corine were practically grown when my grandparents took Raymond in. Nobody knows why they did it. Granddaddy and Grandma had four kids already and were poor and working hard in the G.M. plants, having to stretch things to keep it together when talk of a new child started bubbling around the house. There was a neighbor from Pine Bluff, Arkansas, like my grand folks were, and she had come north, to Michigan, to Flint, to work at the plants with her husband and it had all gone to shit on her. Her husband was dead or gone or something, "wasn't 'round" is how my Uncle Louis the dentist says it. The woman, the neighbor, was coal black and had no job and no prospects and decided she had better go on back to whatever it was she had left behind. She gave Raymond to my grand folks. My grand folks took him in. "It was a different time back then," is how my Uncle Langston the Muslim mumbles it. My mother will say she and Corine raised Raymond and Grandma had no business taking on more than she could.

My mother, who's the first and at least fifteen years older, says for a while everyone in the immediate and extended family thought Raymond was going to outshine all the kids, and even her brothers and sisters and cousin Benella knew it. He was talking before anybody else had, and walking before anybody and had that music; she says he was always good with the music, used to play Sundays for the church and had made the varsity basketball team as a sophomore at Northern and was long, lean and handsome with those almond-shaped hazel eyes like mine and Grandma's. Raymond had lots of friends and girlfriends and was a smart boy going to college. Everyone boasted, talked of him, touched him, sure he'd do the family right.

And then he came apart.

Cousin Benella says Uncle Raymond was losing it even at the end of high school, at Northern. She said he ran with a certain crowd she wouldn't go near, which is one of the things nobody else knows or at least says. Benella says they were watching TV one day and he told her he heard voices sometimes. Sometimes those voices, those people in his head, would come around telling him what to do, not always good things, either. "Oh, now ya don't even want be in the room with me," he said and then "I bet ya all scared, right?" She said no, but as he said all this she was scared of him and his voices, and who can blame her? She said she remembers that and him telling her one day in high school, "Yeah, I don't ever plan to leave Mamma and Daddy. I'm gonna get a factory job and just live on 'em at home." Right on the heels of telling me that, Benella says, "It's not like Raymond ain't really sick but, you know, he ain't tryin' his hardest to get better. And that drinkin' don't help anybody." Benella says she never told anybody that stuff but me. But who knows? He also told Benella that he'd met his real mother, who was light-skinned, too, and rich and Granddaddy was indeed his real father, and he was going to be a professional musician was why he wasn't going to go college like everybody said he had to, or a pro basketball player maybe, which was why he was taking time off, or a singer in Detroit, Motown, he said. Benella says he was always talking big and long about things like that.

Before that, when some say he was still together, he went to visit my mother who wasn't married yet and was living alone in New York. That year, that hot summer in sixty-something right before Raymond was supposed to go to college but didn't, my mother who wasn't a mother yet, brought Raymond back home early to Flint. Raymond was hearing things. Had James Brown up all the way in the living room with his head right next to the speaker—to drown out the voices, he said. In the middle of the night, he'd chain smoke while talking and screaming at folks who weren't there. Waking her sleepover friends with a bright flashlight right in their eyes. My ma had a doctor friend over to look at him, and her friend said Raymond needed help, hospital help.

By all accounts save my grandma's, my mother brought Raymond home and told Grandma he was real sick and needed help. Grandma didn't think so, and that was it for talking about something my grandma said she was done talking about. My ma said that was the exact reason why she moved far away. Grandma's stubbornness. The pushiness. The getting bossed around. My mother was grown and had been through college, and had put herself through her masters in teaching at the University of Michigan the way both Grandma and Granddaddy had wanted her to, but it wasn't enough. One year on the long drive back to New York from Flint, with my mother asleep with her mouth open in the back, my pop told me, "Your ma told your Grandma it wasn't enough and her mother said, 'Well if you think you can do better on your own, you go on ahead and do it.' And so your Mother did and moved to New York. She thinks your Grandma threw her out and they didn't talk for a while after that."

Story goes, my ma was as smart as anybody black or white, old or young and knew she was smart like that, and I guess she decided she wasn't going to knuckle under to anyone but would speak her mind to anyone and everyone who needed to hear it in those days. Seems there were so many who needed to hear it when my mother tells of those uncomfortable times, being a beautiful six-foot-tall, well-educated black woman always standing out, getting stared at everywhere, sometimes wishing she could blend into the walls and be like everyone else. So with Raymond all broken in the head from something, she decided she was going to speak her mind to her mother, my grandma, like nobody ever had, like nobody ever did. She spoke up and told her right there early one morning at that long empty kitchen counter that there was something real wrong with Raymond. Raymond needed help. A New York doctor friend had said so. And a New York doctor certainly knew a lot more than my grandma did.

Some say Grandma's a spiteful woman. Some say that talk with my mother at the kitchen counter, that's the reason why Raymond never saw a doctor. Maybe Grandma didn't care for how she was being spoken to. Maybe it was the tone of voice and that way of arguing my mother had, like she had raised Raymond, like Raymond was *her* baby. After drinking some, my uncle Otis just says, "Ya Grandma's one of those proud high yella women not used to being told about this or that. Couldn't believe anything she had a hand in like her Raymond, someone she'd raised and loved, could be crazy or sick. And ya gotta blame somebody for something like that, and warn't nobody to blame but ya mamma, and there ya go."

I myself don't know. I wasn't there. Nobody was there. What I do know is when I was four my mother took me up Broadway for a long while until we came upon a nodding junkie and she said this is what happens to people like your uncle Raymond who do drugs. Another time, she broke a plastic bottle of wax over the back of my head for a bad word and cut the waxed tuft out of my hair and next day said she hadn't done it. Stepped off a curb one day and broke her ankle and still says I pushed her. But nobody knows that stuff about my ma and me, and she helped all of her brothers and sisters and nieces and cousins and nephews, when they needed her help, wanted to come to New York to stay a while, needed quiet emergency money, sound stern advice when no one else would or could help them like that, and they all love her for it. They all really do. I think sometimes that's why they agree with my mother.

They say she tried telling Grandma that even Raymond was scared, but Grandma didn't think so, and they both argued on and on and came to shouting even, with my mother using fancy college words, *schizophrenia* and the such, to show Grandma, but when Grandma is set on something, she doesn't budge. And at the end of it all, my ma said, "Well, he's not my child and it's not my business," which is maybe what a lot of them say to get themselves through.

A lot of folks say if Grandma had gotten Raymond the proper help back then when my mother stood up to her, maybe Raymond wouldn't be how he is. If you ever get folks talking about it for real, folks in the family who were around and remember the long slow aftermath, they look off in the distance the way Raymond sometimes does, then they get talking full steam and might even get a little angry about it, a little spiteful about it sometimes, a little teary eyed. "It was that LSD," my mother will say on drives back to New York, my father nodding, but quiet. She'll say things like, "Drugs and that angel dust and that LSD, I'm sure. And they could treat that, even then." And other folks say things like, "No reason for it, no reason at all. If Mamma had just budged that once;" things like, "It's a shame;" things like, "It ain't all her fault, but she could a done something when she had the chance;" things like, "Ain't nothin' nobody can do now;" things like, "She gotta lay in the bed she's made." My mother, other folks, say things like that.

Grandma doesn't say anything about it.

"He eat his plate?" Grandma says when she notices me back by the Christmas tree.

"Yes," I say.

"You sit in there with him?"

"Yes," I say.

"What else he say?"

"He said alright," I say, "and he looked like he really liked it."

"And what else?"

"Said he was just going to go to the bathroom and rest for a little while and then he'd come back out soon." And Grandma looks at me and turns away and turns back to look at me, smiling. She seems to feel better with this. I look away.

Food is eaten and everything everywhere is dirty and light gospel is coming over the radio in the living room where I sit, a hymn sort of thing, something Raymond might've played for Grandma way back when he could still do such things. Plates, pots, pans are piled all about the sink, some still in front of the people sitting at the black Santa Claus–patterned tablecloths on card tables all around the house. Raymond is back and sweating with both arms through his coat and white high-tops laced up too tight, head down, quickly finishing up his third plate there at the table and my grandma shoots me a look. Grandma is looking at everybody now, then looking at Raymond, and soon the loud laughing and lying slow to half smiles and murmurs, with people feeling Grandma looking and shifting. Then everybody's up and moving, snapping pants buttons, buckling belts with excuses and reasons and lies to my grandma who's frowning now, glaring at them. Raymond grins and clicks and jerks, sweating all over with that jacket and those headphones blasting, with ash from his cigarette spread across his big belly. He's waiting. Folks up and moving out the door, ignitions being turned over in the driveway and sounds of car engines getting quieter, going further and further, softly over the snow-covered road.

Empty.

A quiet about the house except for blaring headphones and Raymond giggling at the television. It's snowing pretty good outside, the big flakes weighing down all the branches of the evergreens so they droop towards the ground. Raymond is looking out the small window, grinning and laughing at something only he sees as my grandma frowns at him, wanting him to act different and right and not so sick, but how he was supposed to have been. His sneakers are wet and as he jerks they squeak off the metal on the bottom of the stool, and I wonder if he's gone out already or is going out soon, or maybe both.

Grandma just sits and watches him. And if you stick around for a spell, don't go too far, maybe take a seat in the big chair in the living room, after a while you'll hear her sigh and say softly, "Oh Raymond," real quiet, "my baby, my baby," as she rocks up out of her low-chair to hobble down the hall to her room to lie down and close her eyes for a long time.

Brothers and Sisters Around the World

By Andrea Lee

Andrea Lee (1953–), the Philadelphia-born child of a Baptist minister, lives with her husband and two children in Torino, Italy. A regular contributor to *The New Yorker,* she was nominated for a National Book Award for her first book, *Russian Journal.* This short story appears in Lee's most recent book, *Interesting Women.* Like much of Lee's work, it portrays a Black female expatriate attempting to reconcile sexual and cultural tensions.

I took them around the point toward Dzamandzar," Michel tells me. "Those two little whores. Just ten minutes. They asked me for a ride when I was down on the beach bailing out the Zodiac. It was rough and I went too fast on purpose. You should have seen their titties bounce!" He tells me this in French, but with a carefree lewdness that could be Roman. He is in fact half Italian, product of the officially French no man's land where the Ligurian Alps touch the Massif Central. In love, like so many of his Mediterranean compatriots, with boats, with hot blue seas, with dusky women, with the steamy belt of tropics that girdles the earth. We live above Cannes, in Mougins, where it is always sunny, but on vacation we travel the world to get hotter and wilder. Islands are what Michel prefers: in Asia, Oceania, Africa, the Caribbean, it doesn't matter. Any place where the people are the color of different grades of coffee, and mangoes plop in mushy heaps on the ground, and the reef fish are brilliant as a box of new crayons. On vacation Michel sheds his manicured ad-man image and with innocent glee sets about turning himself into a Eurotrash version of Tarzan. Bronzed muscles well in evidence, shark's tooth on a leather thong, fishing knife stuck into the waist of a threadbare pareu, and a wispy sun-streaked ponytail that he tends painstakingly, along with a chin crop of Hollywood stubble.

He loves me for a number of wrong reasons connected with his dreams of hot islands. It makes no difference to him that I grew up in Massachusetts, wearing L.L. Bean boots more often than sandals; after eight years of marriage, he doesn't seem to see that what gives strength to the spine of an American black woman, however exotic she appears, is a steely Protestant core. A core that in its absolutism is curiously cold and Nordic. The fact is that I'm not crazy about the tropics, but Michel doesn't want to acknowledge that. Mysteriously, we continue to get along. In fact, our marriage is surprisingly robust, though at the time of our wedding, my mother, my sister, and my girlfriends all gave it a year. I sometimes think the secret is that we don't know each other and never will. Both of us are lazy by nature, and that makes it convenient to hang on to the fantasies we conjured up back when we met in Milan: mine of the French gentleman-adventurer, and his of a pliant black goddess whose feelings accord with his. It's no surprise to me when Michel tries to share the ribald thoughts that run through the labyrinth of his Roman Catholic mind. He doubtless thought that I would get a kick out of hearing about his boat ride with a pair of African sluts.

Those girls have been sitting around watching us from under the mango tree since the day we rolled up from the airport to spend August in the house we borrowed from our friend Jean-Claude. Michel was driving Jean-Claude's car, a Citroën so rump-sprung from the unpaved roads that it moves like a tractor. Our four-year-old son, Lele, can drag his sneakers in red dust through the holes in the floor. The car smells of failure, like the house, which is built on an island off the northern coast of Madagascar, on a beach where a wide scalloped bay spreads like two blue wings, melting into the sky and the wild archipelago of lemur islands beyond. Behind the garden stretch fields of sugar cane and groves of silvery, arthritic-looking ylang-ylang trees, whose flowers lend a tang of Africa to French perfume.

The house is low and long around a grandiose veranda, and was once whitewashed into an emblem of colonial vainglory; now the walls are the indeterminate color of damp, and the thinning palm thatch on the roof swarms with mice and geckos. It has a queenly housekeeper named Hadijah, whose perfect *pommes frites* and plates of crudités, like the dead bidet and dried-up tubes of Bain de Soleil in the bathroom, are monuments to Jean-Claude's ex-wife, who went back to Toulon after seeing a series of projects—a frozen-fish plant, a perfume company, a small luxury hotel—swallowed up in the calm fireworks of the sunsets. Madagascar is the perfect place for a white fool to lose his money, Michel says. He and I enjoy the scent of dissolution in our borrowed house, fuck inventively in the big mildewed ironwood bed, sit in happiness in the sad, bottomed-out canvas chairs on the veranda after a day of spear-fishing, watching our son race in and out of herds of humpbacked zebu cattle on the beach.

The only problem for me has been those girls. They're not really whores, just local girls who dance at Bar Kariboo on Thursday nights and hang around the few French and Italian tourists, hoping to trade sex for a T-shirt, a hair clip. They don't know to want Ray-Bans yet; this is not the Caribbean.

I'm used to the women from the Comoros Islands who crowd onto the beach near the house, dressed up in gold bangles and earrings and their best lace-trimmed blouses. They clap and sing in circles for hours, jumping up to dance in pairs, wagging their backsides in tiny precise jerks, laughing and flashing gold teeth. They wrap themselves up in their good time in a way that intimidates me. And I've come to an understanding with the older women of the village, who come by to bring us our morning ration of zebu milk (we drink it boiled in coffee) or to barter with *rideaux Richelieu,* the beautiful muslin cutwork curtains that they embroider. They are intensely curious about me, *l'américaine,* who looks not unlike one of them but who dresses and speaks and acts like a foreign madame and is clearly married to the white man, not just a casual concubine. They ask me for medicine, and if I weren't careful they would clean out my supply of Advil and Bimaxin. They go crazy over Lele, whom they call "*bebe metis*"—the mixed baby. I want to know all about them, their still eyes, their faces of varying colors that show both African and Indonesian blood, as I want to know everything about this primeval chunk of Africa floating in the Indian Ocean, with its bottle-shaped baobabs and strange tinkling music, the *sega,* which is said to carry traces of tunes from Irish sailors.

But the girls squatting under the mango tree stare hard at me whenever I sit out on the beach or walk down to the water to swim. Then they make loud comments in Malagasy and burst out laughing. It's juvenile behavior, and I can't help sinking right down to their level and getting provoked. They're probably about eighteen years old, both good-looking: one with a flat brown face and the long straight shining hair that makes some Madagascar women resemble Polynesians; the other darker, with the tiny features that belong to the coastal people called Merina and a pile of kinky hair tinted reddish. Both are big-titted, as Michel pointed out, the merchandise spilling out of a pair of Nouvelles Frontières T-shirts that they must have got from a tour-group leader. Some days they have designs painted on their faces in yellow sulfur clay. They stare at me, and guffaw and stretch and give their breasts a competitive shake. Sometimes they hoot softly or whistle when I appear.

My policy has been to ignore them, but today they've taken a step ahead, gotten a rise, however ironic, out of my man. It's a little triumph. I didn't see the Zodiac ride, but through the bathroom window I saw them come back. I was shaving my legs—waxing never lasts long enough in the tropics. Squealing and laughing, they floundered out of the rubber dinghy, patting their hair, settling their T-shirts, retying the cloth around their waists. One of them blew her nose through her fingers into the shallow water. The other said something to Michel, and he laughed and patted her on the backside. Then, arrogantly as two Cleopatras, they strode across the hot sand and took up their crouch under the mango tree. A pair of brown *netsuke*. Waiting for my move.

So, finally, I act. Michel comes sauntering inside to tell me, and after he tells me I make a scene. He's completely taken aback; he's gotten spoiled since we've been married, used to my American cool, which can seem even cooler than French nonchalance. He thought I was going to react the way I used to when I was still modeling and he used to flirt with some of the girls I was working with, some of the bimbos who weren't serious about their careers. That is, that I was going to chuckle, display complicity, even excitement. Instead I yell, say he's damaged my prestige among the locals, say that things are different here. The words seem to be flowing up into my mouth from the ground beneath my feet. He's so surprised that he just stands there with his blue eyes round and his mouth a small O in the midst of that Indiana Jones stubble.

Then I hitch up my Soleiado bikini and march outside to the mango tree. *"Va-t'en!"* I hiss to Red Hair, who seems to be top girl of the duo. "Go away! *N'e parle plus avec mon homme!"*

The two of them scramble to their feet, but they don't seem to be going anywhere, so I slap the one with the straight hair. Except for once, when I was about ten, in a fight with my cousin Brenda, I don't believe I've ever seriously slapped anyone. This, on the scale of slaps, is half-assed, not hard. In that second of contact I feel the strange smoothness of her cheek and an instantaneous awareness that my hand is just as smooth. An electric current seems to connect them. A red light flickers in the depths of the girl's dark eyes, like a computer blinking on, and then, without saying anything to me, both girls scuttle off down the beach, talking loudly to each other and occasionally looking back at me. I make motions as if I'm shooing chickens. *"Allez-vouz-en!"* I screech. Far off down the beach, they disappear into the palms.

Then I go and stretch out in the water, which is like stretching out in blue air. I take off my bikini top and let the equatorial sun print my shadow on the white sand below, where small white fish graze. I feel suddenly calm, but at the same time my mind is working very fast. "My dear, who invited you to come halfway

across the world and slap somebody?" I ask myself in the ultra-
reasonable tones of my mother, the school guidance counselor.
Suddenly I remember another summer on yet another island.
This was in Indonesia, a few years ago, when we were exploring the
back roads of one of the Moluccas. The driver was a local kid who
didn't speak any of the languages we spoke and was clearly gay. A
great-looking kid with light-brown skin pitted with a few acne
scars, and neat dreadlocks that would have looked stylish in Manhattan. A Princess Di T-shirt and peeling red nail polish. When
we stopped at a waterfall and Michel the Adventurer went off to
climb the lava cliffs, I sat down on a flat rock with the driver,
whipped out my beauty case, and painted his nails shocking pink.
He jumped when I first grabbed his hand, but when he saw what I
was up to he gave me a huge ecstatic grin and then closed his eyes.
And there it was: paradise. The waterfall, the jungle, and that
beautiful kid with his long fingers lying in my hand. It was Michel
who made a fuss that time, jealous of something he couldn't even
define. But I had the same feeling I do now, of acting on instinct
and on target. The right act. At the right moment.

"Mama, what did you do?" Lele comes running up to me from
where he has been squatting naked on the beach, playing with two
small boys from the village. His legs and backside and little penis
are covered with sand. I see the boys staring after him, one holding
a toy they've been squabbling over: a rough wooden model of a
truck, without wheels, tied with a piece of string to a stick. "Ismail
says you hit a lady."

Word has already spread along the beach, which is like a stage
where a different variety show goes on every hour of the day. The
set acts are the tides, which determine the movements of fishing
boats, pirogues, Zodiacs, and sailboats. There is always action on
the sand: women walk up and down with bundles on their heads;
bands of ragged children dig clams at low tide or launch themselves into the waves at high tide to surf with a piece of old timber;
yellow dogs chase chickens and fight over shrimp shells; palm
branches crash down on corrugated iron roofs; girls with lacy
dresses and bare sandy shanks parade to mass; the little mosque

opens and shuts its creaky doors; boys play soccer, kicking a plastic water bottle; babies howl; sunburned tourist couples argue and reconcile. Gossip flashes up and down with electronic swiftness.

I sit up in the water and grab Lele and kiss him all over while he splashes and struggles to get away. "Yes, that's right," I tell him. It's the firm, didactic voice I use when we've turned off the Teletubbies and I am playing the ideal parent. "I did hit a lady," I say. "She needed hitting." I, the mother who instructs her cross-cultural child in tolerance and nonviolence. Lele has a picture book called *Brothers and Sisters Around the World*, full of cookie-cutter figures of various colors holding hands across continents. All people belong to one family, it teaches. All oceans are the same ocean.

Michel, who has watched the whole scene, comes and tells me that in all his past visits to the island he's never seen anything like it. He's worried. The women fight among themselves, or they fight with their men for sleeping with the tourists, he says. But no foreign woman has ever got mixed up with them. He talks like an anthropologist about loss of face and vendetta. "We might get run out of here," he says nervously.

I tell him to relax, that absolutely nothing will happen. Where do I get this knowledge? It has sifted into me from the water, the air. So, as we planned, we go spearfishing over by Nosy Komba, where the coral grows in big pastel poufs like furniture in a Hollywood bedroom of the fifties. We find a den of rock lobster and shoot two, and take them back to Jean-Claude's house for Hadijah to cook. Waiting for the lobster, we eat about fifty small oysters the size of mussels and shine flashlights over the beach in front of the veranda, which is crawling with crabs. Inside, Lele is snoring adenoidally under a mosquito net. The black sky above is alive with falling stars. Michel keeps looking at me and shaking his head.

Hadijah comes out bearing the lobster magnificently broiled with vanilla sauce. To say she has presence is an understatement. She got married when she was thirteen and is now, after eight children, an important personage, the matriarch of a vast and prosperous island clan. She and I have gotten along fine ever since she realized that I wasn't going to horn in on her despotic rule over

Jean-Claude's house or say anything about the percentage she skims off the marketing money. She has a closely braided head and is as short and solid as a boulder—on the spectrum of Madagascar skin colors, well toward the darkest. This evening she is showing off her wealth by wearing over her pareu a venerable Guns n' Roses T shirt. She puts down the lobster, sets her hands on her hips, and looks at me, and my heart suddenly skips a beat. Hers, I realize, is the only opinion I care about. "Oh, madame," she says, flashing me a wide smile and shaking her finger indulgently, as if I'm a child who has been up to mischief. I begin breathing again. "Oh, madame!"

"Madame has a quick temper," Michel says in a placating voice, and Hadijah throws her head back and laughs till the Guns n' Roses logo shimmies.

"She is right!" she exclaims. "*Madame a raison!* She's a good wife!"

Next morning our neighbor PierLuigi pulls up to the house in his dust-covered Renault pickup. PierLuigi is Italian, and back in Italy has a title and a castle. Here he lives in a bamboo hut when he is not away leading a shark-hunting safari to one of the wild islands a day's sail to the north. He is the real version of what Michel pretends to be: a walking, talking character from a boys' adventure tale, with a corrugated scar low down on one side where a hammerhead once snatched a mouthful. The islanders respect him and bring their children to him for a worm cure he's devised from crushed papaya seeds. He can bargain down the tough Indian merchants in the market, and he sleeps with pretty tourists and island girls impartially. Nobody knows how many kids he has fathered on the island.

"I hear your wife is mixing in local politics," he calls from the truck to Michel, while looking me over with those shameless eyes that have gotten so many women in trouble. PierLuigi is sixty years old and has streaks of white in his hair, but he is still six feet four and the best-looking man I have ever seen in my life. "Brava," he says to me. "Good for you, my dear. The local young ladies very often need things put in perspective, but very few of our lovely visitors know how to do it on their own terms."

After he drives off, Michel looks at me with new respect. "I can't say you don't have guts," he says later. Then, "You really must be in love with me."

In the afternoon after our siesta, when I emerge onto the veranda from Jean-Claude's shuttered bedroom, massaging Phyto Plage into my hair, smelling on my skin the pleasant odor of sex, I see—as I somehow expected—that the two girls are back under the mango tree. I walk out onto the burning sand, squinting against the glare that makes every distant object a flat black silhouette, and approach them for the second time. I don't think that we're in for another round, yet I feel my knees take on a wary pugilistic springiness. But as I get close, the straight-haired girl says, "Bonjour, madame."

The formal greeting conveys an odd intimacy. It is clear that we are breathing the same air now, that we have taken each other's measure. Both girls look straight at me, no longer bridling. All three of us know perfectly well that the man—my European husband—was just an excuse, a playing field for our curiosity. The curiosity of sisters separated before birth and flung by the caprice of history half a world away from each other. Now in this troublesome way our connection has been established, and between my guilt and my dawning affection I suspect that I'll never get rid of these two. Already in my mind is forming an exasperating vision of the gifts I know I'll have to give them: lace underpants, Tampax, music cassettes, body lotion—all of them extracted from me with the tender ruthlessness of family members anywhere. And then what? What, after all these years, will there be to say? Well, the first thing to do is answer. "Bonjour, mesdemoiselles," I reply, in my politest voice.

And because I can't think of anything else, I smile and nod at them and walk into the water, which as always in the tropics is as warm as blood. The whole time I swim, the girls are silent, and they don't take their eyes off me.

China

By Charles Johnson

Charles Johnson (1948–) is the Pollock Professor of English at the University of Washington. Born in Evanston, Illinois, he won the National Book Award in 1990 for his novel, *Middle Passage*, and was awarded a MacArthur Foundation "genius grant" in 1998. His most recent book, *Dreamer,* is a fictional account of the last years of Martin Luther King, Jr. In "China," Johnson observes a married couple at midlife.

If one man conquers in battle a thousand men, and if another conquers himself, he is the greatest of conquerors. —The Dhammapada

Evelyn's problems with her husband, Rudolph, began one evening in early March—a dreary winter evening in Seattle—when he complained after a heavy meal of pig's feet and mashed potatoes of shortness of breath, an allergy to something she put in his food perhaps, or brought on by the first signs of wild flowers around them. She suggested they get out of the house for the evening, go to a movie. He was fifty-four, a postman for thirty-three years now, with high blood pressure, emphysema, flat feet, and, as Evelyn told her friend Shelberdine Lewis, the lingering fear that he had cancer. Getting old, he was also getting hard to live with. He told her never to salt his dinners, to keep their Lincoln Continental at a crawl, and never run her fingers along his inner thigh when they sat in Reverend William Merrill's church, because anything, even sex, or laughing too loud—Rudolph was serious—might bring on heart failure.

So she chose for their Saturday night outing a peaceful movie, a mildly funny comedy a *Seattle Times* reviewer said was fit only for titters and nasal snorts, a low-key satire that made Rudolph's eyelids droop as he shoveled down unbuttered popcorn in the darkened, half-empty theater. Sticky fluids cemented Evelyn's feet to the floor. A man in the last row laughed at all the wrong places. She kept the popcorn on her lap, though she hated the unsalted stuff and wouldn't touch it, sighing as Rudolph pawed across her to shove his fingers inside the cup.

She followed the film as best she could, but occasionally her eyes frosted over, flashed white. She went blind like this now and then. The fibers of her eyes were failing; her retinas were tearing like soft tissue. At these times the world was a canvas with whiteout spilling from the far left corner toward the center; it was the sudden shock of an empty frame in a series of slides. Someday, she knew, the snow on her eyes would stay. Winter eternally: her eyes split like her walking stick. She groped along the fractured surface, waiting for her sight to thaw, listening to the film she couldn't see. Her only comfort was knowing that, despite her infirmity, her Rudolph was in even worse health.

He slid back and forth from sleep during the film (she elbowed him occasionally, or pinched his leg), then came full awake, sitting up suddenly when the movie ended and a "Coming Attractions" trailer began. It was some sort of gladiator movie, Evelyn thought, blinking, and it was pretty trashy stuff at that. The plot's revenge theme was a poor excuse for Chinese actors or Japanese (she couldn't tell those people apart) to flail the air with their hands and feet, take on fifty costumed extras at once, and leap twenty feet through the air in perfect defiance of gravity. Rudolph's mouth hung open.

"Can people really do that?" He did not take his eyes off the screen, but talked at her from the right side of his mouth. "Leap that high?"

"It's a *movie*," sighed Evelyn. "A *bad* movie."

He nodded, then asked again, "But can they?"

"Oh, Rudolph, for God's sake!" She stood up to leave, her seat slapping back loudly. "They're on *trampolines!* You can see them in the corner—there!—if you open your eyes!"

He did see them, once Evelyn twisted his head to the lower left corner of the screen, and it seemed to her that her husband looked disappointed—looked, in fact, the way he did the afternoon Dr. Guylee told Rudolph he'd developed an extrasystolic reaction, a faint, moaning sound from his heart whenever it relaxed. He said no more and, after the trailer finished, stood—there was chewing gum stuck to his trouser seat—dragged on his heavy coat with her help and followed Evelyn up the long, carpeted aisle, through the exit of the Coronet Theater, and to their car. He said nothing as she chattered on the way home, reminding him that he could not stay up all night puttering in his basement shop because the next evening they were to attend the church's revival meeting.

Rudolph, however, did not attend the revival. He complained after lunch of a light, dancing pain in his chest, which he had conveniently whenever Mount Zion Baptist Church held revivals, and she went alone, sitting with her friend Shelberdine, a beautician. She was forty-one; Evelyn, fifty-two. That evening Evelyn wore spotless white gloves, tan therapeutic stockings for the swelling in her ankles, and a white dress that brought out nicely the brown color of her skin, the most beautiful cedar brown, Rudolph said when they were courting thirty-five years ago in South Carolina. But then Evelyn had worn a matching checkered skirt and coat to meeting. With her jet black hair pinned behind her neck by a simple wooden comb, she looked as if she might have been Andrew Wyeth's starkly beautiful model for *Day of the Fair*. Rudolph, she remembered, wore black business suits, black ties, black wing tips, but he also wore white gloves because he was a senior usher—this was how she first noticed him. He was one of four young men dressed like deacons (or blackbirds), their left hands tucked into the hollow of their backs, their right carrying silver plates for the offering as they marched in almost military fashion down each aisle: Christian soldiers, she'd thought, the cream of black manhood, and to get his attention she placed not her white envelope or coins in Rudolph's plate but instead a note that said: "You have a beautiful smile." It was, for all her innocence, a daring thing to do, according to Evelyn's mother—flirting with a randy young man like Rudolph Lee Jackson, but he did have nice, tigerish teeth. A killer smile, people called it, like all the boys in the Jackson family: a killer smile and good hair that needed no more than one stroke of his palm to bring out Quo Vadis rows pomaded sweetly with the scent of Murray's.

And, of course, Rudolph was no dummy. Not a total dummy, at least. He pretended nothing extraordinary had happened as the congregation left the little whitewashed church. He stood, the youngest son, between his father and mother, and let old Deacon Adcock remark, "Oh, how strong he's looking now," which was a lie. Rudolph was the weakest of the Jackson boys, the pale, bookish, spiritual child born when his parents were well past forty. His brothers played football, they went into the navy; Rudolph lived in Scripture, was labeled 4-F, and hoped to attend Moody Bible Institute in Chicago, if he could ever find the money. Evelyn could tell Rudolph knew exactly where she was in the crowd, that he could feel her as she and her sister, Debbie, waited for their father to bring his DeSoto—the family prize—closer to the front steps. When the crowd thinned, he shambled over in his slow, ministerial walk, introduced himself, and unfolded her note.

"You write this?" he asked. "It's not right to play with the Lord's money, you know."

"I like to play," she said.

"You do, huh?" He never looked directly at people. Women, she guessed, terrified him. Or, to be exact, the powerful emotions they caused in him terrified Rudolph. He was a pud puller, if she ever saw one. He kept his eyes on a spot left of her face. "You're Joe Montgomery's daughter, aren't you?"

"Maybe," teased Evelyn.

He trousered the note and stood marking the ground with his toe. "And just what you expect to get, Miss Playful, by fooling with people during collection time?"

She waited, let him look away, and, when the back-and-forth

swing of his gaze crossed her again, said in her most melic soft-breathing voice: *"You."*

Up front, portly Reverend Merrill concluded his sermon. Evelyn tipped her head slightly, smiling into memory; her hand reached left to pat Rudolph's leg gently; then she remembered it was Shelberdine beside her, and lifted her hand to the seat in front of her. She said a prayer for Rudolph's health, but mainly it was for herself, a hedge against her fear that their childless years had slipped by like wind, that she might return home one day and find him—as she had found her father—on the floor, bellied up, one arm twisted behind him where he fell, alone, his fingers locked against his chest. Rudolph had begun to run down, Evelyn decided, the minute he was turned down by Moody Bible Institute. They moved to Seattle in 1956—his brother Eli was stationed nearby and said Boeing was hiring black men. But they didn't hire Rudolph. He had kidney trouble on and off before he landed the job at the Post Office. Whenever he bent forward, he felt dizzy. Liver, heart, and lungs—they'd worn down gradually as his belly grew, but none of this was as bad as what he called "the Problem." His pecker shrank to no bigger than a pencil eraser each time he saw her undress. Or when Evelyn, as was her habit when talking, touched his arm. Was she the cause of this? Well, she knew she wasn't much to look at anymore. She'd seen the bottom of a few too many candy wrappers. Evelyn was nothing to make a man pant and jump her bones, pulling her fully clothed onto the daven-port, as Rudolph had done years before, but wasn't sex something else you surrendered with age? It never seemed all that good to her anyway. And besides, he'd wanted oral sex, which Evelyn—if she knew nothing else—thought was a nasty, unsanitary thing to do with your mouth. She glanced up from under her spring hat past the pulpit, past the choir of black and brown faces to the agonized beauty of a bearded white carpenter impaled on a rood, and in this timeless image she felt comforted that suffering was inescapable, the loss of vitality inevitable, even a good thing maybe, and that she had to steel herself—yes—for someday opening her bedroom door and finding her Rudolph face down in his breakfast oatmeal. He would die before her, she knew that in her bones.

And so, after service, Sanka, and a slice of meat pie with Shelberdine downstairs in the brightly lit church basement, Evelyn returned home to tell her husband how lovely the Griffin girls had sung that day, that their neighbor Rod Kenner had been saved, and to listen, if necessary, to Rudolph's fear that the lump on his shoulder was an early-warning sign of something evil. As it turned out, Evelyn found that except for their cat, Mr. Miller, the little A-frame house was empty. She looked in his bedroom. No Rudolph. The unnaturally still house made Evelyn uneasy, and she took the excruciatingly painful twenty stairs into the basement to peer into a workroom littered with power tools, planks of wood, and the blueprints her husband used to make bookshelves and cabinets. No Rudolph. Frightened, Evelyn called the eight hospitals in Seattle, but no one had a Rudolph Lee Jackson on his books. After her last call the starburst clock in the living room read twelve-thirty. Putting down the wall phone, she felt a familiar pain in her abdomen. Another attack of Hershey squirts, probably from the meat pie. She hurried into the bathroom, lifted her skirt, and lowered her underwear around her ankles, but kept the door wide open, something impossible to do if Rudolph was home. Actually, it felt good not to have him underfoot, a little like he was dead already. But the last thing Evelyn wanted was that or, as she lay down against her lumpy backrest, to fall asleep, though she did, nodding off and dreaming until something shifted down her weight on the side of her bed away from the wall.

"Evelyn," said Rudolph, "look at this." She blinked back sleep and squinted at the cover of a magazine called *Inside Kung-Fu,* which Rudolph waved under her nose. On the cover a man stood bow-legged, one hand cocked under his armpit, the other corkscrewing straight at Evelyn's nose.

"Rudolph!" She batted the magazine aside, then swung her eyes toward the cluttered nightstand, focusing on the electric clock beside her water glass from McDonald's, Preparation H suppositories, and Harlequin romances. "It's morning!" Now she was mad. At least, working at it. "Where have you been?"

Her husband inhaled, a wheezing, whistlelike breath. He rolled the magazine into a cylinder and, as he spoke, struck his left palm with it. "That movie we saw advertised? You remember—it was called *The Five Fingers of Death.* I just saw that and one called *Deep Thrust.*"

"Wonderful." Evelyn screwed up her lips. "I'm calling hospitals and you're at a Hong Kong double feature."

"Listen," said Rudolph. "You don't understand." He seemed at that moment as if he did not understand either. "It was a Seattle movie premiere. The Northwest is crawling with fighters. It has something to do with all the Asians out here. Before they showed the movie, four students from a kwoon in Chinatown went onstage—"

"A what?" asked Evelyn.

"A kwoon—it's a place to study fighting, a meditation hall." He looked at her but was really watching, Evelyn realized, something exciting she had missed. "They did a demonstration to drum up their membership. They broke boards and bricks, Evelyn. They went through what's called kata and kumite and . . ." He stopped again to breathe. "I've never seen anything so beautiful. The reason I'm late is because I wanted to talk with them after the movie."

Evelyn, suspicious, took a Valium and waited.

"I signed up for lessons," he said.

She gave a glacial look at Rudolph, then at his magazine, and said in the voice she used five years ago when he wanted to take a vacation to Upper Volta or, before that, invest in a British car she knew they couldn't afford:

"You're fifty-*four* years old, Rudolph."

"I know that."

"You're no Muhammad Ali."

"I know that," he said.

"You're no Bruce Lee. Do you want to be Bruce Lee? Do you know where he is now, Rudolph? He's dead—dead here in a Seattle cemetery and buried up on Capital Hill."

His shoulders slumped a little. Silently, Rudolph began undressing, his beefy backside turned toward her, slipping his pajama bottoms on before taking off his shirt so his scrawny lower body would not be fully exposed. He picked up his magazine, said, "I'm sorry if I worried you," and huffed upstairs to his bedroom. Evelyn clicked off the mushroom-shaped lamp on her nightstand. She lay on her side, listening to his slow footsteps strike the stairs, then heard his mattress creak above her—his bedroom was directly above hers—but she did not hear him click off his own light. From time to time she heard his shifting weight squeak the mattress springs. He was reading that foolish magazine, she guessed; then she grew tired and gave this impossible man up to God. With a copy of *The Thorn Birds* open on her lap, Evelyn fell heavily to sleep again.

At breakfast the next morning any mention of the lessons gave Rudolph lockjaw. He kissed her forehead, as always, before going to work, and simply said he might be home late. Climbing the stairs to his bedroom was painful for Evelyn, but she hauled herself up, pausing at each step to huff, then sat on his bed and looked over his copy of *Inside Kung-Fu*. There were articles on empty-hand combat, soft-focus photos of ferocious-looking men in funny suits, parables about legendary Zen masters, an interview with someone named Bernie Bernheim, who began to study karate at age fifty-seven and became a black belt at age sixty-one, and page after page of advertisements for exotic Asian weapons: nunchaku, shuriken, sai swords, tonfa, bo staffs, training bags of all sorts, a wooden dummy shaped like a man and called a Mook Jong, and weights. Rudolph had circled them all. He had torn the order form from the last page of the magazine. The total cost of the things he'd circled—Evelyn added them furiously, rounding of the figures—was $800.

Two minutes later she was on the telephone to Shelberdine.

"Let him tire of it," said her friend. "Didn't you tell me Rudolph had Lower Lombard Strain?"

Evelyn's nose clogged with tears.

"Why is he doing this? Is it me, do you think?"

"It's the Problem," said Shelberdine. "He wants his manhood back. Before he died, Arthur did the same. Someone at the plant told him he could get it back if he did twenty-yard sprints. He went into convulsions while running around the lake."

Evelyn felt something turn in her chest. "You don't think he'll hurt himself, do you?"

"Of course not."

"Do you think he'll hurt *me*?"

Her friend reassured Evelyn that Mid-Life Crisis brought out these shenanigans in men. Evelyn replied that she thought Mid-Life Crisis started around age forty, to which Shelberdine said, "Honey, I don't mean no harm, but Rudolph always was a little on the slow side," and Evelyn agreed. She would wait until he worked this thing out of his system, until Nature defeated him and he surrendered, as any right-thinking person would, to the breakdown of the body, the brutal fact of decay, which could only be blunted, it seemed to her, by decaying *with* someone, the comfort every Negro couple felt when, aging, they knew enough to let things wind down.

Her patience was rewarded in the beginning. Rudolph crawled home from his first lesson, hunched over, hardly able to stand, afraid he had permanently ruptured something. He collapsed face down on the living room sofa, his feet on the floor. She helped him change into his pajamas and fingered Ben-Gay into his back muscles. Evelyn had never seen her husband so close to tears.

"I can't *do* push-ups," he moaned. "Or sit-ups. I'm so stiff—I don't know my body." He lifted his head, looking up pitifully, his eyes pleading. "Call Dr. Guylee. Make an appointment for Thursday, okay?"

"Yes, dear." Evelyn hid her smile with one hand. "You shouldn't push yourself so hard."

At that, he sat up, bare-chested, his stomach bubbling over his pajama bottoms. "That's what it means. *Gung fu* means 'hard work' in Chinese. Evelyn"—he lowered his voice—"I don't think I've ever really done hard work in my life. Not like this, something that asks me to give *every*thing, body and soul, spirit and flesh. I've always felt . . ." He looked down, his dark hands dangling between his thighs. "I've never been able to give *everything* to *anything*. The world never let me. It won't let me put all of myself into play. Do you know what I'm saying? Every job I've ever had, everything I've ever done, it only demanded part of me. It was like there was so much *more* of me that went unused after the job was over. I get that feeling in church sometimes." He lay back down, talking now into the sofa cushion. "Sometimes I get that feeling with you."

Her hand stopped on his shoulder. She wasn't sure she'd heard him right, his voice was so muffled. "That I've never used all of you?"

Rudolph nodded, rubbing his right knuckle where, at the kwoon, he'd lost a stretch of skin on a speedbag. "There's still part of me left over. You never tried to touch all of me, to take everything. Maybe you can't. Maybe no one can. But sometimes I get the feeling that the unused part—the unlived life—*spoils*, that you get cancer because it sits like fruit on the ground and rots." Rudolph shook his head; he'd said too much and knew it, perhaps had not even put it the way he felt inside. Stiffly, he got to his feet. "Don't ask me to stop training." His eyebrows spread inward. "If I stop, I'll die."

Evelyn twisted the cap back onto the Ben-Gay. She held out her hand, which Rudolph took. Veins on the back of his hand burgeoned abnormally like dough. Once when she was shopping at the Public Market she'd seen monstrous plastic gloves shaped like hands in a magic store window. His hand looked like that. It belonged on Lon Chaney. Her voice shook a little, panicky, "I'll call Dr. Guylee in the morning."

Evelyn knew—or thought she knew—his trouble. He'd never come to terms with the disagreeableness of things. Rudolph had always been too serious for some people, even in South Carolina. It was the thing, strange to say, that drew her to him, this crimped-browed tendency in Rudolph to listen with every atom of his life when their minister in Hodges, quoting Marcus Aurelius to give his sermon flash, said, "Live with the gods," or later in Seattle, the habit of working himself up over Reverend Merrill's reading from

Ecclesiastes 9:10: "Whatsoever thy hand findeth to do, do it with all thy might." Now, he didn't *really* mean that, Evelyn knew. Nothing in the world could be taken that seriously; that's *why* this was the world. And, as all Mount Zion knew, Reverend Merrill had a weakness for high-yellow choirgirls and gin, and was forever complaining that his salary was too small for his family. People made compromises, nodded at spiritual common-places—the high seriousness of biblical verses that demanded nearly super-human duty and self-denial—and laughed off their lapses into sloth, envy, and the other deadly sins. It was what made living so enjoyably *human*: this built-in inability of man to square his per-formance with perfection. People were naturally soft on them-selves. But not her Rudolph.

Of course, he seldom complained. It was not in his nature to complain when, looking for "gods," he found only ruin and wreckage. What did he expect? Evelyn wondered. Man was evil—she'd told him that a thousand times—or, if not evil, hopelessly flawed. Everything failed; it was some sort of law. But at least there was laughter, and lovers clinging to one another against the cliff; there were novels—wonderful tales of how things should be—and perfection promised in the afterworld. He'd sit and listen, her Rudolph, when she put things this way, nodding because he knew that in his persistent hunger for perfection in the here and now he was, at best, in the minority. He kept his dissatisfaction to him-self, but occasionally Evelyn would glimpse in his eyes that look, that distant, pained expression that asked: *Is this all?* She saw it after her first miscarriage, then her second; saw it when he stopped searching the want ads and settled on the Post Office as the fulfill-ment of his potential in the marketplace. It was always there, that look, after he turned forty, and no new, lavishly praised novel from the Book-of-the-Month Club, no feature-length movie, prayer meeting, or meal she fixed for him wiped it from Rudolph's eyes. He was, at least, this sort of man before he saw that martial-arts B movie. It was a dark vision, Evelyn decided, a dan-gerous vision, and in it she whiffed something that might destroy her. What that was, she couldn't say, but she knew her Rudolph better than he knew himself. He would see the error—the waste of time—in his new hobby, and she was sure he would mend his ways.

In the weeks, then months that followed Evelyn waited, watching her husband for a flag of surrender. There was no such sign. He became worse than before. He cooked his own meals, called her heavy soul food dishes "too acidic," lived on raw vegetables, seaweed, nuts, and fruit to make his body "more alkaline," and fasted on Sundays. He ordered books on something called Shaolin fighting and meditation from a store in California, and when his equipment arrived UPS from Dolan's Sports in New Jersey, he ordered more—in consternation, Evelyn read the list—leg stretchers, makiwara boards, air shields, hand grips, bokken, focus mitts, a full-length mirror (for heaven's sake) so he could correct his form, and protective equipment. For proper use of his headgear and gloves, however, he said he needed a sparring partner—an opponent—he said, to help him instinctively understand "combat strategy," how to "flow" and "close the gap" between himself and an adversary, how to create by his movements a negative space in which the other would be neutralized.

"Well," crabbed Evelyn, "if you need a punching bag, don't look at *me*."

He sat across the kitchen table from her, doing dynamic-tension exercises as she read a new magazine called *Self*. "Did I ever tell you what a black belt means?" he asked.

"You told me."

"Sifu Chan doesn't use belts for ranking. They were introduced seventy years ago because Westerners were impatient, you know, needed signposts and all that."

"You told me," said Evelyn.

"Originally, all you got was a white belt. It symbolized innocence. Virginity." His face was immensely serious, like a preacher's. "As you worked, it got darker, dirtier, and turned brown. Then black. You were a master then. With even more work, the belt became frayed, the threads came loose, you see, and the belt showed white again."

"Rudolph, I've heard this before!" Evelyn picked up her

magazine and took it into her bedroom. From there, with her legs drawn up under the blankets, she shouted: "I *won't* be your punching bag!"

So he brought friends from his kwoon, friends she wanted nothing to do with. There was something unsettling about them. Some were street fighters. Young. They wore tank-top shirts and motorcycle jackets. After drinking racks of Rainier beer on the front porch, they tossed their crumpled empties next door into Rod Kenner's yard. Together, two of Rudolph's new friends— Truck and Tuco—weighed a quarter of a ton. Evelyn kept a rolling pin under her pillow when they came, but she knew they could eat that along with her. But some of his new friends were students at the University of Washington. Truck, a Vietnamese only two years in America, planned to apply to the Police Academy once his training ended; and Tuco, who was Puerto Rican, had been fighting since he could make a fist; but a delicate young man named Andrea, a blue sash, was an actor in the drama department at the university. His kwoon training, he said, was less for self-defense than helping him understand his movements onstage— how, for example, to convincingly explode across a room in anger. Her husband liked them, Evelyn realized in horror. And they liked him. They were separated by money, background, and religion, but something she could not identify made them seem, those nights on the porch after his class, like a single body. They called Rudolph "Older Brother" or, less politely, "Pop."

His sifu, a short, smooth-figured boy named Douglas Chan, who Evelyn figured couldn't be over eighteen, sat like the Dalai Lama in their tiny kitchen as if he owned it, sipping her tea, which Rudolph laced with Korean ginseng. Her husband lit Chan's cigarettes as if he were President Carter come to visit the common man. He recommended that Rudolph study T'ai Chi, "soft" fighting systems, ki, and something called Tao. He told him to study, as well, Newton's three laws of physics and apply them to his own body during kumite. What she remembered most about Chan were his wrist braces, ornamental weapons that had three straps and, along the black leather, highly polished studs like those worn by Steve Reeves in a movie she'd seen about Hercules. In a voice she thought girlish, he spoke of eye gouges and groin-tearing techniques, exercises called the Delayed Touch of Death and Dim Mak, with the casualness she and Shelberdine talked about bargains at Thriftway. And then they suited up, the boyish Sifu, who looked like Maharaj-ji's rougher brother, and her clumsy husband; they went out back, pushed aside the aluminum lawn furniture, and pommeled each other for half an hour. More precisely, her Rudolph was on the receiving end of hook kicks, spinning back fists faster than thought, and foot sweeps that left his body purpled for weeks. A sensible man would have known enough to drive to Swedish Hospital pronto. Rudolph, never known as a profound thinker, pushed on after Sifu Chan left, practicing his flying kicks by leaping to ground level from a four-foot hole he'd dug by their cyclone fence.

Evelyn, nibbling a Van de Kamp's pastry from Safeway—she was always nibbling, these days—watched from the kitchen window until twilight, then brought out the Ben-Gay, a cold beer, and rubbing alcohol on a tray. She figured he needed it. Instead, Rudolph, stretching under the far-reaching cedar in the backyard, politely refused, pushed the tray aside, and rubbed himself with Dit-Da-Jow, "iron-hitting wine," which smelled like the open door of an opium factory on a hot summer day. Yet this ancient potion not only instantly healed his wounds (said Rudolph) but prevented arthritis as well. She was tempted to see if it healed brain damage by pouring it into Rudolph's ears, but apparently he was doing something right. Dr. Guylee's examination had been glowing; he said Rudolph's muscle tone, whatever that was, was better. His cardiovascular system was healthier. His erections were outstanding—or upstanding—though lately he seemed to have no interest in sex. Evelyn, even she, saw in the crepuscular light changes in Rudolph's upper body as he stretched: Muscles like globes of light rippled along his shoulders; larval currents moved on his belly. The language of his new, developing body eluded her. He was not always like this. After a cold shower and sleep his muscles shrank back a little. It was only after his workouts, his weight lifting, that his body expanded like baking bread, filling out in a way that obliterated the soft Rudolph-body she knew. This new flesh had the contours of the silhouetted figures on medical charts: the body as it must be in the mind of God. Glistening with perspiration, his muscles took on the properties of the free weights he pumped relentlessly. They were profoundly tragic, too, because their beauty was earthbound. It would vanish with the world. You are ugly, his new muscles said to Evelyn; old and ugly. His self-punishment made her feel sick. She was afraid of his hard, cold weights. She hated them. Yet she wanted them, too. They had a certain monastic beauty. She thought: *He's doing this to hurt me.* She wondered: What was it like to be powerful? Was clever cynicism—even comedy—the by-product of bulging bellies, weak nerves, bad posture? Her only defense against the dumbbells that stood between them—she meant both his weights and his friends—was, as always, her acid southern tongue:

"They're all fairies, right?"

Rudolph looked dreamily her way. These post-workout periods made him feel, he said, as if there were no interval between himself and what he saw. His face was vacant, his eyes—like smoke. In this afterglow (he said) he saw without judging. Without judgment, there were no distinctions. Without distinctions, there was no desire. Without desire . . .

He smiled sideways at her. "Who?"

"The people in your kwoon." Evelyn crossed her arms. "I read somewhere that most body builders are homosexual."

He refused to answer her.

"If they're not gay, then maybe I should take lessons. It's been good for you, right?" Her voice grew sharp. "I mean, isn't that what you're saying? That you and your friends are better'n everybody else?"

Rudolph's head dropped; he drew a long breath. Lately, his responses to her took the form of quietly clearing his lungs.

"You should do what you *have* to, Evelyn. You don't have to do what anybody else does." He stood up, touched his toes, then brought his forehead straight down against his unbent knees, which was physically impossible, Evelyn would have said—and faintly obscene.

It was a nightmare to watch him each evening after dinner. He walked around the house in his Everlast leg weights, tried push-ups on his finger-tips and wrists, and, as she sat trying to watch "The Jeffersons," stood in a ready stance before the flickering screen, throwing punches each time the scene, or shot, changed to improve his timing. It took the fun out of watching TV, him doing that—she preferred him falling asleep in his chair beside her, as he used to. But what truly frightened Evelyn was his "doing nothing." Sitting in meditation, planted cross-legged in a full lotus on their front porch, with Mr. Miller blissfully curled on his lap, a Bod-hisattva in the middle of houseplants she set out for the sun. Looking at him, you'd have thought he was dead. The whole thing smelled like self-hypnosis. He breathed too slowly, in Evelyn's view—only three breaths per minute, he claimed. He wore his gi, splotchy with dried blood and sweat, his calloused hands on his knees, the forefingers on each tipped against his thumbs, his eyes screwed shut.

During his eighth month at the kwoon, she stood watching him as he sat, wondering over the vivid changes in his body, the grim firmness where before there was jolly fat, the disquieting steadi-ness of his posture, where before Rudolph could not sit still in church for five minutes without fidgeting. Now he sat in zazen for forty-five minutes a day, fifteen when he awoke, fifteen (he said) at work in the mailroom during his lunch break, fifteen before going to bed. He called this withdrawal (how she hated his fancy language) similar to the necessary silences in music, "a stillness that prepared him for busyness and sound." He'd never breathed before, he told her. Not once. Not clear to the floor of himself. Never breathed and emptied himself as he did now, picturing himself sitting on the bottom of Lake Washington: himself, Rudolph Lee Jackson, at the center of the universe; for if the uni-verse was infinite, any point where he stood would be at its center—it would shift and move with him. (That saying, Evelyn knew, was minted in Douglas Chan's mind. No Negro preacher worth the name would speak that way.) He told her that in zazen, at the bottom of the lake, he worked to discipline his mind and maintain one point of concentration; each thought, each feeling that overcame him he saw as a fragile bubble, which he could inspect passionlessly from all sides; then he let it float gently to the surface, and soon—as he slipped deeper into the vortices of himself, into the Void—even the image of himself on the lake floor vanished.

Evelyn stifled a scream.

Was she one of Rudolph's bubbles, something to detach himself from? On the porch, Evelyn watched him narrowly, sitting in a rain-whitened chair, her chin on her left fist. She snapped the fingers on her right hand under his nose. Nothing. She knocked her knuckles lightly on his forehead. Nothing. (Faker, she thought.) For another five minutes he sat and breathed, sat and breathed, then opened his eyes slowly as if he'd slept as long as Rip Van Winkle. "It's dark," he said, stunned. When he began, it was twilight. Evelyn realized something new: He was not living time as she was, not even that anymore. Things, she saw, were slower for him; to him she must seem like a woman stuck in fast-forward. She asked:

"What do you see when you go in there?"

Rudolph rubbed his eyes. "Nothing."

"Then *why* do you do it? The world's out here!"

He seemed unable to say, as if the question were senseless. His eyes angled up, like a child's, toward her face. "Nothing is peaceful sometimes. The emptiness is full. I'm not afraid of it now."

"You empty yourself?" she asked. "Of me, too?"

"Yes."

Evelyn's hand shot up to cover her face. She let fly with a whimper. Rudolph rose instantly—he sent Mr. Miller flying—then fell back hard on his buttocks; the lotus cut off blood to his lower body—which provided more to his brain, he claimed—and it always took him a few seconds before he could stand again. He reached up, pulled her hand down, and stroked it.

"What've I done?"

"That's it," sobbed Evelyn. "I don't know what you're doing." She lifted the end of her bathrobe, blew her nose, then looked at him through streaming, unseeing eyes. "And you don't either. I wish you'd never seen that movie. I'm sick of all your weights and workouts—sick of them, do you hear? Rudolph, I want you back the way you were: *sick*." No sooner than she said this Evelyn was sorry. But she'd done no harm. Rudolph, she saw, didn't want anything; everything, Evelyn included, delighted him, but as far as Rudolph was concerned, it was all shadows in a phantom history. He was humbler now, more patient, but he'd lost touch with everything she knew was normal in people: weakness, fear, guilt, self-doubt, the very things that gave the world thickness and made people do things. She *did* want him to desire her. No, she didn't. Not if it meant oral sex. Evelyn didn't know, really, what she wanted anymore. She felt, suddenly, as if she might dissolve before his eyes. "Rudolph, if you're 'empty,' like you say, you don't know who—or what—is talking to you. If you said you were praying, I'd understand. It would be God talking to you. But this way . . ." She pounded her fist four, five times on her thigh. "It could be *evil spirits*, you know! There *are* evil spirits, Rudolph. It could be the Devil."

Rudolph thought for a second. His chest lowered after another long breath. "Evelyn, this is going to sound funny, but I don't believe in the Devil."

Evelyn swallowed. It had come to that.

"Or God—unless we are gods."

She could tell he was at pains to pick his words carefully, afraid he might offend. Since joining the kwoon and studying ways to kill, he seemed particularly careful to avoid her own most effective weapon: the wry, cutting remark, the put-down, the direct, ego-deflating slash. Oh, he was becoming a real saint. At times, it made her want to hit him.

"Whatever is just *is*," he said. "That's all I know. Instead of worrying about whether it's good or bad, God or the Devil, I just want to be quiet, work on myself, and interfere with things as little as possible. Evelyn," he asked suddenly. "how can there be *two* things?" His brow wrinkled; he chewed his lip. "You think what I'm saying is evil, don't you?"

"I think it's strange! Rudolph, you didn't grow up in China," she said. "They can't breathe in China! I saw that today on the news. They burn soft coal, which gets into the air and turns into acid rain. They wear face masks over there, like the ones we bought when Mount St. Helens blew up. They all ride bicycles, for Christ's sake! They want what we have." Evelyn heard Rod Kenner step onto his screened porch, perhaps to listen from his rocker. She dropped her voice a little. "You grew up in Hodges, South Carolina, same as me, in a right and proper colored church. If you'd *been* to China, maybe I'd understand."

"I can only be what I've been?" This he asked softly, but his voice trembled. "Only what I was in Hodges?"

"You can't be Chinese."

"I don't want to be Chinese!" The thought made Rudolph smile and shake his head. Because she did not understand, and because he was tired of talking, Rudolph stepped back a few feet from her, stretching again, always stretching. "I only want to be what I *can* be, which isn't the greatest fighter in the world, only the fighter *I* can be. Lord knows, I'll probably get creamed in the tournament this Saturday." He added, before she could reply, "Doug asked me if I'd like to compete this weekend in full-contact matches with some people from the kwoon. I have to." He opened the screen door. "I will."

"You'll be killed—you know that. Rudolph." She dug her fingernails into her bathrobe, and dug this into him: "You know, you never were very strong. Six months ago you couldn't open a pickle jar for me."

He did not seem to hear her. "I bought a ticket for you." He held the screen door open, waiting for her to come inside. "I'll fight better if you're there."

She spent the better part of that week at Shelberdine's mornings and Reverend Merrill's church evenings, rinsing her mouth with prayer, sitting most often alone in the front row so she would not have to hear Rudolph talking to himself from the musty basement as he pounded out bench presses, skipped rope for thirty minutes in the backyard, or shadowboxed in preparation for a fight made inevitable by his new muscles. She had married a fool, that was clear, and if he expected her to sit on a bench at the Kingdome while some equally stupid brute spilled the rest of his brains— probably not enough left now to fill a teaspoon—then he was wrong. How could he see the world as "perfect"? —That was his claim. There was poverty, unemployment, twenty-one children dying every minute, every day, every year from hunger and malnutrition, over twenty murdered in Atlanta; there were sixty thousand nuclear weapons in the world, which was dreadful, what with Seattle so close to Boeing; there were far-right Republicans in the White House: *good* reasons, Evelyn thought, to be "negative and life-denying," as Rudolph would put it. It was almost sin to see harmony in an earthly hell, and in a fit of spleen she prayed God would dislocate his shoulder, do some minor damage to humble him, bring him home, and remind him that the body was vanity, a violation of every verse in the Bible. But Evelyn could not sustain her thoughts as long as he could. Not for more than a few seconds. Her mind never settled, never rested, and finally on Saturday morning, when she awoke on Shelberdine's sofa, it would not stay away from the image of her Rudolph dead before hundreds of indifferent spectators, paramedics pounding on his chest, bursting his rib cage in an effort to keep him alive.

From Shelberdine's house she called a taxi and, in the steady rain that northwesterners love, arrived at the Kingdome by noon. It's over already, Evelyn thought, walking the circular stairs to her seat, clamping shut her wet umbrella. She heard cheers, booing, an Asian voice with an accent over a microphone. The tournament began at ten, which was enough time for her white belt husband to be in the emergency ward at Harborview Hospital by now, but she had to see. At first, as she stepped down to her seat through the crowd, she could only hear—her mind grappled for the word, then remembered—kiais, or "spirit shouts," from the great floor of the stadium, many shouts, for contests were progressing in three rings simultaneously. It felt like a circus. It smelled like a locker room. Here two children stood toe to toe until one landed a front kick that sent the other child flying fifteen feet. There two lean-muscled female black belts were interlocked in a delicate ballet, like dance or a chess game, of continual motion. They had a kind of sense, these women—she noticed it immediately—a feel for space and their place in it. (Evelyn hated them immediately.) And in the farthest circle she saw, or rather felt, Rudolph, the oldest thing on the deck, who, sparring in the adult division, was squared off with another white belt, not a boy who might hurt him—the other man was middle-aged, graying, maybe only a few years younger than Rudolph—but they were sparring just the same.

Yet it was not truly him that Evelyn, sitting down, saw. Acoustics in the Kingdome whirlpooled the noise of the crowd, a rivering of voices that affected her, suddenly, like the pitch and roll of voices during service. It affected the way she watched Rudolph. She wondered: Who are these people? She caught her breath when, miscalculating his distance from his opponent, her husband stepped sideways into a roundhouse kick with lots of snap—she heard the cloth of his opponent's gi crack like a gunshot when he threw the technique. She leaned forward, gripping the huge purse on her lap when Rudolph recovered and retreated from the killing to the neutral zone, and then, in a wide stance, rethought strategy. This was not the man she'd slept with for twenty years. Not her hypochondriac Rudolph who had to rest and run cold water on his wrists after walking from the front stairs to the fence to pick up the *Seattle Times*. She did not know him, perhaps had never known him, and now she never would, for the man on the floor, the man splashed with sweat, rising on the ball of his rear foot for a flying kick—was he so foolish he still thought he could fly?—would outlive her; he'd stand healthy and strong and think of her in a bubble, one hand on her headstone, and it was all right, she thought, weeping uncontrollably, it was all right that Rudolph would return home after visiting her wet grave, clean out her bedroom, the pillboxes and paperback books, and throw open her windows to let her sour, rotting smell escape, then move a younger woman's things onto the floor space darkened by her color television, her porcelain chamber pot, her antique sewing machine. And then Evelyn was on her feet, unsure why, but the crowd had stood suddenly to clap, and Evelyn clapped, too, though for an instant she pounded her gloved hands together instinctively until her vision cleared, the momentary flash of retinal blindness giving way to a frame of her husband, the postman, twenty feet off the ground in a perfect flying kick that floored his opponent and made a Japanese judge who looked like Oddjob shout "ippon"— one point—and the fighting in the farthest ring, in herself, perhaps in all the world, was over.

Will & Testament

By Malaika Adero

Malaika Adero (1957–) is a senior editor at Atria Books. A dancer, poet, and essayist, she edited *Up South: Stories, Studies and Letters of this Century's African American Migrations* and co-authored (with Lucy Hurston) *Now You're Cooking With Gas*, a book of Zora Neale Hurston memorabilia. Born in Knoxville, Tennessee, she now lives in Harlem. "My father, a gifted and loving person, took his own life at age 42," she says. In "Will & Testament" she evokes the haunting aftermath.

My father's ashes landed on our doorstep
Vacuum-sealed in clear plastic
in a plain brown box.

This was new to us. We *buried* our dead
before.

The family. We drove to the old home place
with the box between us
high up in the mountains
where Grandma and Grandad were born.
We didn't have a map. We followed
the legends on the soles of our feet.

We are native to all manner of death, we think.
But only Daddy could imagine turning
the key in a vacuum-sealed car
running idle until his last breath.

We are destined from now on for great ironies.
Brightest son the star of the darkest day.
A rainbow appears on our decline
against a sky of hammered steel; it mirrors
the hue of winding asphalt way down.

Mother walked a trail of tears
like a warrior mud striped
across the sacred terrain of her face.
The force of her grief deflects the devil's
aim. I am in awe of her power.

We kin and kind find a common ground this day.
An open high place for a man's flesh and bones to feed
the earth.

Where the music of water and wind is heard through
the trees.
Where the music of water and wind is heard through
the trees.
Where Daddy can be at peace.

Mending the World

Momma

By Paulette Childress White

Paulette Childress White (1948–) is the author of two books of poetry, *Love Poem to a Black Junkie* and *The Watermelon Dress: Portrait of a Woman.* In "Momma," she pays tribute to the archetypal "strong Black woman" embodied in the selfless person of her mother.

Momma
Pale as the southern secrets
in her blood
was the princess of morning.

She rose alone
to apocalyptic silence,
set the sun in our windows
and daily mended the world

through the years of never-enough
hiding her dreams
in a typewriter
rusting beneath the kitchen sink.

In weary dresses
that would not survive the Fifties
she gifted us with memory
and created home.

Daddy

By James McBride

James McBride (1957–) won the 1997 Anisfield-Wolf Book Award for Literary Excellence for his bestselling memoir *The Color of Water*. His debut novel, *Miracle at St. Anna*, appeared in 2002. An accomplished saxophonist, McBride has composed scores for musicals and written songs for Anita Baker and Grover Washington, among others. This excerpt from his memoir reveals how a boy's worship of his stepfather allows glimpses of the older man's frailties.

At some point in my consciousness, it occured to me that I had a father. It happened around the time my younger brother Hunter was born. I was five years ahead of Hunter, and while the arrival of a new baby in the house didn't seem to shake anyone—Hunter was the eleventh child—it was the first time that an elderly, slow-moving man in a brown hat, vest sweater, suspenders, and wool pants seemed to float into my consciousness. He picked up Hunter and held him in the air with such delight it made me happy to watch him. His name was Hunter Jordan, Sr., and he raised me as his own son.

As a small boy, I was never quite aware of the concept of "father." My real father, Andrew McBride, died before I was born. I was lorded over by Mommy, my older siblings, friends of Ma's, and relatives on my father's and stepfather's sides whom, years later, I would recognize as guiding forces in my life. Out of this haze of relatives and authority figures loomed a dominating presence that

would come and go. My stepfather worked as a furnace fireman for
the New York City Housing Authority, fixing and maintaining the
huge boilers that heated the Red Hook Housing Projects where we
lived then. He and Mommy met a few months after my biological
father died; Ma was selling church dinners in the plaza in front of
our building at 811 Hicks Street when my stepfather came by and
bought a rib dinner. The next week he came back and bought
another, then another and another. He must have been getting
sick eating all those ribs. Finally one afternoon he came by where
she was selling the church dinners and asked Ma, "Do you go to
the movies?"

"Yeah," she said. "But I got eight kids and they go to the
movies too."

"You got enough for a baseball team," he said.

He married her and made the baseball team his own, adding four
more kids to make it an even twelve. He made no separation between
the McBride and Jordan children, and my siblings and I never
thought of or referred to each other as half brothers and sisters;
for the powerless Little Kids, myself included, he was "Daddy." For
the midlevel executives, he was sometimes "Daddy," sometimes "Mr.
Hunter." To the powerful elder statesmen who remembered their
biological father well, he was always "Mr. Hunter." The older ones
liked to make fun of "Mr. Hunter," the slow way he moved, the
southern accent. "Hrrrrfffff! Hrrrrffffff!" they'd say when he was out
of earshot. But they loved and appreciated him.

When I was about six or seven, he came to our apartment in the
projects, piled us into his car, and drove us out to St. Albans,
Queens, parking in front of a large, pink stucco, four-bedroom
house and disappearing inside while we played on the big front
lawn, tearing out the grass and rolling around in the leaves. It was
fall, and leaves were everywhere. After a while he came outside and
sat on the stoop and watched us play. We tore the grass to shreds,
crushed the neatly manicured bushes, stomped the flowers, and
cracked one of the house's windows with a rock. After ravaging the
lawn for about an hour, one of us had the presence of mind to ask

him, "Whose house is this?" He laughed. I never saw him laugh so
hard. He had just spent his life's savings to buy the place.

He was a gruff man with a good sense of humor, quiet, and stuck
in his ways. He liked neatness, which meant our St. Albans house
was out of bounds for him. However much he loved us, he
couldn't live with the madness in our Queens home, preferring to
keep his old digs at 478 Carlton Avenue in Fort Greene,
Brooklyn. He came home only on weekends, striding into the
living room with bags of groceries, Entenmann's cakes, a pocketful
of dough, and a real live automobile parked outside, in which he
often piled in as many of us as would fit to take us back to his
brownstone for the weekend. We loved staying in his house in
Brooklyn. It was old and dark and filled with antique furniture,
cookies, and Nat King Cole records.

His father was a black man, a railroad brakeman, and his mother
a Native American, so he had a lot of Indian in his face: brown
skin, slanted brown eyes, high cheekbones, and a weather-beaten
outdoor look about him, a very handsome dude. He was educated
in a one-room schoolhouse and raised on a farm in Henrico
County, near Richmond, Virginia, and his family, the Jordans,
were easygoing folks. Beneath their cool exterior, however, was a
rugged breed of black man you did not want to cross—tough, griz-
zled men whose strong brown hands gripped hammers tightly and
whose eyes met you dead on. Those hands could fix anything that
cranked, moved, pumped heat, moved water, or had valves, vac-
uums, or wires.

He fled Virginia around 1927 or so, with Jim Crow hot on his
tail, so to speak. A white sheriff had locked him up for peeking
under the tent of a traveling circus without paying, and when the
sheriff went to lunch and inadvertently left the cell door open,
Daddy eased out of the jailhouse and caught the first thing smokin';
he never returned to Virginia for good until he died. He met up
with his brother Walter in Chicago, where he was fleeced and pick-
pocketed from the time he hit town till the time he left. He worked
in slaughterhouses there, moved up to Detroit, where he shined
shoes with his brother in a barbershop near the Ford plant—he

shined one of Henry Ford's shoes while Walter shined the other—
and on to Brooklyn, New York, in the Roaring Twenties, where the
brothers made a living selling illegal booze for a while. He was out
of his apartment one day when one of his liquor-making stills
broke and spilled so much liquor onto the floor that it leaked
downstairs into the apartment below; the guy living downstairs
held his glass under his light fixture and got dead drunk, wandering into the street while my stepfather tried to reel him in, but
the cat was out of the bag and not long after that he was raided. He
jumped out his back window holding two five-gallon jugs of hooch,
right into the arms of waiting federal agents. He did time for that,
something neither he nor Mommy ever told us about, though I
always wondered how a guy who seemed so unsophisticated could
be so clever at checkers. I never could beat him.

Altogether there were four brothers—he, Henry, Walter, and
Garland—and they epitomized old-time cool: suave, handsome
black men who worked hard, drank hard, dressed well, liked fine
women and new money. Daddy's favorite was Walter, the most fun-
loving and gregarious of his brothers. He'd often take us to Walter's
house in Fort Greene just blocks from his house, where my siblings
and I would play with our cousin Little Mommy while Uncle
Walter, Daddy, and their other brothers partied, drinking and listening to Nat King Cole, Gene Krupa, and Charlie Parker
records. Mommy would never drink at these occasions. She did not
like us to socialize too much with the partying side of Daddy's
family. She never drank or smoked. In fact, drinking was number
one on her don't list, and if my stepfather drank too much, she'd
scream at him on the way home. He'd drive twenty miles an hour all
the way to Queens from Brooklyn, nosing his big sedan through
traffic till he found a city bus, which he would get behind and
follow all the way home. "You can never get a speeding ticket if you
follow one of them," he declared. Car after car of angry motorists
would fly by us, yelling, "GET OFF THE DAMN ROAD!" He'd
ignore them. We'd be in the back seat, shrinking low, laughing,
hoping none of our friends would happen to see us.

Every summer he would take a bunch of us down south to

Richmond to his cousin Clemy's house, where we ate watermelon from Clemy's yard, rode her pony, and watched our other "down south" relatives do wild tricks, like taking their teeth out. We had a cousin who would sit on the couch, drink a beer, and take her teeth out, making them go *chomp! chomp!* and causing us to run from the room. Uncle Henry was a real character. He was a mechanic and a decorated World War II vet who had a gold tooth in his mouth that flashed and sparkled when he smiled, which was often. His stomach had been ruined after he was stabbed in a knife fight, though I couldn't imagine him angry. We loved him. When he laughed, he sounded like a car trying to start, "Heeerrrrrr! Heerrrrrrr!" We used to make fun of his laugh, which amused him greatly, touching off another round of "Heeerrrrrr! Heerrrrrrr!" from him, prompting further outraged giggles from us.

There were so many of us, we'd travel south in two cars, some of us riding with Daddy and Mommy in Daddy's car, some with Walter and Henry in a second car. One night as we began one of our migrations back to New York from Richmond, Uncle Henry got drunk and was driving at a hundred miles an hour in his Oldsmobile with me, my sister Judy, and my Uncle Walter inside. "This baby's a powerhouse!" he roared, stomping the accelerator and flying up Interstate 95 as I watched Daddy's headlights through the back windshield grow dimmer and dimmer, then disappear altogether. As he barreled up the road laughing, Uncle Walter screamed at him, "Henry, slow down, dammit!" Uncle Henry ignored him for a few more harrowing minutes, finally pulling over at a rest stop. Minutes later Daddy's car, full of Mommy and the rest of the kids, screeched up behind us. Daddy jumped out of his car so fast his hat flew off.

"Goddammit, Henry!" Walter had to restrain Daddy, and Henry, the boldest of the brothers, backed off and apologized. Daddy was the most respected of the brothers, and anger was a rarity with him. He had a peaceful, strong manner that did not provoke anger or invite fights. We drove back to New York packed in Daddy's car, while Henry slept peacefully in the back of his own car with Walter driving. Walter offered to take a couple of us with him but Daddy refused. "I had enough of y'all," he said. Walter shrugged.

I thought my stepfather was odd. The fact that he and Mommy seemed to love one another did not help me think differently. He was nothing like my friends' parents, who were younger, drove new cars, followed the Mets, talked about civil rights, and foot-raced with us. He had no idea of what the sixties meant, nor did they seem to interest him. His only interests were my grades and church. He came to my church confirmation alone because Mommy could not, dressed to the nines, shirt buttoned to the top, hat creased just so, and sat in the back by himself, paying no attention to the other, younger fathers dressed in bell-bottoms and hip sixties wear. He greeted my Sunday school teacher respectfully, hat in hand, and she smiled at him, impressed by his handsomeness and cool manner. But when she tried to engage him in conversation he seemed uninterested, taking my hand and backing away, his gestures saying, "Thanks, but no thanks." He went to my eldest brother Dennis's college graduation dressed in his old-timey clothes and walked around the all-black campus of Lincoln University in Pennsylvania beaming, full of so much pride, his family and white wife in tow, as black students and their parents did double takes. I used to look at him and wonder, *What is his problem? Doesn't he know how goofy he looks?* but it never seemed to bother him in the least. Race was something he never talked about. To him it was a detail that you stepped over, like a crack in the sidewalk. He was a person who never seemed to worry. "Everything's gonna be allllllll riiiiight," he'd say. That was his motto.

Then in 1969 he got a letter from the city of New York telling him to move out of his house in Brooklyn. They were planning to build a low-income-housing high rise there. He was stunned. He had renovated that old brownstone from a shell. It was his refuge, his joy, his hobby. They gave him $13,000 and he was gone. Twenty years later when I moved back to Fort Greene—now immortalized by Spike Lee's movies, with gentrification pushing poor, blacks out and brownstones selling for $350,000—I'd walk by 478 Carlton Avenue and look at the empty lot there. Nothing. A total waste.

When they tore down his house, it was like they ripped out half his arteries. He came to Queens and lived with us, converting a piece of the basement into his old-time headquarters; he squeezed in his antique furniture, his windup record player, and a small refrigerator in which he stored his jars of pig feet and cans of Rheingold beer, but his heart was back in Brooklyn. He'd retired by then—he was seventy-two—but he did odd jobs and worked on heating systems with his brother Walter. One night about three years after he moved in with us, he was staggering around the kitchen, cursing and saying his head hurt, and before I knew it, an ambulance pulled up and they were loading him in. "What's wrong with him?" I asked Ma. She said nothing, her eyes red-rimmed, denoting deep alarm, as she climbed into the ambulance with his sweater grasped tightly in her fist.

He'd had a stroke. I was fourteen and didn't know what a stroke was. I thought it was something you got from the sun. For me, the two weeks or so he was in the hospital meant I could hang out with my friends as long and as late as I wanted to, and I avoided going to see him until Mommy forced me to. I went with my sister Kathy, and when we walked into his hospital room, it was a brutal shock. He was laid out in hospital white. His face was slightly twisted. He could not talk. He could not move his right arm or right side. His hand, a strong, brown, veined hand that I'd seen gripping wrenches and tools and pipe fittings hundreds of times, was nearly limp, covered with gauze and connected to an IV. Mommy sat by him in silence, her face ashen. Kathy, who was always his favorite, walked into the room, saw him, and backed away from him, horrified. She could not look at him. She sat on a chair near the window and stared outside, crying softly. He raised his hand to comfort her and made some sort of horrid, gurgling speech noise to get her attention. She finally came over to him and laid her head on his chest and wept uncontrollably. I walked out of the room, wiping my tears, staggering toward the elevator, covering my eyes so no one could see, as nurses and hospital aides backed out of my way.

He came home from the hospital about a week later and seemed to get better. His speech, though slurred, returned. He sat in his basement headquarters, recuperating, while we crept around the house and Mommy walked about silently, eyes still red-rimmed, on edge. One day he summoned me downstairs and asked me to help him dress. "I want to take a drive," he said. I was the oldest kid living at home by then, my other siblings being away at school. He put on his sweater, wool pants, hat, and blue peacoat. Though ill and thin, he still looked sharp. Slowly, he mounted the stairs and stepped outside. It was May and brisk, almost cold outside. We went into the garage and stepped into his gold-colored Pontiac. "I want to drive home one more time," he said. He was talking about Richmond, Virginia, where he grew up. But he was too weak to drive, so he sat there behind the wheel of the car, staring at the garage wall, and he began to talk.

He said he had a little money saved up for Mommy and a little land in Virginia, but it was not enough. He said that since I was the oldest living at home, I had to watch out for Mommy and my little brothers and sisters because "y'all are special," he said. "And just so special to me." It was the only time I ever heard him refer to race in any way, however vaguely, but it didn't matter, because right then and there I knew he was going to die and I had to blink back my tears. I wanted to tell him that I loved him, that I hoped with all my heart that he would get better, but I could not formulate the words in my mouth. We had never spoken that way to one another. We joked and talked, but his chief concern had always been my "schooling" and "church raising" as he called it. He was not a man for dialogue. That was Mommy's job.

Two days later he suffered a relapse. An ambulance came and got him. About four in the morning the phone rang. My sister Kathy and I lay upstairs and listened, and through what seemed to be a fog, I heard my older brother Richie, home from school, telling Mommy, "It's all right, Ma. It's all right."

"It's not all right! It's not all right!" Ma cried, and she wailed and wailed, the sound of her cries circling the house like a spirit and settling on all the corridors and beds where we lay, weeping in silence.

Counting Breaths

By Rosemarie Robotham

Rosemarie Robotham (1957–) was born in Kingston, Jamaica, and now lives in New York with her husband and two children. She wrote "Counting Breaths" during the last months of her father's life, as a tribute to the love her parents shared and to the courage with which they faced the inevitable.

It is a slow, inexorable dance. The conclusion is sure, only the interval is still in question. My father is dying. My mother refuses to lose him. Daddy has fought the internal mutiny of cells for more than a decade, and he is tired now, tired of restraining the invisible march, tired of holding his breath as the doctor shares the newest results of tissue scans, tired of yielding, again and again, to the surgeon's well-meaning knife. And he's exhausted by the way his heart aches at the lines in my mother's face, the tender grooves beside her mouth that belie the determined smile she marshals each time a visitor enters the room.

The cancer is throughout my father's body. It has penetrated the bone—infiltrated skull, ribs, pelvis, toes—and robbed his legs of their ability to propel him forward. Daddy sits in a wheelchair, gaunt, sallow, his preternaturally black hair finally going to gray. His memory skips and falters, and sometimes, in the moment that he awakens, he even thinks he can rise from his bed and walk unaided to the bathroom to perform his morning rituals. But then he tries to move his legs, lying cramped and cold under the sheets, and they betray him. Tears sting his eyes. He averts his face so that my mother won't see. For several moments, he says nothing for fear that his helplessness will cause a ripple in his voice.

I stroke his hair. "To be struck down like this . . ." he whispers. I just keep stroking his hair.

I worry about my mother. She's talking, walking, moving fast, obsessively focused on caring for my father from morning till night. But sometimes, her stomach knits so severely she is forced to lie still. It is the only pause she permits herself. My father watches her flurry of motion with an intimate grasp of its meaning. He is holding on, I think, waiting for her to accept that he must move on. But my mother will not give in to what she sees as defeat. God, she points out, is in their corner: Daddy *will* walk again. He will rebuild the muscles in his wasted legs. He will allow God's healing Spirit to storm his body and repair his wounds. He will get, if not well, then better. He cannot give up. *She* cannot give up.

But lately, there has been so much pain. Flaring, unendurable pain in the joints of his limbs. My mother fumbles with the medicine bottle, her twisted, arthritic fingers fighting the childproof cap. She manages to extract a huge yellow pill. She lifts my father's head, places the painkiller on his tongue and holds the water to his lips. Then she sits at his bedside, counting his breaths, praying silently for the hour it takes for the medication to take effect, for her face to grow fuzzy in his sight as merciful sleep takes hold.

Much later, when he wakes, my mother is in the kitchen preparing a meal. It is her supreme purpose to coax food into my father. She scolds and cajoles him to take feasts as large as my six-foot-two, 240-pound husband regularly consumes. My father's small frame, bird-like appetite, and nausea from the chemotherapy drugs make my mother's task difficult. He complains that he is not hungry. He rebels by pushing the food around his plate, never lifting the fork to his lips. "I am not a child!" he objects finally. "You'd think I was torturing you!" she protests. Once, watching them, I begged them not to argue. They both turned to look at me. A playful light came into my father's eyes, and my mother laughed outright. "Why do you want to begrudge us our fun?" she said. I saw Daddy's hand reach under the table to caress Mommy's knee.

Daddy's only desire, in these months of failing health, is that my mother stay near. In the mornings, when my mother tries to push out of bed to get his 6 a.m. medication and a cup of hot chocolate, he holds on to her. It is far better therapy, he insists with a flash of his old mischief, for them to lie in bed and cuddle. He chuckles as he says it, but he means it fiercely. If my mother goes out, to the grocery store or to get her hair done, my father asks me several times each hour: "Where is Mommy? Isn't she back yet?"

They have been married 46 years. Although they do not say it, they realize that the cherished 50 year mark may not be achieved. My mother will not allow melancholy. She observes that she and Daddy courted for four years before they were married. "This is our 50th year together," she tells him on the morning of their anniversary. My father's mind cavorts in the rooms of memory. His breaths grow full, his chest lifts higher. Robust recollections fill his fragile frame. His groping hand finds my mother's arthritic one and, clasping it, he brings her fingers to his lips and closes his eyes. My father sighs deeply. My mother measures his breath.

The Two of Us

By Alice Walker

Alice Walker (1944–) achieved worldwide recognition with *The Color Purple,* which won both a Pulitzer Prize and an American Book Award in 1983. Born in Eatonton, Georgia, the eighth child of share-croppers, Walker has published eighteen books of fiction, essays, and poetry devoted to exploring the sexual and racial realities of Black women. In "The Two of Us," which she wrote on the occasion of her daughter's twenty-fifth birthday, she reflects on the joy and pain of their relationship.

First I see her smiling face as she stands at the gate to our house, waiting for me to open it. She has forgotten her key. I am always struck by her sunniness. It amused me many a gray day when she was an infant and we lived in a dangerous and dreary Mississippi. There were glowing pussy willows outside her windows and bright posters on the walls; I awakened to the sound of her singing. When I poked my head into the vibrant room, she greeted me with a toothless grin. Now she has become a woman, and a sunny optimism still her fundamental nature, though by now I have seen its other faces of sorrow, anger, cloud and storm.

As soon as she walks through the door we embrace. She sighs deeply, resting her head on my shoulder. I silently thank the Universe she has returned to me once again. I am always shocked she is so tall. My cheek lies just above her heart. I am reminded of her father; he is six feet tall. Of my parents, my mother especially, whom Rebecca resembles, who was five foot seven. I often exclaim,

"You are so tall!" She laughs. Kisses my forehead. "Mama," she says indulgently. She doesn't bother to remind me I am short. For many years she did a curious little dance when we hugged, a kind of flapping of her knees against mine. It was uniquely Rebecca's, and endearing, if somewhat strange. She no longer does that, and I miss it. I think she dropped it as a student at Yale.

She has always been appreciative of our living spaces: In San Francisco, as we walk from the front door through the parlors to the kitchen, she notices every single thing. If there is a new painting, she stops to look at it. A piece of sculpture she'd forgotten, she's delighted to see again. I love how observant and enthusiastic she is; being this way, I know, she will always enjoy life. As I put on the pot for tea, she moves about touching, sniffing, exclaiming and smiling; and I settle into a motherly busyness that expresses the pleasure I anticipate from my daughter's visit home. So many years we've been together. One of my longest relationships and the most important. As I pour our tea I look at her and think: *This completely separate person came out of my body; I have the stretch marks to prove it.* I remember her turning in my womb, sucking her thumb, dragging a bedraggled pink blanket everywhere. Riding her first bicycle. At 2 she read her first word: *book.* By the age of 3 she could pack her own suitcase. I see her flying out the door of our house in Jackson, Mississippi, a straw hat on her head, on her way to Jamaica with her father and me. I remember a dozen or so years later, also in Jamaica, Rebecca lying injured in the middle of the highway, a victim of a motorcycle accident. I remember holding her broken foot in the car all the way back to our hotel, her teenage boyfriend, Brian, who traveled with us, glancing anxiously back at her from the front seat.

A bonus of being Rebecca's mother has been the love I've felt for each of her Significant Others. There was Brian, a boy from the neighborhood, who was an early passion; Omari, a Kenyan from the island of Lamu, with whom Rebecca lived for several months, who used to call me in the middle of the night when she was ill with malaria to tell me not to worry; Bechét, the son of a friend, who seemed so much like my own child that when he and

Rebecca separated I was as sad as she was. Later there was Rhyan, a smart and gentle woman who felt like a second daughter. This attachment to my daughter's partners surprised me; no one had warned me that when they suddenly disappeared from her life they disappeared from mine. And that I would miss them. Or that, while they shared her life, I would feel I had two children to enjoy and worry over, not one.

I have loved being Rebecca's mom. There's no one I'd rather hear from, talk with, listen to. Except for those times when I've had to face the ways in which being her mother made life harder for her. I believed the sunniness because it was real, but also because I thought it meant she was okay. More than a decade after her father and I separated she confronted me with the hurt, confusion, deep sorrow and depression she experienced losing the safety and warmth of our marriage, intolerable for us but a sanctuary for her, and how she'd kept that side of herself hidden, especially her grief, for fear I would not be able to accept it. Accept her. My defense was that I had done the best I could, and I refused to be judged. What she wanted, she said, was my simple acknowledgment, a feeling acknowledgment, of her suffering. I found this very hard, for it seemed to deny the difficulty of my life as her mother, and as a working, creative person who had tried to do the best I could by both of us, sometimes under impossible and unsupported circumstances.

As a child, though my parents stayed together in a marriage that lasted more than 40 years, and seemed to continue even after my father's death, I often felt abandoned, because both my parents worked. By the time I was 10, I was the family's housekeeper during the week, while my mother and sister worked in town; I felt like Cinderella as I attempted to care for a household that consisted of a sexist father and brothers who were not taught to tolerate sensitivity. However, no matter how grim my existence was, I put on a cheerful front for my mother, whose exhausted face at the end of her day cleaning another woman's house and caring for another woman's children made me weep inwardly, just to see her. Her place of solace and renewal was her garden, into which she retreated, leaving me with my fears and worries unheard, unexpressed.

I realize Rebecca and I have reenacted this behavior, for when I became a mother battered by the outside world, my garden was my work: *Having trouble dealing with Mississippi in the sixties? Write your way out of it.* The illusion I'd indulged was that because I'd married someone very unlike my father, and because I was a writer and not a laborer-housewife, and because I was an educated woman, and because Rebecca had been spared siblings, her experience as a child (I thought of her as extremely privileged) bore no resemblance to mine. I was so wrong. Behind the brave smiles she'd given me, during her years of sadness and feelings of abandonment, had slumped the little dejected girl I knew so well, twin to the one I had also been.

This realization catapulted me into a period of intense dreaming that led to partial recall of my own childhood—I had mercifully forgotten whole years of it—and culminated in a series of paintings, both savage and sad, that took me back to my anger. An anger well hidden by depression and thoughts of suicide. When I emerged, my heart broke open to my daughter's solitary suffering, locked in her shining, smiling ways.

I did my best, I was finally able to say, and still I hurt you. I am so sorry. My daughter is compassionate and forgiving. More than that, she is understanding. We sit, sipping our tea, and talk frankly about "the old days" of her growing up—and my inadequate, perhaps, but still fierce-hearted mothering. Rebecca has made me a mother. Because of her, I've reunited with banished bits of my own life. I know again the daughter and the mother I was, and feel pity and empathy for both. I appreciate the admirable daughter courage that, though self-denying and therefore painful, still springs from a valiant solidarity with the mother, who, in this world, always has too much to do and too few to help her. I've also discovered the world is full of mothers who've done their best and still hurt their daughters: that we have daughters everywhere.

The names of Rebecca's significant others have been changed to protect their privacy.

The Good Daughter

By Rebecca Walker

Rebecca Walker (1970–), named by *Time* magazine as one of fifty leaders of her generation, founded Third Wave Foundation, the nation's only activist philanthropic organization for women under thirty. In her books, *Black, White and Jewish* and *To Be Real,* she engages us in the search for identity and acceptance of self. In this companion essay to Alice Walker's "The Two of Us," she arrives at a deeper understanding of her connection to her mother.

The year that I turned 25, my mother called to say happy birthday to both of us. Twenty-five years ago, she said, was our birthday. I will remember our twenty-fifth year as the one in which we both began to understand that what is traditionally considered an adolescent and absolute task of individuation is really a lifelong process of leaving and returning home, of being apart and coming together. That year I pushed hard against some of the rules of the good daughter and learned to really hear the message my mother has given me all my life: "I will be with you always." As in forever, into the eternal hereafter, no matter what. But it has been a long struggle.

When I was just 8 years old, my mother had me crawl into bed beside her before asking me to take some dictation. "When I die," she said as if she were telling me which clothes to lay out for the next day, "make sure I am buried in a simple pine box. And play lots of Stevie Wonder. My funeral should be a celebration!" Dutifully, I began to write—P-i-n-e b-o-x, S-t-e-v-i-e W-o-n-d-e-r—on the yellow legal pad she placed on my lap. I don't remember what I felt then as my mother asked me to prepare for a time when she would no longer be present.

Now, after reliving certain childhood moments in an attempt to understand them and myself better, I imagine that I did what I always tried to do for my mama. I tried to be who and what she needed me to be at the time. Instead of asking her all the hideous questions running scared through my child mind—*Mama, are you going to die? Mama, are you leaving me? Mama, who will take care of me? Mama, what about us?*—I simply memorized the funeral plan to the letter and cheerfully assured her I would take care of everything.

This was the face I would show my mother again and again as I was growing up and she needed space or silence or to go away to do her work. Rather than insist on being with her or tell her that I did not want to be alone, I would nod, smile and say cheerfully, "Okay, Mama."

I am not sure if the pine-box incident marked the beginning of my fear of my mother's abandonment of me, or if it was the first time that I silenced my own apprehensions in order to soothe hers. I do know that this memory captures how I have always felt, deep down, about my relationship with my mother: If I don't do what she wants me to do, she will be gone, she will leave me. The plan I devised in response was simple: I would be too perfect to leave, too indispensable, too wonderful. Thinking I could keep her closer for longer by winning her unconditional love, I instinctively made myself into what I perceived to be a good daughter, often silencing or ignoring my own needs.

Not surprisingly, this is not an uncommon pattern. My mother has told me that she, too, had similar though undiscussed fears about her mother, and together we think that at least three generations of mothers and daughters before us must have been similarly afflicted with the same story of silence and need. Perhaps this mother-daughter code is a legacy of slavery; cultivating a daughter's independence and sense of separateness could be one way our great-great-great-grandmothers protected a child who could wake up motherless, and toughening their own hearts to the needs of a child who might be taken away might have been our foremothers' only defense against unending sorrow.

I have heard similar fears from other women whose working mothers had to leave them alone for greater parts of the day or night, depending on them to "take care of things;" or who, because of some other circumstance beyond their control, usually abuse or neglect, were unable to get the kind of constant unconditional love that young children crave. Listening to their stories, it becomes clear why individuation is often so difficult for young women. We fear that if we go our own way, off into our destinies outside of our mothers' desires, we will surely perish. We will die of aloneness.

All the way through college I lived with this fear of abandonment as one lives with unresolved childhood abuse; it covertly steered my life. It mostly affected my relationships, turning them into struggles for proof of the unconditional love that I longed for. I pushed partners to dire limits to see if they would still love me, and I stayed with partners I didn't necessarily enjoy because I couldn't stand the idea of being walked away from forever. In relationships with my peers, my belief that I wouldn't be accepted as who I was often kept me from opening up and making new friends, and with those who were my friends, I felt an acute need to show a strong, supportive, everything-is-going-to-be-all-right face. In my relationships with older women and mentors whom I loved and respected, I always felt slightly uncomfortable. Was I being what they wanted me to be? Was I giving them the daughter they always wanted?

While I knew that I would have to stop always being the good daughter in order to reach an adulthood I could be proud of, I fretted unconsciously for a few years, taking tentative steps out of my mother's orbit. The most symbolic decision was to move to New York instead of back to San Francisco, where my mother lived, after my graduation from college. In my mind, my desire to cultivate a life full of pollution and urbanity would signify to my mother that my values were questionable, that I was less than pure.

I could hear her wondering what could possibly be worthwhile enough to keep me away from healthy and politically evolved San Francisco. I also worried that because she wanted me home, my move would feel to her like the same abandonment I so feared. If I let her down, she would withdraw, and I would be, as my childhood self understood it, motherless.

As I feared, when I moved, she withdrew, and we have been coming together and letting go ever since. She, trying to let me go my way without judgment, trying to make space for and understand my feelings of fear; and me, trying to make my own way on my own terms, not letting the choices she has made keep me from making important decisions that are mine—according to what I want and not what I imagine she would want. Honestly, it has been a tough road, full of long silences and angry confrontations, teary reunions and sometimes frightening insights into the limits of the daughter-mother bond.

But the great news is this: I have come full out to my mother as myself, cursing sometimes, having widely divergent points of view, making choices I know she wouldn't make, even allowing myself to get angry with her to the point of yelling! And what I have learned is that much of what I fear is in my mind, my psyche, carried over from a child's logic, from another era in both of our lives. By articulating and talking about my childhood fears and feelings with my mother over the past few years, I have tested my childhood assumptions and found that not only are both my mother and my mother's love here to stay, but that the voice inside of me that said I was not loved unconditionally can also begin to change. I am no longer the powerless child at the mercy of my mother's moods. And she is no longer the uncertain mother afraid to love without question. These truths will neither kill nor divide us but will instead set us free. Being honest, being real with each other helps us to be true to ourselves and more accepting of what is real in all of our relationships.

Twenty-five was a year of coming-of-age, in which I realized that there is a point when you have to step out into the world on your own feet and speak from your own mouth. There is no guarantee that most people will like you or even understand you. You must find solace in the fact that you are telling your truth and that when you speak, your words are so much your own that no others could possibly come from your lips. I have learned that mustering that courage, being that true, can only come from unconditional love—of the self.

As I hug my mother at the end of a recent visit, I realize just how long it has taken us to begin to look at the patterns that have shaped our lives. I also feel for the first time that I am not afraid to say good-bye. I don't feel the usual pangs of fear that I may never see her again; I don't doubt the depth and sacredness of our connection. I know that we will be together again, and I feel secure in the knowledge that whenever and wherever we meet, we will pick up exactly where we left off—listening, loving and trying to understand.

The Box

By Diane McKinney-Whetstone

Diane McKinney-Whetstone (1953–), the author of four novels, writes of African-American families caught in the flux of modern life. The fourth in a family of seven siblings, she was raised in Philadelphia and still lives just outside the city with her husband and their twins. In this excerpt from her best-selling novel, *Tumbling*, she evokes the wonder and uncertainty that enfold Herbie and Noon when they find a strange package on their doorstep.

The box sat patiently on the steps as Herbie approached his house. He might have tripped over it except that pink yarn fringes hung over the edges. They rippled in the breeze and startled the night as they moved. They startled Herbie too. "What the hell?" he murmured as he stopped sharply and nudged the box with his foot. He pulled back the pink covering. He peered into the box.

He stood straight up. He pulled at the end of his long, thin nose and rubbed his hand hard across his head. How many beers had he had at Royale? Only two, not even enough to make him miss a step, certainly not enough to make the night do a strangeness on his mind. He reached in his jacket pocket and snatched out a tin filled with red-topped stick matches. He struck a match and cupped his hands to protect the flame from the air that was circling him in wispy drafts. He leaned into the box guided by the fire. A baby. Damn sure was. Somebody had left a baby right here on his steps.

"Noon," he yelled once inside the door. "Noon, you gotta come down here and see this. Noon!" He trod tenuously across the buffed-up shine of the hardwood floor. He held the baby's head to his chest as he walked. He stepped onto the thick circle of a throw rug in the center of the room and yanked the cord that turned on the living room chandelier. He eased the baby's head back in his palm so he could see her in the swaying light of the chandelier.

"Herbie, that you? What you got that bright light on in the middle of the night for? Coming in here talking loud this time of night, what's all the commotion?" Noon's voice was generous like her round face, her bow-shaped hips, and her healthy legs. It was what had attracted Herbie to her in the first place, the hips and the legs. He could see the print of the hips even now as she rushed down the stairs in a thick quilted robe.

"Lord have mercy! Where in Jesus name did you get that baby? Where it come from, Herbie?"

"On the steps. I was on my way in from Royale, and this box was on the steps."

"On what steps? Royale's? Ours?" She pulled back Herbie's arm and gently took the baby from him. "And where's the box? Maybe there's a note or something in there."

"Still on the steps, on our steps, I wouldn't go looking through no boxes left on anybody else's steps." He went back out the front door to bring the box in. The space between his chin and his shoulder still held the warmth of the baby's body right where she had nestled her head.

"It is a girl, right?" he asked as he walked back into the living room and put the box at Noon's feet. She was now on the couch smiling exaggerated smiles and otherwise animating her face as she cooed and clucked and amused the contents of the pink covering.

"Oh, yeah, I done already checked her out, she's a girl for real, a newborn baby girl, can't be more than a week by the looks of the cord, and she's gonna need changing she is." She talked more to the baby than to Herbie.

Herbie hovered over Noon as she undid the loosely knitted blanket and inspected the baby's limbs and fingers and toes.

"Diapers in the box." He said it with authority. "And be careful with her head."

"Scuse me, Mr. Herbie." Noon turned and looked at him, her small, slanted eyes filled with exclamation. "I been taking care of infants since I was ten; I do know how to hold a baby. I'm just surprised you was able to even get her up the steps and in the house without snapping her spine."

"Well, I did. I even stopped her from crying when we were out front. It just came natural. She was good and content with me holding her too till you came and snatched her right outta my hands."

"I declare 'fore God! You seem to have gotten mighty attached to this baby. I thought a baby was the farthest thing from your mind."

"No, it's just that I can hardly get close enough to you to put you in a family way." He saw Noon flinch, even from where he was standing, looking down on her head that she turned from him. He could see her scalp tighten through the brown twisted papers that she used to curl her hair. He stopped and breathed in hard and said, "I'm sorry, Noon, I shouldn't have said that."

Noon's face was round and soft brown, and the print of her cheekbones was usually lost in the roundness, except that they were showing now as she ground her teeth and swallowed hard, trying to swallow the hurt that always surfaced as a ball in her throat whenever he reminded her of her bedroom problem. It was all Noon could do to just pull her defenses up like a girdle to keep him from seeing the hurt.

Right now the baby helped. "Mercy, mercy," she said, ignoring Herbie, "You 'bout the cutest baby I ever did see, look at those eyes."

"The eyes are something, aren't they?" Herbie said excitedly as he pushed into the space between Noon and the arm of the couch. "What those eyes look like to you?"

"Like black diamonds, that's what they look like." Noon took her voice down to a whisper. The baby's eyes held Noon too.

"Wish those eyes could tell me who left you, why they leave you on our steps, who would do such a thing, on a chilly night too, even if they did have you good and bundled. Do they know me, whoever left you, or did they just leave you arbitrarily like?"

The room was completely quiet except for Noon's whispers and the baby's light breathing that sounded like sighs. The chandelier swayed to the hushed rumble of Noon's voice. Herbie pressed himself into the couch and stared in the baby's eyes. He got the same gush of warmth that he had on the steps when she nestled her head along his shoulder.

He fingered the infant's thumb and touched her hair lightly. "Wonder who her parents are, she real light, look to be half white."

"She don't have her true color yet." Now Noon spoke with authority. "Her true color is in the tip of her ears." She pulled the blanket from around the baby's ears. "See, the tips of her ears just a little darker than the rest of her, that's the color she gonna be, good and yellow."

"I done told you bout calling people yellow, woman." Herbie said it playfully, mockingly, trying to soften Noon and make up for his sarcasm a minute ago.

"All right, golden then, she gonna be a golden color, like a piece of cornbread." Noon got quiet then as she looked from the newborn to Herbie. The dark hair, the coal black eyes, the light skin, Herbie and the baby had these in common in a striking way. Noon couldn't think it. Suppose this was Herbie's baby. Suppose this whole business of a box on the steps was a made-up tale. Suppose he had just crept from some hellhole with some harlot and had just finished telling her that his wife will take this baby, she can't have any of her own because she can't mix pleasures with a man. She cringed at the thought. Except that she knew Herbie better than that. Terrible liar he was. Lean face showed off every muscle twitch when he was nervous. Thick dark brows couldn't do anything but recess when he was ashamed, even his lips, which were short and full, tightened involuntarily when he was guilty. She watched him as he sat transfixed by the baby's stare. His wide shoulders were rounded, relaxed. He found the box on the steps, she believed that for sure.

When she spoke again, she said, "Guess we gonna have to turn her over to the authorities come daybreak."

"Guess we will," he agreed. "Sure can't keep her. That could get us both locked up." His words felt like lead coming out. He was hoping Noon would say, "We not hardly turning this chile over. No, no, no."

Daybreak came. The blues went from navy to royal to light with just a speck of pink. Then came the yellow spilling into Noon and Herbie's bedroom. Noon was wide-awake, had been for the past hour. Herbie was snoring, and the baby was between them, fast asleep, looking like butter the way the sunlight was stroking her. The bed was warm. So warm that Noon didn't jump right up when the Saturday morning church bells rang. And when she did get up, it was only because the baby needed feeding. Once that was done, she snuggled back in between the stiff muslin sheets topped with the patchwork quilt that was one-quarter wool. She moved the baby in closer to her body and thought that even though this was the beginning of April, they might need to buy yet one more bin of coal, especially if there was to be a baby in the house. She reminded herself then that they would still have to get in touch with the proper authorities who handled such things like abandoned children. She knew how they would have handled it back home. They would have taken the child to the mouth of the river and dipped her in the name of the Father and the Son and the Holy Ghost and claimed her as their own. No questions about it, none at all. But here in Philadelphia the laws were more complicated. The mother might even come back for the child. City people were so unpredictable; they didn't follow the same rules for living like country folk in the South, where if a thing was done, it was done for good.

The baby squirmed, and Noon leaned on her elbow so she could face her. She pecked the child's forehead and smoothed at her hair and wondered if she could feel any more motherly about her very own child than she did right now with this abandoned baby next to her and the sunlight splashing in through the stark white curtains. She pictured the mothers she used to help the midwives tend. She'd watch them as their babies suckled their high and firm breasts. How complete they must have felt. How devastated she herself felt when she was examined by Lula, the midwife blessed with the gift of healing. And when Lula had mouthed the words "Shame 'fore God what they to did to you," Noon's heart froze. She felt a chill even now as she remembered how Lula's eyes filled up as she'd covered Noon's lower body with the stiff white sheet as if she were covering the mangled face of a dead child. She'd told Noon then that her womb would never issue forth a birth. Despite the praying over her, the sassafras teas, the salves made from this herb or that leaf, the cornstarch soaks to soothe the pain, the scarring was just too thick, too permanent to dissolve.

She pushed her hand down into her pink flannel nightgown and grabbed at her own breasts. They felt flaccid and heavy. "Young as I am, breasts ain't got no business feeling like this," she muttered. At least they were warm now. At night, when Herbie reached for her, they'd go cold and shrivel up like a prune. At least now they were warm and smooth.

The baby was getting hungry again. Noon could tell because her mouth was pursing and smacking and opening and closing with sucking motions. She listened for Herbie's loud and rhythmic snoring. She pulled her nightgown from her shoulder and lifted her breast and just held it in her hand for a while. Then she closed her eyes tightly and guided her breast straight to the infant's hungry mouth. The baby clamped her mouth around Noon's breast and pulled in hard, instinctively, pulling for milk. Noon felt a pain that started at her nipple and ricocheted through her body to her deepest parts. She almost cried out; were it not for Herbie on the other side of the baby snoring soundly, she would have cried out. The baby did cry. Pulling on emptiness, she cried, and twisted her head so that Noon's breast fell from her mouth and hung there, wet from the child's spit and exposed.

The commotion jostled Herbie, who sat up with a start. "What's wrong with her, why she acting like that? She all right, Noon? Noon, is she all right?"

"Just hungry, is all," Noon said as she turned quickly so that her back was to Herbie, and then, covering herself up, rolled out of the bed. "I'll warm her bottle, that's all she needs right now; a little milk and she'll go right back to sleep." She pushed her feet into her soft pink slippers and rushed out of the room before Herbie could see her shame.

In the kitchen everything was yellow and orange except for the white sink-tub, next to the off-white gas-powered stove that had set them back $59.95. Noon ran the water hot over her softest dish towel and pressed it to her breast. Guess even that newborn know these breasts can't make no milk, wonder if she know I don't bleed right either, wonder if everybody knows. Wonder if they can look at me and see the best of my feelings were snatched away. She patted herself dry and started mixing milk and water and Karo syrup into the bottle that had been packed in the cardboard box. Still don't mean I can't be a good mother, she thought. Just 'cause my body ain't ripe for it don't mean my heart and my mind ain't. I could sure be a better mother to that child upstairs than her natural mother. Somebody probably know that too. Probably why they left her out there. Somebody know already I'd be as good as Mary was to Jesus. Humph, takes more than dripping titties to make a good mother.

She scuffed out of the kitchen and through the dining room that was as immaculate as the rest of the house. She walked back into the bedroom, where Herbie stood at the window bouncing the infant along his shoulder. His back was bare, and she thought that his shoulders looked wider with the baby's dark hair peeking over the top.

"Aren't you chilly standing next to that drafty window bare-chested?" "Amazing how much heat this little body sends off," Herbie answered as he turned and smiled as contented a smile as Noon had ever seen.

Noon was struck by the contentment settling in good on

Herbie's brow. She knew then that a baby was exactly what Herbie needed to calm him down some, keep him out of those clubs where the women ogled over his honest smile and half-straight hair and eyes as dark as his skin was light. A baby like this might even get him into a church service or two. She felt as sad for him as for herself that they couldn't claim this child as their own.

"You getting mighty attached." Noon took the baby from him. "It's only gonna make it harder when we got to give her up later today."

"I was gonna say the same thing about you getting attached, you know how sensitive you are about things." Herbie rubbed his stomach as he talked.

Noon looked at the baby so that she didn't have to watch his hands make circles over his stomach, which was hairy and flat. "Well, since we on the subject"—she paused and took a deep breath—"I want to get Reverend Schell over here to pray over the chile, later, maybe, after I get her bathed down, and she gets in another nap. I'll feel better knowing she's leaving here under special blessings."

Herbie agreed quickly, even though he wasn't big on prayer in the public sort of way that Reverend Schell went about it. "Okay, you call Schell, and I'll go around the corner and tell Big Carl from the club to stop by. He hears rumors before they're spoken. Maybe he heard of someone having a baby, and now don't have the baby to show."

"I been thinking too," Noon said as she busied herself changing the baby's diaper. "Since today is Saturday and all, and no one's at work down there at City Hall besides maybe the police—well, I was thinking, she might as well stay the weekend. She's sure no trouble, and Pet milk and Karo sure isn't an extra expense. I can pull out a dresser drawer and empty it and line it, and she can sleep right in there."

"Might as well stay the weekend then." Herbie went to Noon and pecked her on the mouth. "If that's what you want, then she can stay the weekend." He looked down on the bed, and the baby's eyes were dancing as Noon pinned the diaper together. He reached in and pinched the baby's cheek and felt the talc- and cocoa butter-scented warmth he'd felt last night on the steps.

Afternoon came quickly on Saturdays in this part of South Philly. The morning melted from sunrise to afternoon while they scrubbed the steps outside and poured buckets of bleach and hot water through the back alleys. They shined their windows and did their in-the-house work and then shopped on Ninth Street or South Street or Washington Avenue. One to five was catch-up time: to wonder where the morning went, to sew, to fry hair with a hot comb and a tin of Royal Crown grease, to get in on a card game at Rose's, or a special-call choir rehearsal, to go to Bow's for a cut, Royale for a shot, Pop's for a hoagie, or a car ride to Eden to put flowers on somebody's grave. This Saturday from one until five they crowded into Noon and Herbie's because news of the baby spread as quickly as the morning went.

Reverend Schell came, and Noon's choir member friends, the deacons, people from the block, from around the corner, Big Carl from Royale, and Herbie's buddies from the train station. Somebody brought in a crate of fried chicken, somebody else an army pot filled with potato salad; they brought spirits from the club, coffee from the church. One came with a cradle, another with a large wooden playpen, another with a bag filled up with baby clothes. They piled into the neat Lombard Street row house from the kitchen to the front steps. They sat along the arms of the couch and on the steps and the floor. They clapped and sang, danced worldly dances, prayed holy prayers, and chatted excitedly about the baby in the box.

"Just like that, huh? Box was just sitting on the steps, huh?" Reverend Schell asked, as he sipped at his steaming cup of coffee.

"Just sitting like it was waiting for me to see it," Herbie answered, drinking his chilled wine. "Might have tripped over it in the dark, but they had her all in pink that acted like a light as I was on my way up the steps. Then I picked her up and she started to cry, but I rocked her a little and she got quiet and content like she was just waiting for me to come and rock her."

"You thought about calling the police?" asked Dottie, who lived across the street.

"No need to call the authorities. That child is a gift from God," Reverend Schell boomed. "We got to learn how to handle our own affairs without always getting white folks to intervene."

"Wait a minute," Herbie said slowly. "You saying you think we should keep the chile."

"What else you gonna do with her? Where I come from, which is right here in Philadelphia born and raised, we take care of our own."

"But I thought they were stricter with the laws here in Philadelphia," Herbie said excitedly. Then he called into the dining room, where Noon and a roomful of women were passing the baby from hand to hand.

"Noon," he said, "come on in here. Your reverend is saying we should just keep the baby."

"It's been on my heart to suggest that," Noon spouted as she moved through the throng of people into the living room. "I know down Florida it happened to two families that I know of, somebody left children with them and the people just raised them as their own."

"Well, down in Mississippi," Herbie said, taking the baby from Noon, "everybody raised everybody else's children anyhow. At least it was that way with me since my mama died when I was seven and my daddy was a Pullman porter and away for stretches at a time. My brother and me got all the mothering we needed from any of a number of good-cooking women."

"So y'all in agreement then, right?" Reverend Schell looked from Noon to Herbie. "Y'all gonna keep the baby, right?"

Noon looked at Herbie and smiled, almost shyly. "I was gonna suggest it this morning, but I didn't know how you'd take to such a notion so suddenly, having the finances of a baby's upkeep thrust on you."

"You should have spoken it then," Herbie said. "I was thinking along the same lines, but I thought that was a suggestion that should come from you, you being the woman, and the baby's tending to being your responsibility." He moved in close to Noon and handed the baby back to her and then covered his wife's shoulders with his arms. "I just want you to be happy, Noon."

"Seems like it's settled to me," Reverend Schell said. "God bless the new parents."

"Still seem to me like the court or somebody official needs to be involved," Dottie countered. She rested her hand on Herbie's forearm and squeezed it lightly.

"Now let me say something to you, Sister Dottie," Reverend Schell bellowed, raising his hand high. "What's a bunch of white folks gonna do once they get their hands on this baby? They just gonna turn her over to a foster family, and I'm telling you the Lord has already handpicked the family. Noon and Herbie have just had a blessing laid at their doorsteps. No need to be second-guessing the hand of God. Sometimes the Lord's work and man's work don't always mesh. And when that happens, I'm going with the Lord every time." He loosened his tie and cleared his throat for preaching.

Herbie reached up to Reverend Schell, who towered over him, grabbed Reverend Schell's cup, and put his arm around his shoulder. "Now, Rev, you been a good pastor to my wife this past year that we been here in Philadelphia. And I promise, I do plan to visit you in the House of the Lord one of these Sundays. But Reverend, if you fixing to preach right here and now, we got to trade off cups 'cause I'm sure gonna need some coffee and I do believe you could benefit from some wine."

The rooms from the kitchen to the front door exploded with laughter. These were downtown folks. Holy Ghost–filled to whiskey-inspired, bartender to deacon, jazz singer to choir member, the separations fell away when there was an occasion for a grand coming together such as this.

"I will say this," Cardplaying-Rose offered, "you won't have to worry 'bout that mother coming back for the chile. Whoever left that chile cares for her. They know just what they doing. Ain't coming back. No offense to you, Reverend, but I saw Queen of Hearts in my reading this morning. Means motherly love, they ain't coming back."

"Sister Rose, I agree the mother won't return, but my source is more reliable than a deck of cards. It's the word of God—"

"Rev, Rev, Rev," Herbie cut in. "So what we got to do legally? I mean, what about birth certificates?"

"First thing Monday morning"—Reverend Schell placed his hand on Herbie's shoulder as he spoke—"go down to City Hall, to the department that handles birth certificates. Tell them one of your relatives from down South left the baby for you to raise, and you want to do whatever paperwork you need to do so you don't get any of their undereyed looks when it's time for the chile to get enrolled in school. And you sure don't have to worry about anybody gathered here saying anything different. To intercede in the workings of God that way might bring damnation to us all. Am I right, Sister Dottie?" He looked over at his shoulder and squinted his eyes at Dottie.

"I was only saying that the law—"

"Damnation! Sister Dottie, am I right?" Reverend Schell cut her off.

"You right, Reverend," Dottie mumbled, trying to shake off the collected gaze of the roomful of people.

"Now you give me your Bible," Reverend Schell said, "and I'm gonna make it legal right now in the sight of God. That's what I love about my God, we don't have to wait till Monday morning to do our business with the Lord."

"Ain't it the truth," someone shouted, until sounds of agreement rippled through the whole house.

"Now, what you gonna call her?" Reverend Schell asked as he patted his breast pocket and then handed the Bible to Herbie. "Left my glasses home, but you can do this part. Just turn the gold-trimmed pages of this beautiful white leather Bible to the one marked 'Birth Certificate,' and you take this with you Monday, let them put their official stamp to it."

The memory of the early morning fell over Herbie like a wave as he moved his fingers over the thin, soft pages. He thought about the way the air felt at his back as he pushed up Lombard Street right before he stumbled upon the box. And then the eyes, as the air fanned the flame of the match and made the baby's eyes dance in the flickering light.

"Fannie!" he shouted. "Her name's Fannie. The name just came to me; it fits her too. That name allright by you, Noon?"

"Fannie, it is," Noon answered.

"Just put it right there on that top line of that page, then fill in the date and hand it here and let me put my scribble to it." Reverend Schell's voice was filled with jubilation.

They cheered and shouted. Reverend Schell prayed over the infant. Afterward they raised their cups filled with wine, or juice, or milk, or coffee, or vodka, or tea. The merriment even sifted out of the front door, onto the street, where even more people had gathered to hear about the baby in the box.

Noon's round face beamed as she sat propped in the deep green armchair. She ran her hand along the baby's hair and almost seemed to blush. "Fannie," she said again. "Who would've thought it? Noon and Herbie's baby girl named Fannie."

Permissions

Bibliography

The selections used in this anthology were taken from the editions listed below. For more information on selections original to this anthology or never before published in book form, refer to the permissions credits.

Ansa, Tina McElroy. *Baby of the Family*. New York: Harvest Books, 1989.

Clarke, Breena. "The Drill" from *Streetlights: Illuminating Tales of the Black Urban Experience*, edited by Doris Jean Austin and Martin Simmons. New York: Penguin Books, 1996.

Danticat, Edwidge. "The Book of the Dead" from *Giant Steps: The New Generation of African-American Writers*, edited by Kevin Young. New York: HarperCollins, 2000.

D'Aguiar, Fred. "A Son in Shadow" from *The Beacon Best of 2000: Great Writing by Women and Men of All Colors and Cultures*, edited by Edwidge Danticat. Boston: Beacon Press, 2000.

Derricotte, Toi. "Holy Cross Hospital" from *Natural Birth* by Toi Derricotte. Reprinted in *Making Callaloo: 25 Years of Black Literature*, edited by Charles Henry Rowell. New York: St. Martin's Press, 2002.

DeVeaux, Alexis. "Dear Aunt Nanadine" from *Afrekete: An Anthology of Black Lesbian Writing*, edited by Catherine E. McKinley and L. Joyce DeLaney. New York: Anchor Books, 1995.

Early, Gerald. "The Driving Lesson" from *Fathering Daughters: Reflections by Men*, edited by DeWitt Henry and James Alan McPherson. Boston: Beacon Press, 1998.

Hippolyte, Kendel. *Birthright*. Leeds, England: Pepal Tree Press, 1997.

Johnson, Charles. "China" from *The Sorcerer's Apprentice* by Charles Johnson. Reprinted in *Breaking Ice: An Anthology of Contemporary African-American Fiction*, edited by Terry McMillan. New York: Penguin Books, 1990.

Kincaid, Jamaica. *Annie John*. New York: Plume, 1986.

Lee, Andrea. *Interesting Women: Stories*. New York: Random House, 2002.

Marshall, Paule. *Praisesong for the Widow*. New York: Plume, 1983.

McBride, James. *The Color of Water*. New York: Riverhead Books, 1996.

McKinney-Whetstone, Diane. *Tumbling*. New York: William Morrow, 1996.

Olive Senior. *Summer Lightening and Other Stories*. Longman Group UK Limited, 1986.

White, Paulette Childress. *The Watermelon Dress*. Detroit: Lotus Press, 1984.

Wesley, Valerie Wilson. *Ain't Nobody's Business If I Do*. New York: Avon Books, 1999.

Youngblood, Shay. *Soul Kiss*. New York: Riverhead Books, 1997.

ADDITIONAL TITLES

The following works, by authors whose selections in this collection are being anthologized for the first time, may also be of interest.

Adams, Janus. *Sister Days: 365 Inspired Moments in African-American Women's History*. New York: John Wiley & Sons, 2000.

Adero, Malaika, editor. *Up South: Stories, Studies and Letter of this Century's African-American Migrations*. New York: The New Press, 1993.

Cobb, William Jelani, editor. *The Essential Harold Cruse: A Reader*. New York: Palgrave Macmillan, 2002.

Dickerson, Debra J. *An American Story*. New York: Anchor Books, 2001

Robotham, Rosemarie. *Zachary Wings*. New York: Scribner, 1998.

Southgate, Martha. *The Fall of Rome*. New York: Scribner, 2002.

Walker, Alice. *The Way Foreword is With a Broken Heart*. New York: Ballantine, 2001.

Walker, Rebecca. *Black, White and Jewish: Autobiography of a Shifting Self*. New York: Riverhead Books, 2002.

Woodson, Jacqueline. *Autobiography of a Family Photo*. New York: Plume, 1996.

Maya Angelou

Hailed as one of the great voices of contemporary literature and as a remarkable Renaissance woman, Dr. Maya Angelou is a poet, educator, historian, author, actress, playwright, Civil Rights activist, producer and director. Born in St. Louis, Missouri, and educated in Stamps, Arkansas and San Francisco, she is the author of twelve best-selling books, including the groundbreaking *I Know Why the Caged Bird Sings* and her most recent memoir, *A Song Flung Up to Heaven*. In 1981, Dr. Angelou was appointed to a lifetime position as the first Reynolds Professor of American Studies at Wake Forest University in Winston Salem, North Carolina. In January 1993, she became only the second poet in United States history to have the honor of writing and reciting an original work at the Presidential Inauguration.

Pearl Cleage

One of the nation's foremost African-American playwrights, with such staged hits as *Flyin' West, Blues for an Alabama Sky* and *Bourbon at the Border,* Pearl Cleage is also a best-selling novelist whose first book, 1997's *What Looks Like Crazy On an Ordinary Day,* was an Oprah Book Club pick. Her second novel, *I Wish I Had a Red Dress,* was published in 2001 and her third is forthcoming. An essayist, activist, teacher, mother, wife, and grandmother in her other incarnations, she was born in Detroit and now lives in Atlanta. Cleage was the founding editor of *Catalyst* magazine, a columnist for *The Atlanta Tribune,* and is a regular contributor to *Essence* and *Ms.* magazines.

Rosemarie Robotham

Rosemarie Robotham, senior editor-at-large of *Essence* magazine, writes frequently about the Black family. Born in Kingston, Jamaica, she moved to New York in 1975. She holds a B.A. in Literature from Barnard College and a M.S.J. from Columbia University's Graduate School of Journalism. A former staff reporter for *Life* magazine, she also served as a senior editor at Simon & Schuster. The co-author of *Spirits of the Passage: The Transatlantic Slave Trade in the Seventeenth Century,* she is the author of the novel *Zachary's Wings* and editor of the anthology *The Bluelight Corner: Black Women Writing on Passion, Sex and Romantic Love.* Anthologized in John Henrik Clarke's *Black American Short Stories: One Hundred Years of the Best,* Robotham is the recipient of many awards, including a 1997 Unity Award for "Broken Promises," a report on poverty in the Mississippi Delta region, and a 1998 PASS Award from the National Council on Crime and Delinquency for "Gang Girl: The Transformation of Isis Sapp-Grant." A writer-in-residence at Yaddo during 2000, Robotham lives in New York City with her husband, Radford Arrindell, and their children, Radford III and Kai Angela.